I am highly honored
to have this volume
represented in the
Special Collection for
American Studies

William D. Ellis

Cleveland 1970

The Cuyahoga

BOOKS IN THE
RIVERS OF AMERICA SERIES

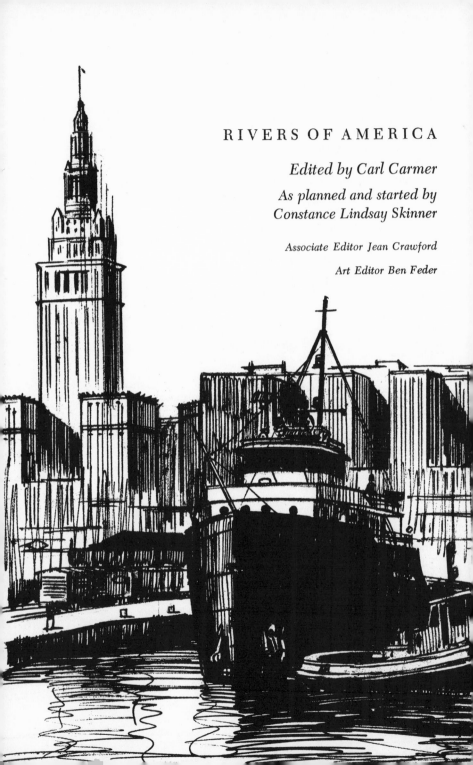

RIVERS OF AMERICA

Edited by Carl Carmer

*As planned and started by
Constance Lindsay Skinner*

Associate Editor Jean Crawford

Art Editor Ben Feder

The Cuyahoga

BY WILLIAM DONOHUE ELLIS

Illustrated by Kinley T. Shogren

Holt, Rinehart and Winston

New York · Chicago · San Francisco

F
497
C 95
E 55

1/26/71 Gift (Mrs. Anthony)

58559

To Bill and Sarah

Contents

"It has always been my opinion that the shortest, easiest and least expensive communication with the invaluable back country would be [to] let the courses and distances be taken to the mouth of the Muskingum and up that river to the carrying place to the Cuyahoga, down the Cuyahoga to Lake Erie."

—George Washington
to Benjamin Harrison
Governor of Virginia
October 10, 1784

The Cuyahoga

The
CUYAHOGA

L A K E

CLEVELAND

KINGSBURY RUN

MORGAN RUN

South New

Garfield Heights

TINKER'S CR.

Elyria

Independence

CUYAHOGA R.

OHIO CANAL

Brecksville

BRANDYWINE CR.

Jaite

Boston

Streetsbo

FURNACE RUN

Peninsula

Hudson

Everett

DICKERSON RUN

Ira

Brady's Lake

Botzum

Cuyahoga Falls

Stow

Kent

YELLOW CR.

Munroe Falls

AKRON

Tallmadge

OHIO CANAL

LITTLE CUYAHOGA R.

TUSCARAWAS R.

1

Cuyahoga Sound Track

EIGHTY MILES WEST of Pennsylvania along the shore line with which Ohio cups Lake Erie, there is a wide gash where the Cuyahoga River cuts its way out through the shore escarpment and enters the lake. In view of its empire-building career the Cuyahoga is a surprisingly small stream.

Smallness, in fact, is the constant surprise about this river. Though it is nearly a hundred miles long, its unique course allows its whole watershed to drain less than seven hundred and fifty square miles. It travels in such an extreme U-shape that its fork-tongued double source is only thirty crow-flown miles east of its mouth.

The U-shaped Cuyahoga meanders through only the four counties of Geauga, Portage, Summit, and Cuyahoga; and, though fed by hundreds of brooks, its major tributaries are sometimes so small they run through culverts. The Little Cuyahoga River at Akron is the largest. Downstream from that flow the waters of Yellow Creek at Botzum, Furnace Run and Dickerson Run at Everett, Tinker's Creek at Independence, and Morgan and Kingsbury runs near the mouth.

Yet the Cuyahoga is one of the pivotal North American rivers. No larger than many a fishing stream of less renown, turbulent in its uplands and impossibly crooked where it flows still and deep, it has influenced several major events in the nation's history.

When the Cuyahoga was the republic's northwest boundary, settlement was working its way too slowly north from the Ohio River, leaving America's northwest corner nervously unpeopled and unpossessed. This corner of the land wore a defense of roadless forests and so the Cuyahoga became the only means of opening the area which General Washington called "the invaluable backland." The opening of this territory, called the Western

Reserve, was carried out under a unique land settlement plan, an intricate lottery system conducted by the stockholders of the Connecticut Land Company. In order to break their way into the the backlands these persons depended upon the Cuyahoga as a water highway.

Once settled, the Western Reserve, in fact all of the then western frontier, faced economic strangulation. It was the Cuyahoga that furnished quick and dramatic escape. At her mouth she had access to New York markets via Lake Erie to New York State's great Erie Canal. At the U-bend, she swirled against the hog-backed divide that cut the south from the north at present-day Akron. Just eight miles from the bend, on the south slope of that hogback, the Tuscarawas River began its flow southward. With a tremendous effort in man-made works, these waters were made to link the entire Ohio country to the Ohio River and thus to the Gulf of Mexico and Southern and Eastern markets. A traffic in people, goods, and money thus opened from New York City, across New York State, across Lake Erie to the Cuyahoga mouth, up the Cuyahoga, across the divide and south to the Ohio River and the Mississippi to New Orleans. And the basic fact that underlay all this traffic was the U-bend in the Cuyahoga.

Moreover, though limited in size, the Cuyahoga mouth became a harbor which launched ships to open the iron country, first the Michigan Upper Peninsula, later the Mesabi, and in this century the vast iron ore fields in Quebec and Labrador. Today the Cuyahoga is a port of call for ships from every registry in the world.

Sometimes the old river seems to be a combination of one-third mud from the still rural headwaters, one-third sludge, and one-third pickle liquor from the great mills, but it continues making history. Mile for mile and drop for drop, it is doubtful that it can be matched by any other river.

East Bank, West Bank

Following the entire Cuyahoga on the map is only the work of minutes. The wandering blue line depicts its flow from the source in Chardon Township, Geauga County, south to Burton, South Newbury, Auburn, Welshfield, Hiram, Mantua, Streetsboro, Shalersville, Kent, Munroe Falls, Akron, and thence sharply north through Cuyahoga Falls, Botzum, Everett, Peninsula, Boston,

Jaite, Breckville, Independence, Garfield Heights, and Cleveland.

But following the stream on the land is another matter. The source is what you would hope. Out of sight of roads or telephone poles, you feel you are the first man to discover it. The East Branch rises near a dairy farm and flows through woods and into East Branch Reservoir, a shining jewel surrounded by young Christmas trees.

The West Branch grows from a score of rivulets coming out of the hollows between the great hilltop houses in the Chardon Woods.

Both these south-flowing sources are *north* of the Cuyahoga mouth at Cleveland. Their confluence is ten miles south of the sources, near Brady's Pond. The river flows thence through beautiful farmland widening from the strength of a thousand brooks.

After wandering by the peaceful college towns of Hiram and Kent in a pastoral valley, the Cuyahoga flows into Munroe Falls where suddenly it strips off its green shore and puts on rust. From here on it is strictly a downtown river. It picks up warehouses and railroad tracks, and then just short of Akron, it runs smack up against the great escarpment which turns it north. Off that hogback, at Akron, the Little Cuyahoga (not to be confused with the Cuyahoga) also runs north to plunge down a stairway of falls to Lake Erie.

After its sudden sharp turn, the Cuyahoga sometimes becomes so narrow that it runs through a lane of trees whose leafy branches meet over it, whispering history. For the Cuyahoga was the key to settlement of all the towns from the bend to its mouth. And the downstream towns of Peninsula and Boston and Brecksville and Independence still cherish their history and preserve it in restorations like the Jonathan Hale House in the area that includes Everett, Bath, and Peninsula. Through these towns the landscape goes natural again with meadows and woods; but it is not farming rural, it is suburban rural. Here and there manicured lawns slant down to the river's edge.

It is this stretch of the Cuyahoga which, with the Portage Path and the Tuscarawas river, formed the earliest known inland road on the continent. It appeared on European maps over four hundred years ago, even before cartographers could draw the Great Lakes or the Gulf or the eastern seaboard correctly. Being the only well-established interior route from the Gulf to the Great Lakes, it suggested military planning to Europeans.

Boundary River

Since it was the only interior line accurately definable it became a boundary river. European kings, needing to state where claims began and ended, made use of the Cuyahoga in their geographic calculations. For many years, too, it was the western boundary of the Republic of America; and it was alternately the eastern boundary of the Wyandots, French, British, and again the Wyandots.

As the river comes out of Independence, Ohio, it changes from lovely and green to loud and red. The change is complete and sudden. For its last six miles flow between refineries, steel mills, and warehouses to Lake Erie. From its ruddy waters arises a pandemonium of sound created by that shoreside workshop that is Cleveland.

Bordering and in the center of the hundred-mile horseshoe here described live a million and a half people contained in three dozen towns and villages most of which orbit Akron and Cleveland.

To come in for close-ups of the Cuyahoga, it is best to start at the mouth, where the river's story starts as far as men are concerned. And it is important not only to look but to listen, because this river talks all day and squawks all night. And in the winter, it's talked *about*.

"Yes, but have you ever sailed the Ka-hawga?"

This is a way of presenting credentials. Most ten-year Great Lakes' seamen have a story that begins, "We were in the Ka-hawga when the fog set in." Such a preamble stills the chatter along twenty feet of brass rail in most dockside taverns from Cleveland to Duluth.

In the six miles from the mouth to the Republic Steel Dock, under the lower Cuyahoga's twenty-one bridges and around seven bends, the nation's greatest navigation tall tales are born. But mixed in with them are fabulous true stories of seamanship, where 650-foot vessels snake horeshoe turns in the narrows to clear cofferdams by a rivet head. During the war when the full iron-ore fleet was in commission, breath-stopping skill in the pilothouses was a daily requirement.

The red of the water is created by iron, mud, sulphur, crude oil, and pickle liquor from the mills. And for a hundred years those who have known which side Midwest bread is buttered on have thanked God . . . also Sam Mather, John D. Rockefeller, Ben Fairless, Cyrus Eaton, and many early iron men who sailed out of the Cuyahoga basin up to the Michigan, Menominee, and Mesabi ranges to find the red dirt that feeds Cuyahoga's iron furnaces and colors its waters.

The vessels which traffic the lower Cuyahoga are enormous blunt-bowed, powerful hulls which at first seem boxy, then turn beautiful before your eyes. And they are so long that one may take a quarter hour to pass you as you stand among the squash and sunflowers planted behind the harbormaster's office.

A Brace of Lions

River entrances have traditionally been guarded by a pair of forts and shore batteries astride the mouth. But the mouth of the Cuyahoga is watched by two powerful old bull lions.

On the east bank, Admiral Khoury used to look down from the

Rockefeller Building at the mouth of the river. There his ore boats, largest fleet on the Great Lakes, were hauling millions of tons of Mesabi range red dirt to the Cuyahoga's blast furnaces.

Those furnaces feed iron to conversion furnaces which feed steel to the valley's strip and bar and rod and wire mills. This activity tears up the valley somewhat. It leaves a certain kind of wreckage alongshore, and the kind of riverside slums that haunt industrial valleys. Famous and gamey resorts grew here as colorful as coal-acid flowers, and so did diseases and orphans.

Across on the west bank of the Cuyahoga sits the other lion, irascible Ernie Bohn, the toughest practicing sociologist the region has produced. And he is steadfastly repairing the damage along the river with public housing that has become the nation's pilot model.

To do it, he has had to change the laws of the state (and nation) to allow him to use public money to tear out slums and build fit dwellings. He has sometimes had to go across the river to get the iron and steel men to help.

So when ships enter the river, the crews look up to the Rockefeller Building on the east bank, traditional headquarters of Great Lakes shipping. And each trip they look up the steep west bank to stare at the every-lengthening levee of beautiful brick housing Ernie Bohn is stretching from the mouth southward to build a kind of Eden-on-Cuyahoga.

Man-Made River

You should not read about or travel the Cuyahoga neatly from source to mouth or vice versa. On this winding river, events have broken out here and there, as men of different flammability touched off fires along the banks.

For this is uniquely a man-made river. Not only figuratively, but literally; its mouth and delta and navigable slack-water courses were man-made. Its stature and importance were man-made and by specific men. This fact necessitates that the teller of the river's story jump from the mouth to the big bend to the headwaters—and possibly to points between. It also requires that he be chronological, yet not precisely.

While the upper river is wandering and charming, the lower

river is busy and snarling. It is always in a half dozen fights, battling with railroads twenty times its size, or shipping companies whose boats are nearly half as beamy as the river is wide. It is scrapping with the railroads because they charge more demurrage on the Cuyahoga than they do, say, on the Mississippi at New Orleans.

It is in the middle of the pilotage war. Ever since the opening of the Seaway, there have been efforts to bring the International Rules of the Road to the Cuyahoga. But the river has her own rules.

The Cuyahoga is always in heavy combat with bridge builders, smoke and silt and pollution and riparian lawyers.

The Cuyahoga is in court every month. The fights are in the daily paper if you know where to look. At this writing, magazines are making it "the example" in the national water pollution problem.

Many a man is made by a river. But the Cuyahoga was made by men. It does not flow through oil fields, rubber plantations, nor iron-ore regions, but men have made it the capital of oil, coal, rubber, and iron. Men who built refineries along its banks pulled the crude oil in from Pennsylvania, and the Cuyahoga became oil headquarters.

Alfred Kelley made it the link between New Orleans and New York City by burrowing a canal from the Cuyahoga to the Ohio. Over that canal, men from around Massillon hauled coal up into Cleveland. Other Cuyahoga men sailed vessels out of that narrow channel to cross Lakes Erie, Huron, Superior to bring down iron ore. The iron met the coal on the Cuyahoga banks, and Cuyahoga ironmasters made this river mid-America's steel headquarters.

Upstream at Akron, a group of men with secret recipes in their pockets used Cuyahoga water to give power to so many rubber factories that this town without a single rubber tree became the rubber capital of the world.

Valley Music

I wish this book had a sound track so that as we fade in on the Cuyahoga you could hear the various inflections of the talk along the banks. This river is pronounced differently depending on what the speaker uses it for.

Those who live *on* this red and yellow water merely call it the River. Those who live *off* it, professionally, call it the Ka-hawga, and pronounce it with respect.

You fish in it, it's the Cuya-hoga. You farm it, it's Kyawga, spoken like a 1928 side-mounted autohorn.

Those who make cause of smoke abatement, water depollution, and human salvation call it "Ohio's Big Problem."

Especially do I wish this book had a sound track so you could hear the sounds within its valley.

I don't mean anything sentimental. The Cuyahoga has no songs, ballads, or poems, and it discourages romantic emotion because it has so much work to get done. Yet it does have a cacophonous symphony.

It opens with a tarantara of tugboat whistles scolding at a six hundred-foot ore bulker, segues to contrapuntal tug bell signals from pilothouse to engine room as the tug squares the monster up in the channel, and then the heavy music rolls.

The vessel blows for the bridge—one long blast you hear through your chest bones. The bridge pipes a long and a short. The ship answers with a short blast so percussive that, when it cuts out, the world is empty for seconds.

The Number One bridge rises like a stage curtain and the bulker moves upstream amid tug whistles, railroad brakes, coal dumping, and engine surges as twenty thousand tons of ore move against the current, the bridges, and the clock.

The Number Three drawbridge opens up a stretch of tawny water about as busy as any in America.

To make the boat ready for the first bite of the unloaders when it finally reaches the dock, hatch covers screech open and hit their stops with cymbal crashes as the vessel rounds Collision Bend at Jim's Steak House.

At the head of navigation at one of the steel mill ore docks, there's a hush as the captain whispers his twenty thousand tons up broadside to the dock with just enough touch to crack a walnut.

"Make fast!"

The unloader buckets lower into the holds to the drum roll of cable paying out.

That's music—on the mightiest little river in the nation.

2

The Sculptor

IT WOULD BE fanciful, would it not, to say that a man should be careful what kind of fold in the land he lives on because some magnet in the land itself reaches up and bends or moves the men to fit the landscape or gives them orders what to do or how to go? Especially strong-willed men like the Eries, Ottawas, Mohawks, Captain Bradys, Captain Bradleys, Kelleys, Crosbys, Carters, Mathers, Pichands, Rockefellers, Goodyears, Seiberlings, Firestones, Bohns, Eatons, Humphreys—a wet crack in the rocks like the Cuyahoga could hardly command their destinies.

Yet, perhaps it's not beyond the great scheme of things, when we consider that shaping the Cuyahoga was the work of a half a thousand million years.

Even a scant few thousand years ago only the barest traces of a Cuyahoga river course were visible, here a rock tossed by the glaciers to turn the flow, there a valley etched by some river of the past. But until very late, there was nothing to suggest that this stream's headwaters would originate just fifteen miles from the lake into which it should empty, nothing to indicate it would ignore the proximity of its Lake Erie goal by flowing in exactly the opposite direction, south, then west, *then* north in its hesitant hundred-mile wandering.

However devious the river's course may seem today, nature's steps in sculpting the land in the way she did are more so. The geological clues to these ancient events are numerous, and their sheer multitude leaves a trail into the past so complex that even yet it has not been completely cleared. But it is said by the men who read the rocks that roughly five hundred million years ago great volcanoes spewed out their molten rock and mineral to form the first solid foundation on which nature's modeling could begin.

9

It began immediately. With wind, rain, heat, and cold for tools, she ground the rocks into a plain. Then she poured oceans over the land and let them stand several million years. They say the sea here was shallow by the standards of those ages, a mere hundred to two hundred feet.

At its shores, the sea stored away the volcanic rock, ground it to silt, and spread it as mud and gravel over the rocky floor. Rivers and weather pulverized whole mountain ranges and added them to the shallow depths. After ages of this activity, nature heaved the continent above the waters to let the primordial accumulation of muck dry into sedimentary rocks and shales. Again and again, the area was deluged by inland seas. They raised the rock at intervals to let the weather wear it away (and to confuse geologists), then submerged it once more to collect the ooze that would eventually become earth's blanket.

Sometime in the midst of this ebb and flow of sea and land, a spark created swimming creatures, some of them made in the macrocosmic image of that era; others were created so small that hosts of them could live in a drop of the monstrous sea. Among these were tiny creatures that spun limey shells, then died and left their bodies to collect into two to four hundred foot thick layers of limestone. Eons later these would create along the Cuyahoga River some baronies and barons, and the town of Independence. Settlement was to follow these limestone outcroppings.

During the dry intervals, the waters marshed and puddled over the land, giving root to great ferny forests which flourished, overgrew the swamps, died and were buried again beneath the seas. Thus coal, which would someday seem to be the invention of Mark Hanna and other Ohioans on the river, was added to the foundation.

Finally, as if to show superiority over the ever encroaching water, the land made one last heave so magnificent that it peaked in a towering Alplike mountain range . . . The Appalachian. It shuddered then and ruffled the surrounding surface into foothill ranges, rippling west, well out into what would become eastern Ohio.

Now, we can just see the beginnings of those features which would one day reveal a crack of dampness, the Cuyahoga. The elements attacked the mountainous wrinkles on the surface of the land, grinding away at the rocks. The softer rocks to the west fell readily before the rainy gales of centuries, the freezes and thaws, while those resistant rocks to the east were spared, wearing down only to a flat plateau.

Strangest of all was the division line between these two areas. It was as if the roughly square-shaped state of Ohio had been folded diagonally from the northeast to the southwest corners, and half the state had received the same erosion as the Allegheny-Appalachian highland. The other half, however, had been worn smooth into what scholars call the Erie Plain—and nonscholars call corn-hog country. But the fold or division line between the two areas remains even today as one of the astounding features of Ohio's landscape. It rises in a sheer escarpment two to five miles wide, a jagged scar from northeast to southwest. Beginning near Erie, Pennsylvania, it runs along the shore of Lake Erie to Cleveland. There it forms Cedar Hill at University Circle and the cliff border of North Park Boulevard. Thence it jogs erratically southwest to the Ohio River and on into Kentucky and Tennessee.

The Portage Escarpment, as it is called by geologists, is important to the story of the Cuyahoga because it forms a basin for the river's headwaters in the northeast corner of Ohio. Here the Cuyahoga rises and meanders, looking for a lip that will allow it to pour into Lake Erie.

But we are ahead of our story. The four hundred million years we have covered so far have merely set the stage for the second act of nature's gigantic drama; and the watershed divide is an elusive changeling on this stage.

The divide might be visualized as a wavy ridge running roughly east to west. Like the ridgepole of a cabin, it tips the land so that all waters below it flow south to the Ohio River; every drop above flows north to Lake Erie. In the days before the glaciers of the ice age began their descent, the rivers collected their waters and flowed without turns or twists in straight, uncomplicated torrents, almost like troughs. One in particular, geologists of the preglacial history name the Dover. It could be called the grandfather of our Cuyahoga. Roads, towns, grapes, schools, and a hardware store have been named for Dover. It began its mighty flow, 116 miles from Lake Erie and ran due north. During the several million years of its existence, it sliced a channel everlastingly into the land.

And then there was ice.

Two miles high it came, smashing down mountains, filling the valleys, rivers, and lakes with debris plowed up from its path. The wars of nature were brutal. Rocks, soil, hills, and forests were fused into the hulking ice until it resembled a great, dirty mountain of frozen earth. Along the forward edge of it some say there was always deafening noise, a cracking of rocks, snapping of trees, a sliding of land. Others say, "How could there be noise—with no ear to hear?"

We trace the progress of the ice across Cuyahoga country by the glacial scratches, drift, till, and the great hard heads or lost rocks strewn about on farms. The Cuyahoga is not granite country, yet occasionally the glacier dropped great granite boulders from the Adirondacks here.

In some areas, the glacier seems to have been guided in its southward progress by the Portage Escarpment, but here and there the ice broke down the wall of rock to wreak its havoc in the Allegheny foothills to the east.

The rivers received the worst of the devastation. The frozen hulk jammed billions of tons into the north-flowing rivers, blocking their waters, collecting them into vast lakes that were forced to find new outlets south. When the southern suns checked the glacier's progress at last, the silent task of melting billions of tons of ice began. Now waters gushed forth, carving new valleys into solid rock and carrying acres of ground-up boulders, sand, and gravel over the land.

This period postdating the first glacier is sometimes referred to as "deep drainage," during which the rivers, now released from their ice dams, rushed *north* again, furiously seeking their old beds. You can imagine the energy of these gushing waters, gouging their old troughs into deeper, narrow canyons. In draining the land, the ancestor of the Cuyahoga sliced a line straight north, its canyon walls towering fully a thousand feet straight up, its turbulent waters all of a mile across.

Drive to see the canyon at Cuyahoga Falls today—and multiply the whole, including the sound, the width, the depth of the canyon, by one hundred, and you may get an idea of how the scene once looked.

The valley of this river was spared the next invasion of ice which covered only the western half of Ohio, but the last great glacier filled the river. Sweeping southward, the ice turned the waters once more.

As the ice unveiled its handiwork, our present network of rivers was revealed. The southward-flowing stream was named the Muskingum and that farther to the north, draining the melting glacier, the Tuscarawas. But now the elusive watershed divide was revealed at last. During each glacier, its position had been bent, twisted, raised, and lowered. Now it had reached a new position, like a hogback ridge running east to west, just eight miles above the head of the Tuscarawas.

This divide was not enough to block the turbulent waters melting from the receding glacier. As the ice backed into the Great Lakes, these waters rose and fell with the melt. To release the floods from the basin, exits were found, first near Fort Wayne, then northward at the Grand River, then the thumb of Michigan. Later, the waters drained to the east through Niagara, pouring down through the Mohawk valley to the Hudson and at long last unblocking the channel of the St. Lawrence leading to the sea.

In this final aquatic act, the Cuyahoga was born.

As the waters of Lake Erie fell, they left a lake which formed in that basin bounded on the north and west by the wall of the Portage Escarpment and on the east by the Appalachian foot-hills. The south boundary of the basin was the watershed divide. The water spilled right over this to join the southbound Tuscarawas.

But as the outlets of Lake Erie seesawed from east to west, as the waters rose and fell and finally settled into the general boundaries we know today, the waters of Lake Cuyahoga also receded. They dwindled to a river. Almost like a lost child, it wandered aimlessly over the glacial fill of the basin, turning this way and that seeking least resistance. As though confused, it sought the opposite direction from its natural northern outlet, dropping about nine feet per mile of flow. Finally, it uncovered what was left of the old river valley, now packed with rocky gumbo left from the glacier.

Joyously, the Cuyahoga begins to run at Akron, then leaps into a series of rapids at Cuyahoga Falls to rush north through the mile-and-a-half gorge. After this one wanton leap, the Cuyahoga slows down to meander. The sides of the buried canyon form a margin; the river tries the limits of its prison, touching first one wall and then the other while scooping its own flat bed in the glacial fill. The twisty little river winds its way toward the lake, dropping two feet to the mile. In the final reach, the Cuyahoga leaves the old bed, audaciously looping away to cut a new and kinky path to the lake it has sought for ninety miles.

And now, because it was made as it was, men who live on it, astride it, and beside it, will live their lives in a certain way.

Many different strata can be seen and used in the Cuyahoga Valley and in the gorges leading into it. About a hundred feet of soft argillaceous shale is found from Peninsula north. Just above it in the stratification is Cleveland shale, black and highly bituminous. This erodes quickly, producing cascades.

Above that layer is Bedford shale (first found in Bedford), and above that, Berea grit, white fine-grained sandstone which built a grindstone, curbstone, building stone industry along the Cuyahoga shore line.

Above Berea grit, a ten-foot layer of Berea shale. Above that, Cuyahoga shale, as seen exposed below Cuyahoga Falls, runs 175 feet thick some places. Near the top of this is a layer of impure limestone which gave the canal builders a fair water lime for below-water-level masonry.

Above that, a layer of carboniferous conglomerate comes here and there in a handsome iron oxide red. Used for construction, it was quarried extensively at Cuyahoga Falls and Boston. This building stone conglomerate is the foundation for the coal rock layer which will in turn become the foundation for several industries.

At Cuyahoga Falls and downstream from it, the soft clayey shale under the sandrock disintegrated, creating a precipice once over a hundred feet high. The fall of water would start some men dreaming of harnessing the power.

So the folds in the river lands reach up to influence the lives of men walking alongside.

And these men will want a name for it.

Caujahoga appeared on an ancient European map and correctly placed, just north of a short trail marked *The Carrying Place*. It showed some Indian villages, one at Akron called *Caujahoga Town*. Some say it was an Erie Indian village.

Moravian missionaries were the first whites in the valley, settling where Tinker's Creek joins in. They wrote in records *Gajahaga*.

Cayagaga is what the Mohawks called it. Crooked river is what we believe they meant by that. We must say that with reservation, because displaced Senacas living there called it the *Cuyohaga* which meant to them *place of the jawbone*. It is recorded that in early days the skull and jawbone of a mastodon were discovered five miles from the Cuyahoga mouth. It is understandable that men might make a legend from the fact that they had found a jawbone twenty times bigger than the jaw of a large horse. Yet after the jawbone had disappeared, men looking at the river could assume it was *crooked like a jawbone*.

Diohaga was the name given the stream by the Delawares. Other works called it *Cauahogue*. Heckwelder, the missionary, said *Cujahaga*.

Now what of that great Cuyahoga Lake that receded and receded until it became the Cuyahoga River? It makes a man want to go back to the source to see if anything there speaks of those tumultous eons. In a way the source of a river may be the closest a man can stand to the six days and six nights of creation. So you go to look again.

Fifteen miles south of the Lake Erie shore in the middle of a field in Geauga County, there is an oval-shaped half acre of cattails, elderbushes, high weeds, and small trees, 1370 feet above sea level, perhaps the vestige of the Cuyahoga Lake.

In the middle of that tiny marsh, the wondrous thing takes place.

You push your way in through the reeds and briars. The ditch you find is a foot wide, half that deep with an inch of water. It is hard to believe what you're looking at, because less than a hundred miles downstream, this water will float twenty thousand tons of cargo in a six-hundred-foot hull.

It is hard to remember it took five hundred million years to build this; that it became the once west border of the Republic of America; that it became the once main route from Canada to Mexico.

You are at the fountainhead of the West Branch of the Cuyahoga.

3

The Signal Tree

THE LAND was shaped and ready for men.

Naturally they were red men. But the Indians of the Cuyahoga Valley came in two waves. The second wave will seem almost contemporaneous because it is so much more recent and vivid than the first. There are men alive today in northeastern Ohio who can bring out old letters from great-grandparents they remember, letters speaking of workaday relationships with Senecas, Mohawks, Wyandots, Ottawas, and Delawares.

But before these tribes came into the Cuyahoga Valley, the place belonged to a grand and ancient race of Indians so remote in time that not even the names of their greatest men come down to us. They are vague in our texts and museums. Yet there remains a mystic and living link which chills the blood if the mood is right. If you drive down Peck Road in Cuyahoga Falls to the Goudy Farm, you come to the Signal Tree. You'll know it immediately, for I do not believe you will ever have seen one like it anywhere.

It probably can't last much longer; parts of it are already dead, and you can see where it has shed dead limbs before. The sap flows to parts of it through a hollowed trunk. This tree has a massive four-foot trunk like other multi-hundred-year-old white oaks you have seen. But at the very base, growing out horizontally on either side, are two massive arms. Symmetrically they grow out perhaps thirteen feet, then both make a sharp right-angle upturn and grow straight up alongside the main trunk.

This towering three-pronged oaken candelabra marked the Indian trail to the Old Portage Path. And as you stare, you get an uncommonly strong relationship to another time and another race of men and women.

You know that tree was made in only one way. An Indian had

to reach down to a small triple-shooted oak sapling, break the two side branches just so, and bind them in position. But what will take your breath: That same tree which was alive when the Indian touched it is partly alive today when *you* touch it. It is the strongest sensation of a handshake across hundreds of years. Of course, the handshake from us might not be returned.

The Cuyahoga valley is an Indian story, but a sad one.

Long before real white settlement began along the river, the French Jesuits found an intelligent and powerful people along

the south shore of the lake which they named for them—the Eries.

The men who can read bones today say these Indians were a tall, gaunt and handsome people. The men who can read artifacts say they were formidable in war. The men who can read shrines say they were not inclined toward the worship of any gods, but that they had the gentleness of undisputed power.

Though they fronted the entire south shore of the lake, the Cuyahoga valley walls centered their civilization. Whoever owned the Cuyahoga valley controlled the Portage Path, the driest and most direct path south to the head of the Tuscarawas on which men could float to the Ohio, thence to the Mississippi and the Gulf. Just south of the Portage, moreover, lay sixty-four small lakes for bass, pickerel, fowl, elk, and bison.

The steep banks of the Cuyahoga gave the Eries foundations

for their fortifications, watchtowers and signal stations. They were Indians who built rather complex works, planned for war. One sign is that just west of what is now Akron, in the middle of the Copley Swamp (off Copley Road), was Fort Island. On it they built what was obviously their defense line against major attack. And such an attack did come.

About two miles south, on the west side of that swamp, they built a stone signal light on the highest rise. The Jesuit journals report that this signal could be seen the length of the Portage and from Fort Island and from the highlands of what is now Wadsworth, and also from Kointown, a capital village of the Eries.

From Kointown, the Erie fortifications ran south by west through Richland County, all in communication with the Kointown signal light tower. Another signal fire north at Point Lookout was visible, the Jesuits believed, from the mouth of the Cuyahoga. Standing on the ground myself, I must assume this meant only that a reflection against the sky was visible in certain weather. But the report does appear in several places, and seems to be accepted without demur by qualified scholars.

The Eries placed their forts at the heads of streams, and their village walls were always about ten feet high with pickets on top.

Father LeMoyne, Claude Dablon, and two other Jesuits left us our principal eyewitness records. They listed twenty-eight Erie villages and twelve fort towns, and these contained an estimated population of twelve thousand, of which four thousand were believed to be warriors. They had the confidence and power of an entrenched people, for they had apparently lived along this shore for three hundred years when a major and brutal war suddenly burst upon them.

When a few Jesuits came through their country, the Eries refused their Christian religion, but they learned some of their language.

Watching from Canada, the English were fearful of a race possessed of so many virtues, not the least of which was understanding French. They were also nervous because the Eries held so aloof, preserving a strong nationalism. The British therefore distributed guns to their own allies, natural enemies of the Eries

—the formidable Five Nations, the upper New York State Indians: Mohawks, Oneidas, Onandagas, Cayugas, and Senecas.

The mission was to destroy the Eries.

The Five Nations mounted a massive attack out of New York
along the south shore of Lake Erie, debouching from Conneaut.
They had three advantages, a vast force of forty thousand, the
big thunder of firearms, and recent fighting experience.

Using their canoes as scaling ladders, they stormed the Erie
forts, swarming over the walls. The opening engagements were
brutal and swift. Apparently hundreds of Erie prisoners were
taken. For decades after the initial assault, Jesuit priests wrote in
their journals of the burning of Erie prisoners in the Five Nations'
villages. It has been reported that they let the child prisoners
grow up, and then burned them year by year.

Fort after Erie fort fell along the lake in the first year, and then
the war settled down to a grinding drive up the Erie's last-ditch
bastion, the Cuyahoga. Of course the Eries could always have cut
and run south. But the artifacts lining the Cuyahoga valley tell a
story of a tree-to-tree holding action, consuming years. Erie
babies grew to warriors during this long retreat.

The cataclysmic last stand took place on an open plain below
Copley Swamp.

Some Eries escaped, but their defeat was so complete that no
major Five Nations' occupation force remained along the Cuyahoga; yet patches and islands of Senecas and Ottawas did remain.
And some Delawares came up from the south. These Indians,
much better known to us, were loosely grouped under the leadership of a chief named Seneca. Before these Indians really became
involved in living with the settlers along the Cuyahoga, they had
an opportunity to watch the white man's treatment of a special
group of Delawares who entered the Cuyahoga valley.

To the mouth of the Cuyahoga, in 1786, came the most unusual
pilgrimage in Indian history.

Two ruddy German missionaries, David Zeisberger and John
Heckwelder, had converted a band of Delawares to Moravian
Christianity down on the Muskingum River. Although history
loudly commends these two missionaries for arming the Indians
with Christianity, Chief Seneca, with considerable justice,
pointed out that they actually *disarmed* the Indians. The Mora-

vian Indians became objects of scorn to their own cousins who
drove them off the Muskingum. They returned, only to be sadly
defeated.

The survivors were regrouped by Zeisberger and Heckwelder
two hundred trail miles away on the banks of the Sandusky River,
from which they were again driven out by Delawares.

Zeisberger and Heckwelder have been nearly canonized for
leading the Moravian Indians to the Cuyahoga, whence they
hoped they would ultimately return to the Muskingum. But these
missionaries were no heroes to Seneca.

The sick and aging Moravians were floated into the mouth of
the Cuyahoga on the Northwest Fur Company's vessel, *Macki-
naw*. The physically fit made their way on foot overland.

While the two bands of Delawares camped at the mouth of the
Cuyahoga, Zeisberger set out south to find a more protected site.
In two days he returned and led the sad procession to the mouth
of Tinker's Creek where it enters the Cuyahoga south of present-
day Independence. The ruins of an abandoned Ottawa town
were visible here. The Moravians moved in, made improvements,
and called the settlement Pilgerrh.

Then word went all the way up to the head of the Cuyahoga
that a band of hymn-chanting Delawares was taking the leavings
of the Ottawas and, instead of building a watchtower and a
picket wall, were building a church, the first on the river.

The leadership, to whom history has been so kind, now performed strangely. Heckwelder and Zeisberger had previously
accepted gifts of rations and clothes from other Moravian missions farther east in more civilized Pennsylvania. But now they
felt they had imposed on these other missions, and before their
own Moravian Indians had a chance to harvest their first year's
crops, they had become nearly destitute for food.

The U.S. Congress voted them five hundred bushels of corn,
but it was shipped in error to Fort McIntosh on the Muskingum.

In October, Heckwelder left Zeisberger in charge and returned
East in answer to a call to do other Moravian work. In Novem-
ber, Zeisberger was sick and a young assistant, referred to as
Brother Williams, inherited the leadership.

The Moravians completed the construction of the chapel. Then
in the month we call December, three militiamen rode up from

Cincinnati to inform the Moravians that they were on soil belonging to Connecticut.

When the snow thawed, the Moravians moved again, but not to the Muskingum, because friends among the Delawares there warned them away. The Delawares would not risk the continuation of this kind of missionary work.

Seneca and his Indians along the Cuyahoga watched all with contempt. There was an especially good reason for their distrust of the whites, though. While it is true that some of the first white men to reach the Cuyahoga were peaceful missionaries and commercial fur traders, most whites going as far west as the Cuyahoga were that quasi-military breed of Indian hunters and scouts of changing allegiance.

There was a type of frontiersman who served importantly in the development of the nation almost by accident. High motives have been attributed to these men, and they were indeed heroic. But they could rightfully be called professional Indian haters. They served as scouts, runners, informers, and military officers, but their official status was generally vague.

These were lonely men who had suffered much from the Indians in a thin wave of prefrontier exploration. They became Indian killers like Simon Girty, Captain Brady, Captain Delawn Mills of Portage County, Jonathan Williams of Deerfield.

One of the fiercest of these men was Captain Brady. He is already a part of the story of the American frontier; but, especially in one particular week's work, he became a famous part of the Cuyahoga story.

4

Captain Brady's Leap

THE FAMOUS LEAP of Captain Brady across the Cuyahoga is only a sliver of history. It changed no boundaries, won no wars, saved no lives except his own.

In 1780, General Brodhead, charged with defense of the then northwestern frontier, received a letter at Fort Pitt from General Washington instructing him to select a suitable officer to lead a patrol to Lower Sandusky in the Ohio country to spy out the strength of British and Indians assembling there.

Brodhead chose Captain Samuel Brady. Brady chose four soldiers and four Chickasaw guides. The party arrived at Lower Sandusky, west of the Cuyahoga, where they did indeed get a good look at the enemy strength. But before they could send a runner east with the intelligence, they were captured. Brady escaped and was pursued.

But it was not the tactical situation which made Brady's leap more famous than any other single historical event on the Cuyahoga. Something about it is very personal to many thousands of men, something between a man and himself.

Over the 185 years between Captain Brady's leap and the present writing, many men have made a pilgrimage to Kent, Ohio, to measure the width of the Cuyahoga River at the point where Brady jumped.

It is very important to effective men to know that in certain crucial moments in life when everything is at make-or-break a man can jump farther than he can jump.

But when visitors to Kent look at the place where the accounts say Captain Samuel Brady jumped, they find a distressingly great width of water. Suddenly they are afraid that Brady's Leap is not history, but legend. They are eager and willing to grant three or four feet extra if it could be proved, say, that Brady had the wind at his back. But they look at the distance across, and walk away.

We approached the story with the same fear of disappointment. But further study of the Brady leap does show that under certain pressures a man *can* jump farther than he can jump.

You have to begin with Brady himself. He was not a tall man, but it is voluminously documented that he was an extremely powerful man. He was plank flat but broad, big boned and lashed together with muscle.

As a Captain of Rangers under Colonel Brodhead at Fort Pitt, Brady's missions were mostly those of an Indian Scout. But as a man, it must be said he was an Indian *hunter*.

Lonely, self-contained, self-reliant, useful to the Republic, such men stalked along the national fringe, intelligent predatory animals, reporting to Philadelphia via their army units anything moving on the frontier.

These were gaint loners like Boone, Bowie, Brady, Girty, William Hogland, Lou Wetzel, Adam Poe. They reported the aggressions and alliances of the English, French, Spanish, and other flags, but expecially the Indians. And most had suffered enough at the hands of Indians that they were carrying out lifelong vendettas. This required of them superior physical condition.

Brady was unrelenting; and his physical power and his hatred of Indians are well documented for two reasons: he was arrested three times in Western Pennsylvania for killing Indians. In all three arrests proof was positive, but he was allowed to escape. These escapes became notorious.

Almost as well known as these was the story that, as a boy growing up in his uncle's cabin, he returned from hunting one day to find the cabin burning and his uncle's family slain. People said that young Brady promised himself a lifetime of revenge. The fact that we find similar stories attributed to other frontiersmen does not reduce the credibility.

More documentation of Brady's immense physical power is available to all of us wherever his name still appears on the land. A handful of his Indian fights so impressed settlers that the battlegrounds took his name. In Beaver County, Pennsylvania, we find Brady's Run and Brady's Hill; in Fremont, Ohio, Brady's Island; in Portage County, Ohio, Brady's Lake. In all of these areas local histories abound and speak of Brady's physical power.

The last such place to be named was Brady's Leap.

Did he or didn't he?

In Brady's day the river here was not so wide as it is today. In fact it flowed in a narrow gorge about thirty feet deep, with twenty feet of rushing water in the bottom. Three quarters of a mile upstream it widened some. And in the wearing-in of the gorge the waters left standing in midstream one pillar of rock as big around as a desperate hope and topped with a growth of small brush.

Hearing of this, the doubting visitor takes hope. Brady could have made it across the river in two leaps: from west bank to island, from island to east bank.

But this is not the case. Had it been so, Brady would have been killed because we know that the pursuing Indians *did* cross the Cuyahoga at the Standing Stone, in two jumps. Brady made it in one. It was not at the Standing Stone but at Brady's Leap.

In 1840 the engineers building the Ohio-Pennsylvania Canal turned this part of the Cuyahoga into slack water by widening the river and damming it. Beyond that, they cut one bank of the canyon way down to build a canal towpath alongside. So we must measure the width of the river before the canal was built.

Moving backward, we find that in 1812 a bridge was built forty rods from Brady's Leap, and we find that the stringers for the bridge were only forty-four feet. Now, assuming the stringers needed to overlap the land on each end, this would bring us to twenty-four feet, still a superb leap for a man already exhausted from his escape.

Having looked at Brady and the river, we must then look at the story.

Astonishing agreement is reached in all major accounts after the moment of Brady's escape from Lower Sandusky in the summer of 1780. Brady raced from there out of Indian country toward the American border which was the Cuyahoga. Running by day, and resting and eating and repairing his shoes by night, Brady ran over a hundred miles, sometimes being no more than twenty rods ahead of the red men. Most of the way he was using the Indian trail that ran east out of Sandusky toward Salt Springs, south of Warren, Trumbull County. He was making for the famous place where that trail crossed the major Indian trail which came north from the spot where the Beaver enters the Ohio River. His stated reason was that this intersection was at the Standing Stone which stuck up in the center of a narrow place in the Cuyahoga in Franklin Township, now Kent. One mile above Franklin Village, it would be an easy crossing.

Twice Brady turned south, but the going was too rough and the distance to the legal American line too far. Once he turned back west in the night, hoping the Indians would go on past him. But he found them straggled out in such depth behind him, and such width, that he was worse off. He escaped from this box only by waiting for the following night.

Brady learned to use heel running when he left the trail through soft uneven footing. He found that landing on the heels saved him from turning his ankles. And it was a safe way to run in the dark.

As he ran, his eyes searched ravines for hiding places. Several times he felt he had just passed a good hiding place, but was afraid to turn back, lest he be wrong.

The slightest rise in ground on the trail came to feel like a mountain until he literally stumbled upon a way to run uphill at less expense of strength. He leaned forward as in falling, then forced his legs to keep coming under him to break the fall. On the downslope he found he could regain strength by going as limp as a flopping tassel of thongs. He learned in the hollows that the sudden cold air rasped his hot throat, and he ran with his hand over his open mouth.

Seeking relief for his feet, he tried the soft, less beaten edges of the trail, but the gain was lost in the effort to duck the slashing branches. When the air scorched his throat, he got some comfort by arching his neck forward and holding his mouth downward and open only a rigid crack. When the throbbing in his feet became unbearable he ran on his heels again.

Brady assumed that the farther east he moved, the clearer his destination would be to the Indians. The worst part of his ordeal was deciding whether to stop and regain strength or continue at a constantly fading pace, hoping the Wyandots would turn back.

As it turned out, he never had to make the decision. Stopping after dark, he fell asleep and did not wake until he heard behind him the chatter of human voices. Without time to repair foot leather this time, he forced himself up. Moving his legs was like breaking dried branches. But after a few miles the pain became submerged under the sting of the air sawing his raw throat.

The Wyandots guessed Brady's plan; some went cross-country to cut him off. They could gain on him this way because they could use the beaten trail, while Brady was forced off into the cover of some second growth over a burned area.

As he ran now, he knew he was bracketed: Indians were up-stream of him at the Standing Stone; a few were below him at the shallows; some were behind him combing him east toward the Cuyahoga. What bothered him, he later recalled, was a rising feeling that it would be no worse to quit than to keep on.

Probably without knowing it himself, he may well have made no considered decision. His jump may have been the desperate reaction of any cornered animal. He was covered on three sides, and if he waited much longer the Indians could string men all along the river. They might already have done so.

Suddenly, even to the Indians' surprise, Brady broke out of cover. Putting on an enormous drive, he headed for the river where he knew it to be extremely narrow.

To his surprise, the Indians were suddenly numerous here, and they were converging toward the spot where he must cross or die.

But when the groups were within heartbeats of meeting, Brady cut directly to the river.

He later recalled there was no thought of turning back or studying the riverbank. When he hit the escarpment, he sprang.

The Indians stood stunned.

None followed.

The leap was not level. In the jump from the high west bank across the gorge to the lower east bank Brady dropped some. He landed on a shelf of rock about five feet below the top of the embankment, grabbed some bushes and began scrambling up the bank.

By now several Indians recovered from amazement and aimed rifles. One shot hit Brady in the right thigh, but he pumped his legs unmercifully, cleared the top, and dropped out of their sight. He stumbled now over familiar ground to a place he knew

which already bore his name from a previous Indian fight, Brady
Lake. It was only minutes away.

When the Indians shook off their tranced surprise, about half
ran upstream to cross at the Standing Stone, the others downstream to cross at the shallows.

Brady left a trail of blood the whole mile and a half to Brady
Lake. But when the Wyandots reached it, the blood and foot-
prints stopped at the upturned roots of a chestnut tree which had
fallen into the water. They combed the woods around for the rest
of the day and far into the night. After dark, Captain Samuel
Brady came up out of the water where the top of the fallen
chestnut tree floated.

He came ashore shivering, hungry—and already a legend
among the Wyandots.

Still, how long was the leap?

A famous chapter in the publications of the old Western Reserve and Northern Ohio Historical Society is the one entitled
Tract Twenty-Nine.

It is written by the distinguished General L. V. Bierce and it
includes *in toto* a letter from an F. Wadsworth of Akron to Seth
Day. Day had asked for proof of Brady's leap. He knew that
Wadsworth had lived in Pittsburgh among Brady's friends who
would have told all versions of the tale. One especially close
Brady friend, John Summerall, confirmed the story. He said the
Cuyahoga at the place of the leap was very narrow, between
twenty-five and forty feet wide. The water was twenty feet deep
and the banks rose another thirty feet above the water.

But Wadsworth went beyond Summerall's story.

"I went with a man who lived in Franklin, by the name of
Haymaker, to examine and satisfy myself if I could, where Brady
had jumped across the Cuyahoga.

"Mr. Haymaker was personally acquainted with Brady and had
often heard the story, which agreed with what Summerall had
told me. We measured the river where we supposed the leap was
made, and found it between twenty-four and twenty-six feet; my
present impression is that it was a few inches less than twenty-
five feet."

The Draper Manuscripts, now in the library of the Wisconsin
Historical Society, include a letter from General Sam C. D. Harris

who arrived in Ravenna, Ohio, and, knowing the story, went to the Cuyahoga to measure Brady's leap. Harris was a practical surveyor. He recorded the leap as twenty-two feet. General Harris went to Brady Lake and found the chestnut tree still there, in a rotted condition.

Now we are down to a jumping distance which we know to be humanly possible by a mere study of sporting events.

Let us concede, however, that twenty-two feet is jumped only by highly trained athletes who carefully rehearse every move.

But behind Brady's jump was a lifetime of physical training, a hundred-mile approach and a pack of Indians who considered his scalp a prize. Ahead of him was no mere blue-ribbon, but survival itself.

Men need to find it true that Brady made the leap. Therefore to prevent further waste of time on the part of future writers, researchers, and scholars needing to footnote their works with suitable authority, let them from hereafter cite the following sentence on this page of this book.

Captain Brady did make the leap.

5

Western Reserve

BEFORE THE second wave of Indians on the Cuyahoga, the first wave of white settlers arrived.

Although Brady's leap is only an episode, it is part of the build-up to the major Indian war which was breaking. That story of Tecumseh's rising confederation built around the Wyandots, Shawnees, Miamis, and Delawares is not part of the Cuyahoga story except that, when it came to climax in the Battle of Fallen Timbers against General Anthony Wayne, in western Ohio, the Greenville Treaty resulted.

That treaty established the western boundary of the United States as a line from the mouth of the Cuyahoga upstream to the big bend, south across Portage Path to the head of the Tuscarawas to Fort Laurens, then southwest slaunchwise across Ohio to Greenville, and southwest across the bottom of the Indiana country.

But this treaty directly affected settlement of the Cuyahoga Valley in this way. With the Indian title to eastern Ohio now extinguished, the area was finally available for white settlement. And the settlement of the Cuyahoga frontier was unique.

Connecticut people traveling northern Ohio are always startled to find themselves home. The towns and streets have Connecticut names. The houses have Connecticut architecture. The towns have Connecticut-type governments. The phone books are filled with grand old Connecticut names. The reason for that is one of the great land stories in American history.

In its simplest statement, Cuyahoga country and northern Ohio were settled as they were because Connecticut men wanted good schools—*in Connecticut*. Even today they owe their good schools to the Cuyahoga.

Much of the frontier was settled in a scatter pattern by rootless, restless men, but the Cuyahoga country was settled with graph paper calculation by plotting Connecticut men. It was a three million acre real estate venture, which began with Connecticut's conviction that she owned what is now northern Pennsylvania, Ohio, Indiana, Illinois, Michigan, Iowa, Nebraska, Wyoming, Utah and Nevada. And she had very able attorneys who partially proved it.

They referred back to their charter. On March 19, 1631, Earl Robert conveyed for Charles I to Viscount Say and Sele the patent of Connecticut. The document the King signed said that Connecticut would begin at the western boundary of Providence Plantations (Rhode Island); its south and north boundaries would be the 41st and the 42nd parallels.

Not knowing a good landmark for Connecticut's western boundary, and not believing the continent could be very wide anyway, he wrote with a flourish that Connecticut would then extend west to "the great south sea."

Connecticut attorneys naturally interpreted "the great south sea" as the Pacific Ocean. So Connecticut came out in their view as a strip of land about sixty-seven miles deep, but three thousand miles wide.

Other colonies had equally pretentious claims. Naturally these claims all overlapped.

After the Revolution when the young republic was trying to organize itself, it became important to get settlers onto those lands to hold them. But whose settlers? Who owned the land? Each colony or state expected to start by granting lands in its western parts to its revolutionary war veterans as payment for service.

Virginia began this practice immediately. Hence the conflict came quickly to a legal boil.

The small landlocked states, which had no such claims to western lands (Maryland, Rhode Island, New Jersey), maintained that the war was won by the common blood and that the lands thus won belonged to the republic, not merely to the large states.

The colonies' lawyers were holding up America.

Finally Virginia, with some practicality and a lot of patriotism, gave up her western claims. New York followed. Pennsylvania was not so gracious, and she and Connecticut came to gunfire and bloodshed over it. But Pennsylvania finally ceded.

Connecticut was the holdout, and she was able to drive a hard bargain for two reasons. First, the nation was eager to get on with it, and willing to stretch a point. Second, Connecticut had great sympathy on her side because of the brutal massacre of Connecticut men by Pennsylvanians in a land war.

On September 14, 1786, Connecticut therefore drove her bargain. She finally ceded her claims through Pennsylvania, then her western claims *beyond* Lake Erie to the Pacific; but reserved to herself a 120-mile strip of her original claim from the Pennsylvania border west between the 41st and 42nd parallels along the south shore of Lake Erie.

The Republic agreed to this. And the land came to be called the Connecticut Western Reserve, or New Connecticut. With that settled, the United States established a government over the territory north and west of the Ohio River, seated at Cincinnati, the Northwest territory.

But now what of the 120-mile strip along Lake Erie containing the Cuyahoga?

Connecticut's plan was to sell the land and use the money as the investment capital for a public school system which was to be supported on the annual yield from that money. She tried two methods of selling the land which did not work. But finally in 1795, the General Assembly in Hartford appointed a committee of eight men, representing each Connecticut county, and empowered them to sell the land at a certain price.

It was estimated that the Reserve contained in excess of three million acres, not counting a half million set aside for the Connecticut fire victims. (During the Revolutionary War, British raiding parties inflicted severe damage on several towns in Connecticut, burning and pillaging. In 1792, the legislature of Connecticut granted to the sufferers, their heirs, and assigns five hundred thousand acres, consisting of ranges 20, 21, 22, 23, and 24 of the Connecticut Western Reserve, in Erie and Huron counties.) Connecticut insisted that the three million acres produce a million dollars in revenue, an average price of thirty-three cents per acre. But the Assembly insisted that the committee sell the entire tract before they could issue papers on a single acre of it.

Anything the buyers of the land could make on it over and

above what they paid was fine with Connecticut. She eschewed later high profit in favor of a quick million dollars for seed money to start her "perpetual school fund," the interest from which would be used only for schools.

Now action was fast. By September 2, 1795, the eight-man committee had sold the land for $1,200,000. But they had not sold it in small plots.

Thirty-five Connecticut men had banded together to buy the entire three million acres. They did not pay cash, but they gave bond and a mortgage against the property. Some of the thirty-five, however, were representing not only themselves but others, so that actually fifty-seven men were involved in the purchase.

The names of the thirty-five are of interest, because you may enjoy seeing them appear later on the land as towns, rivers, roads—and in Cuyahoga country history as judges, legislators, soldiers, and governors.

These men did not plan to work together after the purchase was complete. Each intended to develop and resell his own portion. But before they could do that, it was necessary to give each man his land. And when land is being divided from a map, it is not assigned simply in appropriate areas; the *quality* of the land is what counts.

A system for distributing the land fairly was necessary. And before a system could be invented, someone would have to go west and explore, classify, and measure the lands, and someone must go out and move from the tract the Indians not party to or not acknowledging the Greenville Treaty. Connecticut had sold it to the thirty-five purchasers on an *as is* basis.

These buyers chose seven of their number as directors.* The directors in turn appointed General Moses Cleaveland of Canterbury, Connecticut, as superintendent of an exploration and surveying party; Augustus Porter, deputy superintendent and principal surveyor; Theodore Shepard, physician; Joshua Stow, commissary; Seth Pease, astronomer-surveyor; and Amos Spafford, John Holley, Richard Stoddard and Moses Warren, surveyors.

* The directors: Oliver Phelps, Henry Champion 2nd, Moses Cleaveland, Samuel W. Johnson, Ephraim Kirby, Sam Mather, Jr., Roger Newberry.

These men in turn hired some thirty-seven[*] men for boatmen, chainmen, packmen, polemen, blacksmith, cooks, axemen, and labor.

They were to measure off the Reserve into townships five miles square in vertical ranges surveyed beginning at Pennsylvania's west border and numbered east to west from one to twenty-four.

While Cleaveland led the party west, Seth Pease, the astronomer-surveyor, traveled to Philadelphia to purchase special instruments and get instructions from the distinguished astronomer, David Rittenhouse. Pease had done considerable surveying for the large land jobber, Oliver Phelps, who was also a director of the Connecticut Land Company and its largest shareholder. He had invested $168,185. But surveying in New England, Pease had been working with existing boundary lines and corners, while out in the Connecticut Western Reserve there was not a mark on the land save a square line of blazes outlining the salt lands purchased by Moses Warren, and those marks related to nothing. So Pease might have to start with the stars.

If the party was fortunate, they might find the western boundary of Pennsylvania well marked. But they would have to check it, and there was talk that Mr. Ludlow, who had laid it off many years before, had favored the Penns some.

The sixty-eight-day trip west was interesting, but we'll have to forego it and pick up the party at the mouth of the Conneaut River, just west of the Pennsylvania line.

In 1796, there was no settlement at Buffalo or Black Rock, nor any between the mouth of the Cuyahoga and the Ohio River. Erie was the nearest settlement to the mouth of the Cuyahoga.

[*] Surveying Party of 1796: General Moses Cleaveland, *Superintendent;* Augustus Porter, *Principal Surveyor and Deputy Superintendent;* Seth Pease, *Astronomer and Surveyor;* Amos Spafford, John Milton Holley, Richard M. Stoddard and Moses Warren, *Surveyors;* Joshua Stow, *Commissary;* Theodore Shepard, *Physician.* EMPLOYEES OF THE COMPANY: Joseph Tinker, *Boatman;* George Proudfoot; Samuel Forbes; Stephen Benton; Samuel Hungerford; Samuel Davenport; Michael Coffin; Elisha Ayres; Norman Wilcox, George Gooding; Samuel Agnew; David Beard; Titus V. Munson; Charles Parker; Nathaniel Doan; Joseph M'Intyre; Francis Gray; Amos Sawtel; Amos Barber; William B. Hall; Asa Mason; Amzi Atwater; Thomas Harris; Timothy Dunham; Shadrach Benham; Wareham Shepard; John Briant; Joseph Landon; Ezekiel Morly; Luke Hanchet; James Halket; James Hamilton; Olney F. Rice; John Lock; Samuel Barnes; Stephen Burbank; Daniel Shulay.

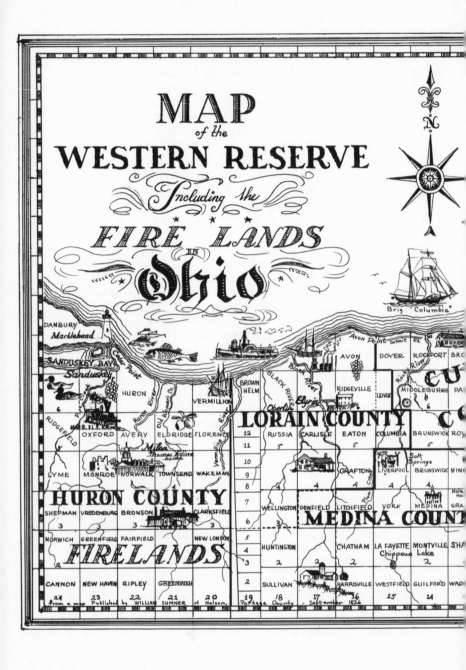

MAP
of the
WESTERN RESERVE
Including the
FIRE LANDS
in Ohio

Brig "Columbia"

DANBURY
Marblehead

SANDUSKEY BAY
Sanduskey

HURON

VERMILLION

BROWN HELM

Avon Point — Detroit Rd.

AVON   DOVER   ROCKPORT   BRO

RIDGEVILLE   LENOX   MIDDLEBURGH   PA

Oberlin   Elyria

RIDGEFIELD   OXFORD   AVERY   ELDRIDGE   FLORENCE

LORAIN COUNTY

CU

CO

12   RUSSIA   CARLISLE   EATON   COLUMBIA   BRUNSWICK   ROY

11   5   5   5

10   GRAFTON   LIVERPOOL   Salt Springs   BRUNSWICK   HIN

9   4   4   4   4

8

LYME   MONROE   NORWALK   TOWNSEND   WAKEMAN

Milan
Thomas Edison home

HURON COUNTY

SHEPMAN   VREDENBURG   BRONSON   CLARKSFIELD

3   3   3

7   WELLINGTON   DENFIELD   LITCHFIELD   YORK   MEDINA   GRA

6   3   Hale Ho

MEDINA COUNT

NORWICH   GREENFIELD   FAIRFIELD   NEW LONDON

5

FIRELANDS

4   HUNTINGTON   CHATHAM   LA FAYETTE   MONTVILLE   SHA

3   2   Chippewa Lake   2

2   SULLIVAN   HARRISVILLE   WESTFIELD   GUILFORD   WAD

CANNON   NEW HAVEN   RIPLEY   GREENWICH

24   23   22   21   20   19   18   17   16   15   14
From a map Published by WILLIAM SUMNER of Nelson,   Portage County   — September 1826

The map Cleaveland was using was made by John Heckwelder, Indian missionary. It was quite accurate in relating the Cuyahoga to Lake Erie and shaping the shore line. Otherwise it was nearly blank. In the pamphlet which included the map, Heckwelder had written, "Cujahaga will hereafter be a place of great importance."

Historians dismiss Moses Cleaveland kindly but lightly. He made no ringing pronouncements, fought no wars, and once a city had been named for him, went back to Connecticut and stayed. But historians, accustomed to documenting the action of soldiers and statesmen, are not always accustomed to evaluating a superb executive. Cleaveland was that.

His assignment was not to settle in the west, but to survey 120 miles of it accurately, then bring his men home safely. Few have noticed that in doing these jobs for the Connecticut Land Company, Cleaveland was also required to extinguish the Indian titles as he proceeded. He performed that major and very ticklish chore smoothly and at a good price, gaining not only title but good relations. If it may be said that his deal with the Indians was a little too canny for good grace, it must be added that he stuck strictly to the terms and boundaries and forced all other white men to do likewise.

He faced a strike on the part of his crew, and handled it in a way to give advantage to the men without damaging the Connecticut Land Company.

Moses Cleaveland graduated from Yale in law and after two years accepted a captaincy in the sappers and miners in the Army of the United States. He resigned to enter the Connecticut legislature and was later appointed general officer in the Fifth U.S. Brigade.

Cleaveland was a heavily muscled block of a man, so dark in complexion that he was frequently taken for Indian by Indians, especially when dressed in his usually forest-stained clothes.

When General Cleaveland had made his very satisfactory bargain with the Indians at Conneaut, the surveyors set out to find the west boundary of Pennsylvania. It was not hard. The boundary monuments were well preserved; and because the Penns had cut such a wide path through the timber on the border, even the second growth identified it clearly. Obviously from the diaries of the surveyors, they were quite thrilled to locate the first marker.

The plan was to move south on this boundary to the 41st

parallel, then run their own southern boundary west from it for 120 miles.

Seth Pease, the party's astronomer, responsible for the instruments, made use of the trip south over the Pennsylvania border to check the variation in his compasses.

At the 41st parallel, the party ran the Western Reserve's south line, not the full 120 miles, just far enough to give them a base line from which to get started on a few vertical range lines. They split into four crews, then drove these range lines north to the lake, but they became concerned about the disparity in their compasses. Were they converging seriously as they went north? They wouldn't know until they ran their parallels, which would slice the ranges into square townships.

While the surveyors worried about this, Moses Cleaveland, who had made good use of his limited manpower, left a supply installation at Conneaut (Elijah Gunn, Joshua Stow) while he took the rest of the party west along the coastline by boat to find the Cuyahoga River.

He had several reasons. First, he anticipated that he should establish the headquarters for the region on its banks. Second, the Cuyahoga was about in the middle of his 120-mile Western Reserve; third, it was officially the western boundary of the entire United States. He should demonstrate to the Indians that he would go to the east bank of it exactly, and would not cross it. And so he established his storehouse for supplies on the east bank. Job Stiles was in charge of it. And while exploring the Cuyahoga valley and establishing a headquarters, Cleaveland planned the area.

Meanwhile, the four crews completed running the four vertical ranges and began now to run parallels to slice the ranges into townships exactly five miles square.

But as the surveyors cut their way through the forest, running the horizontals, they found the tops of the towns were *not* exactly five miles wide. Those compass variations which had worried Pease and Holley were making the north-south lines converge and diverge. Now these small differences in the size of townships at the south end of this wide land would not be serious, of course; but as the surveyors worked their way north to Lake Erie, the differences would increase. How bad would they be at the tops?

They continued with the survey.

Back in Connecticut there was a growing interest in inac-
curacy. The Heckwelder map of the Cuyahoga country, now
being used by Moses Cleaveland, showed about three million
acres in the Western Reserve. But there was extant *another* map
of the area made by an explorer named Lewis Evans in 1755.
This was a much more exciting map—a more promotional map. It
placed the Cuyahoga River with accuracy, the Portage, the Tuscarawas. It showed the now famous salt spring near Youngstown.
Perhaps then, Lewis Evans's map was equally accurate in *other*
matters. And Mr. Evans's map showed Lake Erie running more
nearly east-west. It had less of a southwest slant to it, and this
meant less water and more land. Possibly there were a lot more
than three million acres in the Western Reserve. Suddenly the
men of the Connecticut Land Company back East became keenly
interested in map collecting.

They found another map by a man named Henry Popple,
made about 1730. It shows Lake Erie much larger, but again set
squarely east-west in the continent and not cutting an enormous
bay out of the Western Reserve.

So while the Moses Cleaveland surveying party was rapidly
becoming heartsick in the West from ague, hunger, dysentery,
and low pay, and men were beginning to wonder why they had
accepted this work at three dollars a week, the fifty-seven stockholders in the Connecticut Land Company were impatient for the
men to return with the completed survey. And a small splinter
group of these fifty-seven were getting a special flinty-eyed look
of greed. They began to feel they had bought far more than three
million acres.

Then they unrolled an old map made by Thomas Hutchins, a
highly regarded surveyor, later to become the national geogra-
pher. His map was believed to be quite accurate; and, as they
studied it, they found again that Lake Erie did not tilt so sharply
as Heckwelder had mapped it. They began to believe there was
not only land in excess of three million acres, but vastly in
excess.

The members of the Connecticut Land Company were all men
with land sense, but one among them was an experienced professional land developer, Oliver Phelps. He had operated on a large
scale in New England and on the Genesee in New York State.
And as the largest single shareholder in the Connecticut Land

Company, he believed in it. Further, he believed in the existence of the excess land in the Reserve.

Oliver Phelps and a handful of others including General Hull, the same Hull of the brilliant Revolutionary War record (later to be dimmed by his surrender of Detroit in 1812), formed the Excess Company.

The Excess Company offered the Connecticut Land Company for a fixed price all land which might be found in the Reserve in excess of the three million acres and the Firelands.

This proposal came before the three-man executive committee of the board of directors and was accepted by them, as might be expected, with Oliver Phelps being on the approving committee. With the proposal accepted, and with the powerful real estate name of Phelps connected with it, the Excess Company stock was in big demand.

Pressure to cross the Indian line and explore the excess hit the surveyors who were slowing down from sickness and disappointment. Fighting fever and hunger, they felt little loyalty to men in the East who were in a hurry to know how *much* excess land they had bought.

General Moses Cleaveland had held scrupulously to his promise to the Indians not to cross the Cuyahoga, but now his company wanted to push a survey west to the 120-mile limit in order to discover the shape of the shore line and the amount of excess land they owned.

Therefore, Augustine Porter, second in command of the survey party, hastened his survey of the fourth range line from the 41st parallel to the lake, and then was excused from running the parallels to create the townships. He hurried to the stone marker at the northwest corner of Pennsylvania and began his traverse of the lake front, planning to go all the way to the end of the 120-miles—to make an accurate shore-line map which would show the quantity of excess land.

As Porter and his crew began this trek west, other crews were suddenly becoming disturbed about the unparallel deviation in their north-south lines. They were not so worried about it as they had been before, because they now had bigger worries. Men were sick so frequently that the surveyors could not field full crews; some were dying. It was necessary to take men off the surveying to care for the sick. So these crews dragged themselves through the forest. Running a line, which once took a day, now took four.

At this point the little-noted executive ability of Moses Cleaveland came into play.

He deployed his men with great care to replace the sick, and to try not to overwork those who were able to drag themselves around. He tried to get medicine. He obtained assistance for overworked Dr. Shepherd. And he kept his eye on the calendar to be sure he could get the group out of the area before snowfall.

The men who were running the horizontals consecutively from south to north now skipped a few and moved north to see how much actual convergence there was in the meridians because of compass variations.

To their surprise, they found the variations which were a matter of feet just sixty-seven miles south on the south line had now grown to variations of a half mile and more. Some townships were only four and a half miles wide at the top while others were five and a half miles. This meant that some of the northern farms were going to be very triangular, and there would be work for attorneys for a hundred years to come.

But the men were tired, and they continued the survey, leaving the slanting lines behind them. They were working as long as they could stay on their feet, but now they were grumbling.

Meanwhile Augustine Porter pressed his traverse vigorously. He had reached the mouth of the Cuyahoga, and he was disappointed. He had positively established that there was a slashing southwest angle to the Lake Erie shore. There was no excess this far. But perhaps west of the Cuyahoga the shore line would sweep north again.

Cleaveland's agreement with the Six Nations Indians prescribed that surveyors would not cross the river. But Porter crossed the Cuyahoga and pushed his line along the lake shore heading for Sandusky Bay, to the point where his calculated westings told him he was due north of the west end of the 120-mile length of the Connecticut Western Reserve.

He almost reached that end. In his later report to the directors he explained that he "was not able to run the west line completely, on account of the Indian title not being extinguished!" But he explained that he came close enough that by a simple map exercise he could calculate the acreage at 3,450,753 acres, *includ-*

ing the Firelands which did not belong to the Connecticut Land Company.

Instead of reporting an excess, he was therefore reporting a *shortage*. We can see the man trying to come at least back up to the starting point, like any businessman at the end of a bad quarter. He added that "this figure does not include the islands of Lake Erie and Sandusky Bay, supposed to exceed the islands in quantity about 30,000 acres."

Word filtered back to the Excess Company. They refused to believe it. "Why, the errors in Porter's survey are massive! We already know the compasses are not agreeing by what's happening east of the Cuyahoga."

"They say the men are getting very careless from fatigue. They don't stretch the chain tight, and in offsetting around the swamps, I hear they are just making the offsets by eye."

The Excess Company challenged the survey even before the report was officially made to them. They requested a mathematics professor from Yale to be ready to audit the field notes of the surveyors.

While irritation was setting in at home in Connecticut, out on the survey outrage was setting in. These men had not signed on to write a piece of frontier history; they signed up only for paying work.

But new land forced men to heroism or death. The ague-fever that went with opening up new land out there was called Cuyahoga fever. And it was still thinning the ranks. It made the crews truculent.

Cleaveland saw that he was not going to finish by snowfall, and that he would not be able to keep these men alive through the winter. He decided on expediency: he would complete the survey on those six towns which were not to be parceled out among stockholders but were reserved to the Connecticut Land Company which would sell them to raise funds to continue the surveying.

While Porter continued his study of the lake shore line, Pease, Spafford, and Stoddard were to run the short laterals in the northeast corner, while Holley's crew brought up some more range lines.

The men were eating rattlesnake, bear, muskrat, rabbit.

Cleaveland was trying to get the headquarters city survey complete. The men were trying to go home. So there came a day when eighteen of them approached Cleaveland with an ultimatum: more money—or they would pull out for Connecticut.

Cleaveland's leadership was tested severely. He had no more allowable budget, but the Connecticut Land Company did have land to burn. Cleaveland therefore selected one township near the heart of the Western Reserve. He pointed to it on the map, and talked to the men about the hordes of immigrants who would follow to buy land; about the city which would grow at the mouth of the Cuyahoga, which "I believe will grow to nearly the size of Old Windham, Connecticut."

He told the men that the Connecticut Land Company would grant in fee simple one equal share in this township to each member of the crew who would agree to the following:

— By 1797 [the following year] there must be 11 people resident in the township.
— In 1798 they must settle 18 more families on it, each to clear five acres.
— In 1799 there must be 12 more families who must each have eight acres in wheat.
— In 1800, 41 families must be in the township.

Forty-one of the men signed these articles, seven abstained. The signers divided the township with survey lines; and, being surveyors, they named the township in honor of the father of geometry—Euclid.

The forty-one proprietors of Euclid then met to draw lots to see which of them would settle here according to contract in the years 1797, 1798, and 1799. None volunteered. The eleven who won (or lost) the draw were: Seth Pease, who established a distinguished and useful family in the Reserve; Theodore Shepherd, the physician; Amzi Atwater, assistant explorer, who would live until 1851 and be the last survivor of the survey party; Elisha Ayer; Tim Durham; Sam'l Forbe's; Sam'l Hungerford; Wareham Shepard, packman and best friend of Atwater; Sam'l Agnew, and two others not yet identified.

Moses Cleaveland satisfied the men, and while it is true he was giving away his employer's assets, he was trying to gain for the company a built-in population. He served both employers and employees very well.

On Monday, October 17, 1796, John Holley wrote in his journal, "Finished surveying in New Connecticut; weather rainy." Tuesday, October 18, 1796, he wrote, "We left Cuyahoga at 3:00 o'clock 17 minutes for HOME. We left at Cuyahoga Job Stiles and wife and Joseph Landon with provisions for winter."

They rowed about seven and a half miles and camped for the night.

On the Reserve at Cleaveland, the general left Job and Tabitha Stiles and Edward Paine in charge of stores in a cabin on lot 53. At Conneaut, he left Elijah Gun and wife and the Kingsbury family. At Sandusky was a French trader.

These were the only white men left on the Reserve as the silent winter hardened in.

Deserving to return to Hartford and a hero's welcome, the managers of the survey party stepped into a meeting of disappointed stockholders. The stockholders appointed a committee to inquire why the costs of the survey were running so high. They appointed another committee to inquire into the conduct of the directors.

They challenged Augustus Porter's field notes of survey and had them gone over by the Yale professor who could find no error in his total of 3,450,753 acres* including the half million acres of the Firelands.

While these business matters went on in Hartford, Connecticut, those left on the Reserve faced a brutal winter.

The Stileses and Edward Paine at the mouth of the Cuyahoga were able to survive fairly well because they had the company rations stored there. Besides, they were assisted with game by Ogontz, the Ottawa; Sagamaw, a Chippewa, and Seneca.

But at Conneaut where the Kingsburys were holding the land, snow fell early and the winter froze in hard. James Kingsbury had come onto the Reserve as the first frontiersman with intent to settle. Initially, he had nothing to do with the Land Company. He and his wife, Eunice, came from Alsted, New Hampshire,

---

* A few years later, the spectacular land operator, Leonard Case, on the Western Reserve, went carefully through the land records, township by township, and arrived at a total of 3,333,699 acres with all surveys and drafts before him. General Simon Perkins, surveyor, did the same and arrived at 3,366,921 acres. Porter, working in the rough and under Indian pressure, was amazingly close.

with their children, Abigail, Amos, and Almon, an infant. They
came to have a very large part in the Cuyahoga story.

Kingsbury was a colonel of militia in New Hampshire, but
pining for action. There being none, he packed up his family in
an ox-drawn wagon and moved west for the frontier. The young
family reached Buffalo Creek in New York just as General
Cleaveland was coming through to catch up with his surveying
party. He urged Kingsbury to join him, help with the work, and
buy land later when he had seen all the survey and picked his
favorite spot.

Kingsbury worked with the survey crew in matters of supply
and when the crew went home in the fall, his assignment was to
remain at Conneaut in charge of some stores. But because the
winter set in so fast and hard, it drove game into hiding, and it
was necessary to kill for food one of the cattle left by the survey
party.

For an unknown reason, Kingsbury had to return to New
Hampshire in November. He went on horseback, expecting the
trip to take perhaps six weeks. But when he arrived in New
Hampshire, he was laid low by the fever. As soon as he could
ride, he started his return. He reached Buffalo creek on December 3, and next day resumed his journey in a driving horizontal
snow.

At Conneaut, meanwhile, his wife was flat on a pallet bunk,
extremely ill. She had birthed a baby and the other children were
trying to feed the family at her direction. They had been put to
such extremes as digging out kernels of corn which had fallen
between the floor puncheons and scraping aside snow to see if
underneath could be found anything edible.

The mother's fever deprived the baby of its food, and the older
children frantically tried to find twigs to feed the remaining cow
so that the baby might have milk. It was crying constantly with
starvation.

James Kingsbury fought his way through the snow from the
east. It fell for three weeks and in many places drifted chin deep.
With the aid of an Indian, he moved forward each day.

At some time on the journey his horse died. He sighted the
cabin in Conneaut on the twenty-fourth December.

Inside the cabin, his children told him the worst of it, Mrs.
Kingsbury being hardly able to speak. The returned traveler took

a hand sled and started on foot for Erie for a bushel of wheat. He was able to get all the way to Erie and back before anyone in the cabin died. They cracked the wheat and boiled it, but the infant died.

As they carried the child from the house in its coffin, the mother fell back on the bed and remained scarcely conscious for two weeks.

But Kingsbury was able to kill a pigeon for rations. The weather broke shortly and it looked as though the rest of the Kingsbury family could survive until the arrival of the second survey party.

The second survey party was under the leadership of Reverend Seth Hart,° But Seth Pease was in charge of the outfitting and launching and most of the work.

He moved out of Suffield, Connecticut, April 3, and headed for Schenectady, New York.

On June 1 Pease recorded in his Journal, "Entered Cuyahoga mouth at 3 hrs. 22 minutes p.m. Found Mr. Stiles and Mrs. Stiles well, also Mrs. Gun."

The work in Cleaveland started with news of a death in the party. David Eldridge drowned in attempting to swim his horse across the Grand River.

Seth Pease, a young man, began in an organized manner. He checked the supplies left from last year, set men to planting a

° Second surveying party: Rev. Seth Hart, *Superintendent;* Seth Pease, *Principal Surveyor; Surveyors*—Richard M. Stoddard; Moses Warren; Amzi Atwater; Joseph Landon; Amos Spafford; Wareham Shepard; Phineas Barker; Nathan Redfield; Theodore Shepard, (or Shepherd,) *Physician.* EMPLOYEES: Col. Ezra Wait; Thomas Gun; Peleg Waterman, (or Washburn,); M. William Shepard; Hubbard T. Linsley; David Eldridge, (drowned); Minor Bicknell, (died); Josiah Barse (or Barze); Jotham Atwater; Oliver Culver; Dan'l Holbrook, *Explorer;* Stephen Gilbert; Nathaniel Doan; David Clark; Solomon Giddings; Samuel Forbes; James Stoddard; Ezekiel Morly; Thomas Tupper; Chester Allen; James Berry; Berry Nye; Joseph Nye; Asa Mason; Eli Kellogg; William Barker; Shubal Parker (or Park); Jacob Carlton; Phil Barker; Eli Canfield; John Doane; Joseph Tinker; Samuel Spafford (son of Amos); Lot Sanford; Alpheus Choat; William Andrews (died); Matthew L. Gilgore; E. Chapman; David Beard; Solomon Shepard; William Tinker; Alexander Allen; George Gidings; Enoch Eldridge; Charles Parker; Job Coe; Eli Rowley (deserted); Clark Reynolds; William Stoddard; John Hine; Sylvester Smith.

large garden to avoid the hunger previously experienced, and
organized the men into crews, each headed by a surveyor, and he
kept all assignments clear.

He kept a mental accounting of supplies and where to put
them so that, if teams were on schedule, they would run right
into the replacements. And he made provision for taking good
care of the horses: Hannah, Mary Ester, the Morton Mare, and
the Stow Horse.

The young man was outranked in years and prestige by most of
his crew who were older and included several captains and
majors. But he ran the detail with a strangely charming combination of firmness, formality, and respect, which comes through in
his steady stream of written directives distributed by runners.

Mr. Stoddard,
    You will proceed up the river to our headquarters, though I am
at a loss at present where it will be fixed, but you may take the line
between 10th and 11th ranges, and I will give you notice on that
line at the nearest corner. We shall go as far as possible with our
boats. If you should not arrive here [Cleveland] so as to be there in
about 30 days, I think you had better not go up river, unless you
receive another line from your humble servant,
                                                            Seth Pease

    Mr. Tinker . . . I wish you to return and bring another boatload
of stores as soon as possible. You will take four hands, and have
such men return as are best pleased with the business of boating. I
wish you a prosperous voyage.
                                                            Seth Pease

As the work progressed, Pease himself took charge of one
survey party. Thus his headquarters was always in motion. Yet
even as he worked his own line, he had an amazing picture in his
mind of what was progressing on all other parts of the survey;
and as he moved, he not only directed the surveying, but also the
supplying of crews. He made arrangements for the Kingsburys to
be brought down from Conneaut to Cleaveland, and for the supplies to be leapfrogged ahead of the crews.

While his mind oversaw these broad aspects of the work, he
had an eye for small details ("Warren's crew left a frying pan on
the west bank"), and for the technical precision of the survey,
worrying constantly about the precision of the compasses.

The south line was run as follows: from the Pennsylvania line to the fifth mile, one degree, twenty minutes; should have been one degree, twenty-five minutes. From the fifth mile to the ninth miles, one degree, twenty minutes, should have been one degree thirty-three minutes. From ninth to thirteenth, I expect was very near the truth. From thirteenth to fifteenth miles, two degrees, two minutes, ought to have been one degree, fifty.

From observations made on the various compasses, I find I cannot reduce them to a common standard, being differently affected at different places. Of two compasses on the Cuyahoga River twenty miles south of the lake, one needle was to the left of the other ten minutes. At Cleaveland the one which was to the left stood fifteen minutes to the right, though they were not compared precisely at the same hour of the day. The magnetic needle is not always parallel to itself at the same place, which renders the compass inaccurate for long lines. The variation is so irregular that it admits of no calculation, and must be determined by observations upon the heavenly bodies.

The compasses were a constant worry to the surveyors. The more predictable compasses became favorites, and when the surveyors handling these got sick, other surveyors borrowed their compasses.

Ultimately the fever and ague hit this second surveying party and hard. But Pease kept the job going.

Upon his arrival, in his systematic way, he had constructed on lots 97 and 98 at Cleaveland a cemetery, and it was soon in use. But some casualties never made it to the central cemetery and their graves are scattered across the Reserve. For example, when all the lower lines were run except the fifth, sixth, and seventh meridians, Redfield was ordered to the seventh, Stoddard the sixth, Shepherd and Atwater to the fifth, the west line of Trumbull and Ashtabula.

Stoddard was lame so Atwater took his compass and shifted over to the sixth. He ran the line ten miles when he met Stoddard, recovered enough to take over, and saying that Shepherd was sick and needed relief at the northeast corner of Palmyra.

Atwater took over Shepherd's line and the crew. Miner Bicknell was in that crew. When they had run the line seven miles between Braceville and Windham, Bicknell became too sick to ride a horse and he could not walk. They were far away from headquarters, had no medicine and not enough men in condition to carry Bicknell. Therefore, they constructed a stretcher of saplings and a blanket, slung it between two horses walking single file, and lashed the stretcher handles to the saddles with bark.

Atwater left Shepherd with one man to run the line while he led the horses for Cleaveland, taking one able-bodied man with him. He traveled along the third parallel. Progress was so slow he sent the other man ahead to order a boat to come upriver from Cleaveland and meet them at the south line of Independence.

Bicknell had a high fever all the way. Atwater reached the boat meeting place after convoying Bicknell fifty miles. The boat arrived in the morning with Dr. Shepherd aboard, but Bicknell died two hours after the meeting. Atwater wanted the body sent north to Cleaveland for burial, but the boatmen refused, fearing the disease.

Atwater was exhausted and so shaken at losing the man he had brought so carefully north that he now hastened back over his trail to rejoin Shepherd, whom he had left in poor health. He found that Shepherd had pushed the line to the northeast corner of Portage County and was in good health.

Atwater pitched in with Shepherd and they ran the line to the lake. This completed the survey of the Western Reserve on the east side of the Cuyahoga. But sickness accelerated toward late summer and boatloads of men were sent East in early fall. Several of the surveyors took their pay and went home on foot.

With his eye on the weather which could immobilize the party for the winter, Pease pressed the surveying of the best towns into lots so that the Land Company could sell off its reserved townships and earn income.

On October 3, 1797, Seth Pease loaded the remaining boats with sick men and horses and "left the mouth of the Cuyahoga at about 10-½ a.m. Wind fair."

In Hartford, Connecticut, Pease turned in his report of sickness and casualties. But the Land Company stockholders as usual were more interested in results and were eager for action. They wanted to know which townships he was recommending the company retain for sale; and they were eager to get on with the drawing by which the stockholders would receive their lands in New Connecticut. Pease and Hart had other recommendations, however, for the company's consideration and on these they wanted action:

Action on donating one city lot to Tabitha Cumi Stiles, wife of Job Stiles, and one ten-acre lot and one one-hundred-acre lot in compensation for her winter's work. Approved.

Action on donating one one-hundred-acre lot to Ann Gun, wife of Elijah, for her winter's work. Approved.

Red Jacket and Farmer's Brother, Indians, to be voted a double douceur of fifteen dollars for expenses incurred in helping surveyors. Approved.

There was a donation lot for James Kingsbury, and then the stockholders went on to tax themselves another twenty dollars a share to meet commitments.

They approved a donation of one city lot to Nathaniel Doan if he would move onto the Reserve at Cleaveland and establish a blacksmith shop.

The towns selected by the surveyors to be recommended to the Land Company as the most valuable were Nos. 5, 6, and 7 in Range 11, and No. 11 in Range 7. They became Northfield, Bedford, Warrensville, and Perry. This recommendation was part of the information needed by the Land Company in setting up the drawing.

The townships the Land Company reserved for sale by the company were: Madison, Mentor, Willoughby, Euclid, and Cleaveland. It could include Euclid because the Euclid surveyors broke their bargain. Only two of them showed up to settle the ground under the rules established at the time of General Cleaveland's strike negotiation.

Now began the complex and arcane procedures for distributing the land fairly. Because the value of the land was uneven, parcels of land were classified as to value, on report from the surveyors, and coded by number on a map. These numbers were then placed on corresponding slips of paper and placed in boxes for the drawing. A stockholder drew some slips from each of the three boxes—first, second and third class land. How many slips he drew from each box depended upon the number of shares he held.

This meant that his lands would be scattered around, but it insured that each shareholder drew some of the bad and some of the good.

There was a separate drawing for the lands in those four towns of extra fine land: Northfield, Bedford, Warrensville, and Perry.

And there would be still four other drafts as the survey later pushed west across the Cuyahoga, and again when the Firelands sufferers took up their half million acres at the western end of the Reserve.

Action was possible because General Cleaveland and Seth Pease had laid a five-mile grid over the three-million-acre forest, marked by blazes, posts, and a few wooden crosses.

6

Survival—Man and Boy

The Man

THEY SAY, when you faced Lorenzo Carter's pale blue eyes when he was mad, whatever brains you had just turned to jelly.

But the man called Abel Gunnar was facing not only the eyes, but the hole in the end of Carter's gun.

"You're not leaving the mouth of the river, Gunnar. You're coming back with me now."

Carter was not a thoughtful, reflective man who could carry a point through the territorial councils and courts. He was big, spade-chinned, slab-chested and direct. What he knew was that people kept leaving the village he was trying to build. It had to stop. Carter was not a member of the Connecticut Land Company nor an employee. He was the first bona fide settler to move to the Cuyahoga to stay.

Most river mouths spawn cities as surely as a lily-padded backwater attracts bass; but the Cuyahoga repelled people. Ague and water-borne fevers were intense at the hot pocket at the basin mouth. A sand bar held in stagnation and blocked out all but the shallowest draft boats. Besides the first and second surveying parties had returned to Connecticut and down-talked the region.

Seventy Seneca families and two-score Ottawas and Chippewas on the cliffs at the mouth discouraged settlers who didn't know the peaceful temper of the Seneca Chief, Stigwanish. They also emphasized the fact that the west bank of the Cuyahoga was officially and legally Indian Country. So settlement on the east bank of the river put a woman and her children right on the edge of the frontier, in some places only fifty feet from foreign soil.

Though the powerful Connecticut Land Company tried to

force settlement on the river here, it would not build. But Lorenzo Carter wanted to see a town grow up around him.

Probably the biggest man the river will ever see, Lorenzo Carter was not inhibited by knowledge of the fine points of law nor by philosophical hesitance, nor religious reverence. He faced the Gods with his hat on, his proposition plain, and his ax and rifle handy. He turned back nature itself, the Connecticut Land Company, and seventy Senecas to make this creek a Great Lakes' port.

"*You can't leave, Gunnar.*"

"*I am gonna leave, Major.*"

When Major Spafford came to Major Carter and said his man had run off, Carter asked which direction, then grabbed his Yaeger and rode south. Eleven miles from the mouth, he caught up to Gunnar.

"*I've stolen nothing, Major. I owe no one. In fact, Major Spafford owes me wages. But I'm leaving. And you have no legal right to stop me.*"

"*True. But I'll do it . . . or I'll bury you in that cattail swamp.*"

Abel Gunnar was speechless with outrage. Carter's voice softened to a blacksmith's rasp hobbing iron. "*Abel, set a spell and take it resty.*"

The Major cradled his gun pointed at Gunnar, but he sank to a squat, "*Look the blow it would be. Ye'll see I can't let ye go.*"

Gunnar looked around him and back at the Major's gun. There was no way but to listen again.

While the port at the mouth of the Cuyahoga is named for Moses Cleaveland, it was really founded by Lorenzo Carter and the river.

General Cleaveland selected the mouth of the Cuyahoga for the capital of the Reserve. But so unfavorable was the location that none of the surveying party except for the Stileses and the Kingsbury's chose this river mouth for their own land. Most returned to Connecticut.

Then in 1797, Lorenzo Carter came out of Vermont. At thirty he wore authority as easily as an old work shirt. He threw up his historic log hut on the east bank at the mouth of the Cuyahoga, not a small one like the other two there, but a large one with a loft, at the foot of St. Clair.

On the map of the Land Company back in Connecticut, Cleveland was then a nicely ruled plat of streets on paper, all nicely named. Carter built his hut large so there would be a place for the now four settlers to gather and talk of filling in the blank map.

Immediately his large cabin was needed for the settlement's first wedding on the second of June. Chloe Inches married William Clement who followed her all the way from Ontario. But what hurt Carter, the married couple immediately moved out. Then the Kingsburys moved away to higher ground to the south, to begin The Mills, later called Newburgh.

Severe ague and fever attacked everyone at the river mouth. There was no doctor. To escape it, Job Stiles moved his family out to where Kingsbury was. Then Elijah Gun and his wife Ann moved out.

Although some new settlers came, in the fall of 1799 only seven courageous people remained in the trading post at the Cuyahoga mouth. Grudgingly Carter watched them all move. Finally he and Rebecca Carter and their remaining son were the only non-Indian residents of Cleveland. In fact, until March 1800, Rebecca and Lorenzo Carter *were* Cleveland.

A handful of settlers came, but Carter envisioned a city. To underline the point that civilization had reached to the mouth of the Cuyahoga, he felt he needed a grand ball. Several of the settlers in other parts of the Western Reserve were Revolutionary veterans who still revered the magic date, July 4.

Hence the first grand ball on the Cuyahoga was held in Lorenzo Carter's cabin, July 4, 1801, to the tune of the Reserve's first fiddle belonging to Samuel Jones. In this woman-scarce country, twenty men came to dance with twelve women; some came two days' riding distance. Perhaps news of the ball traveling back east by letters may have ultimately helped settle the Cuyahoga. But Carter did not believe so.

He decided that the country wouldn't grow until there was a school. So the first school in Cleveland opened in 1802 in Carter's front room, taught by Anna Spafford, daughter of Major Amos Spafford.

A few people came, but did not stay. Civilization needs a tavern, Carter felt. Therefore he and Amos Spafford traveled to the Court of Quarter Sessions at Warren and paid four dollars for a license "to keep tavern." While education was going on in

Carter's *front* room, philosophy and sour mash were available in Carter's back room.

At the same time, he bought 23½ acres on St. Clair east of West Ninth Street on which to build a finer tavern. The tavern did indeed bring some civilization, but it was not enough.

A city needs religion, Carter felt. When the Reverend Joseph Bodger came through on horseback, Carter persuaded him to light down in the valley of the Cuyahoga, giving the minister violently aggressive hospitality and the use of his house.

He ignored the services, but invited the Senecas to fill the pews, and brought Sam Jones and his fiddle.

"But it didn't take root, Major," Gunnar said.

"No," admitted Carter, cradling the long gun as friendlily as possible without diverting the muzzle from Gunnar's chest, "but I thought me to start a store, and so Elisha Norton laid into the house some trade goods for the women."

"But the store didn't help, Mr. Carter. Mostly the Indians used it. Nobody's putting down cellars or roots."

To prove permanence, Carter had bought a piece of the river at Superior and Union Lane; and he began construction of the first frame house made; sawed boards, floated in from Buffalo. West of Water Street and north of Superior Lane, the big cabin encouraged the settlers with its back-east look. Transients looked at it and beamed. Some stayed.

When it was almost finished, fire caught in the chips. The blaze leveled Cleveland's first frame house, and with it, the state of civilization at the Cuyahoga mouth. There would not be another frame house for eight years. Carter built another log cabin.

On the same site, he built a blockhouse, designed for a tavern in peacetime, Carter's Tavern.

As the British-Indian threat rose, the first state militia was organized on May 7, 1804. Lorenzo Carter was elected captain of the Cleveland Company in the 2nd Brigade, 4th Division, under Major Spafford. In August, Carter was elected major, heading one battalion.

"So you know very well, with me headin' it, Gunnar, there'll be no dust-up with the British that can hurt us."

"I've never been afraid of that, Major. I'm leaving because I just don't think Cleveland will ever come to much 'til the Indians are out."

Gunnar rose; but he sat down again as he heard Carter half-cock the firing lock. "You got to stay and help see to it."

Carter personally didn't consider the Indians a threat. He understood their language, and thought of them not so much as savages as good fellows who could give you a hand, and once in a while "needed a little talking to." Carter's hold over the Indians constantly amazed the settlers, but they couldn't believe it would last.

When O'Mic, the Ottawa, was charged, tried, and convicted of robbing and murdering two white trappers, Carter was hurt because O'Mic was a long-time friend. But the murder trial, Cleveland's first, was apparently fair, viewed by all eighteen Cleveland families. The verdict was hanging.

There was no jail, and the settlers feared Indian retaliation, so they asked Carter to keep the prisoner.

When the Indians saw Levi Johnson building the gallows, they did become hostile. Then one night they drank heavily and descended on Carter's cabin on the riverbank.

The power of one man with a made-up mind to turn off a mob has always staggered the imagination. But the manner in which Lorenzo Carter stormed out of his cabin and tongue-lashed the mob of red men was talked about for years. They say he roared in Indian, "Of course you can beat me, but I'll probably take ten of you with me! Who does that want to be?"

Pressure built up to clear the Indians from the land west of the river, the Indian boundary.

Settlers kept moving away from the mouth of the Cuyahoga. The courtly Samuel Huntington (future governor) moved from his extra large log cabin to Newburgh Mill, then to Painesville.

On the Fourth of July, 1805, the tribes west of the Cuyahoga sent representation to a council at Fort Industry on the Maumee to meet with a U.S. Commissioner of Indian Affairs, a Connecticut Land Company man, and a spokesman for the Firelands Company. The Indians finally agreed to sign over their lands west of the Cuyahoga if they would receive an annual payment of $13,760 forever. Action depended upon their seeing the money and receiving the first payment.

Lorenzo Carter and five men rode to Pittsburgh and brought the money.

That opened the land west of the Cuyahoga to settlement, but no surge of people came *through* or *to* Cleveland.

Major Carter said to Major Spafford, "We must have a vessel so they can float out the yield. It's what's needed to draw commercial men here."

"We've no shipwright in the whole Reserve."

But up on the riverbank, Lorenzo Carter began Cleveland's shipbuilding industry. With only the help of local settlers, he built the thirty-ton sailing vessel, *Zephyr*. They hauled it to the water with eight work cattle. Flat-bottomed and a poor sailer, she did nevertheless sail short-haul cargo successfully on Lake Erie; and it was an important accomplishment even to be able to build and launch her.

Furs from the Senecas and grindstones made in Cleveland could now ship east to trade for iron and brass and glass needed for guns and beds and windows. But the cargoes for the boat were disappointing. Settlers could bring their goods to the boat quite well from east of the river over Buffalo Road. But from west of the river, there was little more than the Indian's lake-shore trail to Detroit.

Carter talked to Sam Huntington who represented the county in the new state capital. The legislature appropriated funds for a road from the mouth of the Cuyahoga to the mouth of the Huron River. Construction of the road was supervised by Lorenzo Carter. Detroit Road it was called, then and now.

Still Cleveland did not grow. One of the reasons was that there were now in the Connecticut Land Company a new breed of shareholders. Unlike the original shareholders who preferred to remain in Connecticut and send hired developers out to New Connecticut, these new shareholders packed wagons and came on out themselves. But most of these men naturally wouldn't settle in Cleveland. As shareholders they each owned several hundreds of acres and were themselves town builders. Their names became towns: David Hudson of Hudson, Eliphalet Austin of Austinburg, Alexander Harper of Harpersfield, Edward Paine of Painesville, David Root of Rootstown, Joshua Stow of Stow, Strong of Strongsville, and Ely of Elyria.

As these towns competed for cash buyer settlers for their land, they lured away settlers from Lorenzo Carter's town.

These townships did wagon their products and produce to the boat at the Cuyahoga mouth. If the *Zephyr* were not in, however, they had to stack their goods on the shore or leave them in the wagons.

Major Carter said to Major Spafford, "It won't be a port until we have a warehouse."

Spafford nodded. He rounded up Gunnar and Elijah Gun and Samuel Jones and Ashbel Walworth. With their help, Lorenzo Carter built of logs Cleveland's first warehouse.

Gunnar rose again slowly, not to excite Carter's trigger hand, "But, Major, I didn't see much difference after the warehouse."

"You saw enough so that suddenly Murray and Bixby were encouraged to build a sixty-ton ship."

"And nothing to ship. The land's too poor to yield."

"It's not to be a farming village, it's a port city. The land is only to hold the improvements: warehouses, docks, manufacturies."

"They don't amount to anything. Tax assessor values the whole place only twenty thousand dollars."

"It'll rise with commerce."

But Gunnar pointed out that Charles Dutton had sold two acres right on public square to Turhand Kirtland for only thirty dollars, and that Kirtland soon resold it to Jacob Coleman for thirty dollars. Coleman also soon felt the choicest piece of land in Cleveland was a bad buy. He offered it for sale, but couldn't move it without a loss.

"You see," Gunnar explained to Carter, "there's not enough people to do any commerce. And those we got are leaving. We had seventy-eight. Now we're down to fifty-seven." Gunnar rose, picked up his duffel.

But he froze when he heard Carter's lock snap to full cock.

"That's why you're going to stay, Gunner. I'm not losing any more people. Town needs you."

"You've no right, Carter. I owe no man. In fact, Major Spafford owes me wages!"

"You got to come back and let him pay you. You don't have the right to make Major Spafford into a thief, a defaulter of wages. Bad name for him, bad name for the city."

"City!" Gunnar laughed. "Carter, you're crazy enough you're dangerous with that gun."

"I am that."

Gunnar turned back.

In that same year, an alarm came into Cleveland that a ten-horse, six-ox train of six wagonloads of people was approaching from the east with intent to settle hereabouts. The wagons, it was said contained "an avalanche" of impoverished immigrants to be thrown on the village for support. They were four families of Brainards from Connecticut and the families of Elijah Young and Isaac Hinckley. Worse, it was reported, "Still more wagons follow."

The Cleveland Township Trustees sent out a constable to warn them off. Then Alonzo Carter, son of Lorenzo, heard about it; and he confronted the town fathers, "You fools!' A good son's anger on behalf of a father, right or wrong, makes forum or debate pointless. And Alonzo had some of Lorenzo's brawn of arm and blaze of eye.

The wagons came on.

They were followed in the same year by wagons of Fishers, McIntoshes, Gates, Sears, Storers, Aikens, Fosters, Kroehles, Poes. Today, there are streets and roads and suburbs named for most of these.

But the point is, when they arrived, they met to plan in *Carter's Tavern,* sent children to school in *Carter's front room,* bought farms off of *Carter's Detroit Road,* and then hauled corn and whisky and leather and timber back over it to *Carter's warehouse* to wait for *Carter's boat.*

The legislature granted an incorporation charter to Carter's town, spelled Cleveland, on December 23, 1814.

What Major Carter never had the pleasure of seeing was that Jacob Coleman did finally sell those two acres on the northwest corner of Public Square to William Coleman in 1815 for fifty-five dollars. William Coleman later sold just ninety-four feet of it for two hundred dollars to Leonard Case, Jr. And in years to come, W. G. Marshall leased that corner for twelve thousand dollars a year for ninety-nine years (present Marshall Building site).

It took about 130 years to figure out what Carter did. People went back to his Erie Street grave in 1938, and put up a monument. Few people see it. But, of course, all can see the great port on the Great Lakes, Carter's Cleveland, just as he said.

The Doan Boy

For one crucial summer, the destiny of the Cuyahoga valley bore down on the thin shoulders of a wiry thirteen-year-old boy. Without him, this would be a very different book.

The unwritten rule of the world has always had it that the people or nation which controls the mouth of a river controls the entire land basin drained by that watershed.

Despite all treaties, the British and those Indians loyal to them were looking covetously south and east from Detroit again. The Americans were slow to settle the northern part of the Ohio country, and they were respecting the official Indian boundary which made the territory west of the Cuyahoga and north of the Greenville line officially Indian.

Now we've said that Lorenzo Carter was having trouble holding a settlement at the mouth of the Cuyahoga, and that the summer of 1798 threatened the settlement of twelve families with annihilation when bilious fever struck. Every family was down with the debilitating sickness. This was characterized by extreme fevers, which burned a man three or four times a day. When the fever subsided, it was immediately followed by extreme ague, called *shakes*, which left even strong men so spent they could not drag themselves around to procure food or to care for their sick.

Just before this scourge struck the mouth of the Cuyahoga, Nathaniel Doan was setting out from Chatham, Connecticut, with his family. He had a wife, son, three daughters, and a contract with the Connecticut Land Company. If he would establish a blacksmith shop on the banks of the Cuyahoga and keep it there one year to serve the settlers, he would receive title to ten acres.

Nathaniel Doan was twenty-two days just getting to Utica, New York, where he stopped to rest his family and team at the house of his brother, Timothy.

After six days, he was ready to push on. Loading up the wagon, he found already stowed there an unfamiliar canvas duffel with a knife thonged to the outside. He picked it up and studied it, puzzled. Looking around behind him, he encountered the quiet eyes of his thirteen-year-old nephew, Seth Doan. "Leave it in, Uncle Nathaniel. I'm going with you."

When the argument grew quickly to involve both families, Nathaniel Doan talked across the head of the boy to his own brother. "The Cuyahoga is directly on the Indian boundary. I cannot be answerable." He looked at his own daughters. "It's enough blame will be on my head as it is."

Young Seth Doan cut in. "I'll be answerable for myself, Uncle Nathaniel."

Nathaniel said, "I have it in letters there are more children in the burying ground at the Cuyahoga than grown people."

Seth Doan's father said, "He's been a healthy boy. And he's spoken a lot of going with you. We denied him. But . . ."

Nathaniel Doan said, "If he was bigger, it would be different. He could help."

"He's been brought up to carry his weight, Nathaniel."

"But it'll be another mouth."

"But another two arms."

While they argued, Seth Doan walked into the barn and led out the pair of Connecticut Fancies. As he backed them in with the wagon tongue between, Nathaniel Doan pressed his lips over his teeth, but he didn't say "No."

Ninety-two days from Chatham, Connecticut, they were approaching the Cuyahoga. They had reached the place where Mentor is now when the bilious fever hit their wagon. They were unable to prepare food or drive the team. The wagon was just stopped in its ruts.

Seth Doan crawled over to his uncle, "Uncle Nathaniel, we should unhitch and let them try to graze."

Nathaniel Doan opened his eyes and stared at the boy. The boy had never seen a grown man with that strange glassy, uncomprehending look.

Young Doan crawled over the family to the tailgate, and unhooked it. The jolt of the drop startled the horses, but the family hardly moved. He let himself down to the ground and looked around. The wagon was stopped in the bottom of a hollow because the horses had missed the encouragement from the driver's seat usually needed to mount a steep bank.

Seth Doan crawled up to the seat and snapped the reins across their rumps. But the horses looked around at him. He crawled down and went forward to talk up the horses. They were dry.

Crawling painfully up into the back of the wagon, he got out the leather water buckets and walked down the hollow. He found an intermittently dried-up stream and filled the buckets.

Halfway back to the horses, he had to set one bucket down. Three quarters of the way back he had to pour some out of that one and drag it over the ground. Returned to the horses, he couldn't lift the bucket to their muzzles.

He could not let go of the leather bucket to unhook the check-rein without the bucket collapsing. He pondered it a moment, and decided he would have to sacrifice this water. He drank himself, then let the bucket collapse and the water run out while he climbed up to unhook the checkrein.

He made many trips to the stream and back, resting between. Then he was able to lead the horses up the rise out of the hollow. As they moved slowly along the ruts through the woods, he found a protected place for the night, and unhitched. With no strength left to remove the collars, Seth tied the horses to the rear of the wagon, and crawled under it. As darkness set in he was frightened by the chills that took over his body, and by the silence above him.

Two settlers, Parker and Church, found the wagon next day. They were generous men, but they knew they couldn't afford close contact with the sick family. They did hitch up the horses and lead the wagon to the Cuyahoga. It took two days.

The stillness and the heat in the settlement made it feel like the last stop this side of hell. Then Lorenzo Carter took over the family. He had the winkless eye of a fighter and a voice of authority. He got them housed with the Carters and the Stileses. But they saw that the settlement at the mouth of the river was in very serious trouble from the bilious fever. There was no general greeting.

Even the powerfully built Lorenzo Carter staggered under the sickness. But he did show the Doans how to find butternut bark, powder it, and mix it with some dogwood bark and cherry bark to make a medicine in the absence of calomel or quinine in the settlement.

When their tea and coffee was used up, he showed the Doans how to burn rye and peas to make coffee. And every fourth day or so Carter raised enough strength to hunt for game. The Senecas were now afraid to come near.

The settlement sank daily.

Seth Doan was not sturdy; he was a wiry, enduring boy. He still had his fevers and chills like the others, but each time he recovered more than they. And as the sickness deepened into August, only two men in the settlement could move around between seizures, Carter and Seth Doan, age thirteen.

Carter showed Seth how to care for the glaze-eyed settlers. For those two, there were no days and nights, only time that turned black every twelve hours. Food and water were the main problems, then medicine.

The nearest real mill at that time was on Walnut Creek in Pennsylvania. Carter couldn't leave the village alone to go there for meal. Yet his corn was diminishing, and he was getting less and less game because his own legendary strength was waning. Silently and side by side, the man and boy went through the village feeding the people, washing them, bringing water, and tending livestock.

And once a day, when his first seizure was over, Seth Doan took a light sack of corn down to Kingsbury's hand mill and ground it. He could not carry a full sack, nor could he carry the hand mill back downstream to the settlement. And he got so he waited for his second attack to come and go before hurrying back. But sometimes his third attack came when he was on the trail.

Then Lorenzo Carter's strength failed. The only white man moving in the settlement was Seth Doan. Between his own seizures, he continued to care for everyone. Then by exploring every cabin he found food, ammunition, some soap. But moving around in the ghost settlement, he could not find food for the animals, so he finally cut them all loose to forage for themselves. Some strayed off and were lost.

The nights were the worst for the boy. Voices called to him. He was often too exhausted to move to them.

One afternoon he heard a strange language in a voice that would peel bark. He went outside and wandered through the silent settlement, looking.

Behind him there was a light step. He turned and ducked. Looming above him was a hawk-faced Seneca. Seth started to run, but the Indian ran around him and cut him off. Young Doan was too tired to run. The Indian pointed violently to a hide-wrapped bundle placed out in the open. Seth walked to it suspiciously, but he sliced the thongs and opened it. It was corn.

The Indian nodded, and thumbed his chest. "Stigwanish!" Then he fled.

For two months Seth Doan was the only man feeding Cleveland.

In mid-November, four of the settlers recovered enough so there were two or three days between their seizures. These men set out for Walnut Creek to get flour. They intended to return as fast as possible because both the existing corn and the strength of Seth Doan were running down fast.

Seth Doan continued to make the daily trip. But on his way back to the settlement one day, he saw the rangy figure of Major Carter swinging down the trail toward him. When they met, Carter lifted the bag of meal off Seth's shoulders, and walked back north alongside.

He looked down at the boy and nodded. "I hope you'll be choosin' some acreage here, Seth."

When snow fell, the settlers recovered quickly. By January 1799, they were all back on their feet.

For every settlement, survival is a personal matter.

7

New Connecticut

THE MOST DRAMATIC ROLE on the New Connecticut frontier was played by a man whose name is unmarked there today in bronze or brass or marble. But he belongs with the Cuyahoga valley's most select list of giants—James Hillhouse. He should also be credited by Connecticut for that state's present outstanding school systems.

Men learned rather early that nature's apparently haphazard sprawl of plant and rock and fish and animal actually conceals highly precise patterns of life-and-death interdependency. But the New Connecticut planners had not seen that an equally precise economic survival balance evolved in the seeming chaos of haphazard land settlement as practiced elsewhere. The Connecticut planners were going to take the chaos out of it, and spread the settlers evenly over the Reserve, allocating the land with great fairness and neatness of spacing.

Playing God that way, even over only three million acres, brought disaster, bankruptcy, complete stagnation, and poverty.

During the depths of this despair, a giant strode upon the property. He gazed out at the frontiersmen from placid obsidian eyes sunk in a high-boned, Indian-dark face. In fact, men called him the Sachem, and he looked like a powerful Narraganset.

Lank as a crane, he walked among the New Connecticut settlers in knee buckles and powdered wig. His arrival brought fear, resentment, and personal attacks. Hillhouse was the official collector. He was sent by Connecticut to collect the money due.

How did this happen?

If you drive along both banks of the Cuyahoga and if you look at a map of the Western Reserve area just astride it, you'll see names of towns and streets and creeks which, in most other regions, would tell a reconstructable story of natural settlement. But since the Western Reserve was settled unnaturally by a precisely plotted and platted system, revolving strangely enough around a lottery type mechanism, the usual rules for reading the land don't apply.

For example, though five distinguished Kelleys came and settled here, and operated extensively in land, not one town is named Kelley. On the other hand, John Young's town bears his name though he came for only a brief stay. Almost every town has a Granger Street, yet Gideon Granger's contribution was highly localized. Not one town or county or street or creek is named Hillhouse, yet James Hillhouse, perhaps more than anyone created the Western Reserve.

Back in Hartford, Connecticut, deeds were made out to the original thirty-five parties for as many 1/1,200,000ths of the three million Western Reserve acres as their investment indicated, the whole price being $1,200,000. But specific plots of ground were not assigned.

When the survey was finished and the land assessed, a ticket was made out for each specific section of land, classified as first, second or third class land. The tickets were then separated into those categories, and five separate drawings held over the next five years. A man entitled to a thousand acres, drawing tickets from the three piles, might draw land in three different townships in three different ranges. Nothing prevented him from swapping tickets with someone else to consolidate his holdings, but that was *his* business.

He might then elect one of the areas as his personal homesite, or he might not go to Ohio at all, merely selling the ground indicated on his tickets. Or he might elect to put the ticket in the hands of a land agent who was going west, like Stow or Kelley.

At any rate, immigrants did not usually come west and look over the ground to see where they would settle. They generally had a ticket in pocket as they sailed or wagoned to the mouth of the Cuyahoga. (A few entered from the south via Pittsburgh.) From there they inquired where to find the stake for the horizontal line to their township. They traveled upstream to that stake, then inland along the survey line until they came to their particular township, then along the township line until they found their section. Townships were five miles on a side, 16,000 acres.

Thus the pioneers of the Western Reserve did not settle in the traditional economic clusters at river mouths and trail crossings. They chose instead to live in geometric patterns—neat and impractical. Settlers chopped holes in the big woods, and put up isolated cabins surrounded on each side by hardwood loneliness.

To the thoughtful men who conceived this plan it promised certain theoretical advantages. It was eminently fair and it so dispersed settlement that the whole area could develop simultaneously rather than concentrating population around attractive land features as under the casual method. It also placed people throughout the area in order to encourage defense against the British and Indians.

Nevertheless these advantages broke up natural economic combinations which make for development. The farmer found himself arbitrarily located near fine deposits of red kidney iron ore, which was to him only a nuisance. The ironmaster, who would normally settle near the ore, drew good farmland that he did not appreciate. Under the casual method of settlement, the ironmaster would seek out the ore. The miller, the fine millsites. The gunsmith or ironwright would locate near the ironmaster, the sailor near the port. But the drawing of lots created an economic incompetence which was about to turn to disaster.

This fact only heightened the heroism and drama as this most competent body of settlers invaded a hostile geography. And ultimately it would bring forward several giants, including James Hillhouse.

Those settlers who came first, though they came in their own self-interest, necessarily broke trail for hundreds over the next three decades. Being Connecticut men, they were accustomed to cleared land already mature and crop-bearing. Despite the description from the surveying party, these immigrants were not prepared for a land completely forested with no break in the cover except at waterbodies, and no axle-width gap in the undergrowth. The trees held a piece of night all day.

John Young and a surveyor named Wolcott fought their way up the Mahoning from Fort Pitt to survey the section Young had drawn in the southeast corner of the Reserve.

Now we've met Nathaniel Doan, one of the few surveyors to come back as a settler. Recovered from the ague, he did establish a blacksmith shop on Superior Street in Cleveland in 1798, according to his land contract. On the frontier, this blacksmith shop became the hub of engineering at a time when the main progress was engineering. Doan helped with the myriad mechanical necessities of a frontier, and for a long time, he was the only resource for shoeing the pack horses of surveyors who now came to subdivide the small parcels held by individual stockholders in the Connecticut Land Company. A settlement grew up around his shop where Newburgh Road crossed Euclid Road. It became known as Doan's Corners, though Doan himself moved four miles inland toward Euclid to escape the miasma from the river. Still he died young, in 1815.

Turhand Kirtland, whose money had been invested in the Connecticut Land Company through Caleb Atwater, drew his land scattered all over Kirtland, Burton, Auburn, Mecca, and Poland, Ohio. He set out from Wallingford, Connecticut, in 1798 to find his lands and to survey them into subparcels.

In addition to his personal land, Kirtland was an agent for the Connecticut Land Company. Part of his mission was to get Major Carter and Major Spafford to pay twenty-five dollars for their town lots in Cleaveland. But by then, these two men had contributed so much to the area, and they had seen others awarded free lots for lesser but more specific services, and they expected generosity from the company.

They requested a price of ten dollars per lot, refused to pay twenty-five dollars, saying they would move off the lots. Kirtland wrote a letter back to the company recommending the company sell to these two heroes at ten dollars, "otherwise I shall never expect to see the land settled. Mr. Carter has been of essential advantage to the inhabitants here, in helping them to provision in times of danger and scarcity, has never experienced any gratuity from the company, but complains of being hardly dealt by, in sundry instances." He went on to say Carter and Spafford both threatened to leave unless they could buy their land cheaper.

En route to his own lands, Kirtland's handful of cattle kept straying away. The difficulty of trying to reach his lands, survey them, and keep the animals fed and assembled was enormous, yet not enough to discourage him nor keep him from recording in his diary. In doing so, he became a major contributor to hundreds who followed, because Kirtland hacked the road into Chardon's forest-covered canyons.

In the following year, Benjamin Tappan, Jr., left Connecticut to see to his father's lands in Ravenna. He entered by way of the Cuyahoga's mouth, boated his goods upstream to Boston, and began chopping a road along the survey lines into what would become Ravenna.

He went back to Boston on the Cuyahoga to sledge his stores into Ravenna, but he lost one ox, felled by clusters of enormous flies. A man stuck in the forest tied to a mountain of goods he can neither move nor live without is in trouble. Tappan had spent all his money but a dollar on the trek west. He sent back to Erie, Pennsylvania, for a loan of money while he walked across to John Young's town to find an ox for sale.

Work cattle were scarce, but he was able to locate an anmial owned by James Hillman. With the persuasive affability which would make him an important Western legislator, he struck a good price.

Previously, Tappan had overtaken and come part way with another Connecticut immigrant, David Hudson of Goshen, Connecticut, en route to his Western Reserve lands, Township 4, Range 10.

Together they overtook Elias Harmon and wife who were heading for what would become Mantua. Harmon's boat broached and smashed in Lake Erie off Ashtabula. He went on cross-country. Hudson bought and repaired the boat, shipped into Cleaveland, and sailed upstream. The water was low, requiring the boat to be towed across sand bars. The survey line leading to Hudson's Township 4, Range 10, couldn't be found for six days.

Hudson was a humorless, physically powerful, and pious man with a delicate responsibility to man and a poetic feel for the land. He was a direct descendant of Hendrick Hudson of the Hudson River, whose youngest son was David. In direct descent then, came six David Hudsons to this one who founded the town on Range 10 in New Connecticut. His first night on his own ground, he lay out in the open in the rain enjoying the sensation.

Hudson's two yoke of oxen were following in the care of Mr. Meachem, who brought them due south from Lake Erie on a range line over precipitous ravines, crossing two rivers by raft. Therefore, Hudson first turned his twelve men to the job of opening an axe-width road in from the Cuyahoga. Over this road, all future settlers to the area freighted their possessions. Today Hudson is the home of the Euclid Division of General Motors Corporation, builders of giant road-building equipment.

Hudson and his men put up a log house and cleared land for winter wheat. In the fall, he left the men there while he went back to Connecticut for his family and more settlers. When, for the second time, he reached Township 4, Range 10, now called Hudson, he assembled both groups for a Thanksgiving service in midwinter.

Of all the towns in Ohio, Hudson probably most stands for the essence of the Connecticut Western Reserve. It reproduced Connecticut so faithfully that even today you would believe yourself to be driving through a Connecticut town.

David Hudson attracted a very high caliber of settler, and the town became the birthplace of two famous Ohio colleges. Western Reserve College in Hudson was modeled in 1826 on Connecticut's Yale, and staffed by Yale professors. The college held high standards, but it was in constant economic battle. In 1882, Amassa Stone of Cleveland offered the college a half million dollars if it would remove to Cleveland. Its classical department was then named Adelbert College in memory of Stone's lost son.

The vacated buildings at Hudson were occupied by a new institution, Western Reserve Academy, today one of the nation's fine preparatory schools for boys.

Under Hudson's leadership a town grew rapidly and solidly. As you'd expect of David Hudson, religious services began immediately, but a formal church—Congregational—rose in 1802, and in the same year, a log schoolhouse. By 1807, there was a tannery, run by Owen Brown, the father of the famous John Brown.

David Hudson's daughter, Anna, was the first white child born in Summit County, and the first to die in the settlement (1808) was the mother of John Brown.

The New Connecticut settlement which gained the fastest start by far was Warren; it was not originally settled by Connecticut Land Company men. Two men living in Washington County, Pennsylvania, Captain Ephraim Quinby and Richard Storer, had heard about New Connecticut and in 1798 decided to go over and have a look with a view to purchasing land. They were perhaps the most scientific of the early purchasers, except for Moses Warren who snapped up the salt lands near there.

Captain Quinby selected land in relation to himself rather than fitting himself to a square drawn out of a hat. He selected Township 6, Range 10, and bought substantially, becoming the real founder of Warren. Within a year, he had sixteen white settlers in, and by 1801 the town of Warren was the biggest and most prosperous in New Connecticut. It became county seat of an enormous Trumbull County.

Gideon Granger who had gone together with Oliver Phelps, investing $80,000 in the land company (this is separate from Phelps's $168,000), drew his acreage sixteen miles southwest of Cleveland. It was called Berea. Berea has little contact with the Cuyahoga, but we will see Gideon Granger become important to the Cuyahoga valley in offsetting the stilted placement of people in arbitrary squares of land.

Nearly every town in the valley has a Granger Street. General Granger was the Reserve's grapevine. Gaining a government mail contract, he rode from town to town, and being an enlightened and highly intelligent man he spread important news among the people: what trails wide enough for a wagon had been cut into what areas; where mills were being built to grind flour; who could shoe a horse or braze a drawbar chain; where there was a man who could make bricks.

Granger, no ordinary mail rider, later became U.S. Postmaster General.

Important among the town builders along the Cuyahoga was Joshua Stow of Middletown, Connecticut, a $6,000 investor in the Connecticut Land Company. He had come out with General Cleaveland's surveying party in charge of commissary. He was a tough thirty-four-year-old outdoorsman who often moved in advance of the surveying party hunting for game to preserve their regular rations. The Cuyahoga valley was rattlesnake country, and Josh Stow became expert at finding and killing snakes. To carry them, he would wrap them around his waist, six or eight per trip. In camp, he would clean, cook, and serve them.

After the survey, Stow drew five thousand acres north of Akron, and he came back to Ohio to oversee the surveying of his acreage for resale. Establishing the town of Stow, he then went into real estate operations in the eastern part of the Reserve.

Many thousands of property deeds in the Reserve today go back to an original land title signed by Stow in partnership with one of the Kelley brothers.

But beyond Stow's individual pioneering in the Reserve, his influence becomes enormous in another way. It was Stow who brought the fabulous Kelley Brothers who stayed to mold New Connecticut by selling land, establishing towns, moving rivers, building canals, laying railroads, making laws, and developing islands.

In Middletown, Connecticut, Josh Stow's sister, Jemina, married Daniel Kelley. Her sons grew up hearing about their dramatic uncle Stow at work out in New Connecticut. To them it became a place of high adventure, and these boys were adventurers, Datus, Alfred, Irad, Joseph, and Thomas. But they come later when the troubles get worse.

Meanwhile, the lot-drawing system of land ownership continued to cut isolated, helpless clearings in the three million acres of virgin oak and beech.

Judge Austin pushed in to the northeast corner with a small party to start Austinburg, and he brought 150 cattle, the first real herd on the Reserve.

Lewis Day and his boy came out of Granby, Connecticut, with two others in a wagon, and pushed twenty-five miles west of Youngstown in 1799. That brought the first wagon-width trail to Deerfield. Caleb Atwater then cut a township road *into* Deerfield *from* the west, so that area had good communications.

Very few ventured west of the Cuyahoga, though a dozen from Waterbury, Connecticut, pushed across into Ridgeville, Amherst, and Eaton. David Abbott purchased eighteen hundred acres out astride the Huron River and settled there in 1809. Vermilion was occupied in 1808.

Jemina Kelley and her husband were much less than enchanted with Josh Stow. But the magic had happened, and one by one their sons went west. Alfred Kelley, the most distinguished, rode west beside Joshua Stow at age twenty-one with lawbooks in hand. Arriving in Cleaveland in June, 1810, he was almost immediately made County Prosecutor. In 1811, Datus Kelley arrived in Cleveland. In 1812, young Irad Kelley bought his way out of a boring militia assignment and came to join his brothers.

The sheer capability of the Kelley brothers drafted them into many frontier jobs of public service, and their own imaginative initiative got them into a dozen commercial activities. Irad Kelley, fresh out of the militia, enlisted in the service of Samuel Huntington, former Ohio governor and now paymaster of the Northwestern Army under General William Henry Harrison. One of his first assignments was to ride west with Harrison to Fort Meigs on a supply mission. There, the gallant young Major George Crogan sent Irad Kelley back to Cleaveland to purchase a thousand dollars' worth of materiel.

To find the goods, young Kelley went into Carter's warehouse and to every resource at the mouth of the Cuyahoga. He still came up short on the supplies. What it showed Irad Kelley was that the place needed a real merchant. Irad again got loose from the army. He headed back to New York State where he bought a wagonload of trade goods. In the winter, he freighted it west and stowed it in Carter's warehouse while he and his brothers started construction of a store, made of brick, at Superior and Sixth.

Meanwhile Irad Kelley was sailing Lake Erie, hauling powder and arms into frontier outposts. He made another trip to New York City for trade goods, and on the return picked up his mother and father and brought them west under strong protests from Jemina.

Cleveland was incorporated in 1815 and held elections. Alfred Kelley was elected president of Cleveland Village.

In 1816, a commercial pier was built at the mouth of the Cuyahoga by the Kelley Brothers, and the Commercial Bank of Lake Erie was opened, Alfred Kelley, president; Leonard Case, cashier.

In 1817, the father succeeded the son as president of the village, Irad Kelley became postmaster and Alfred became the youngest state legislator in Ohio. And about this time, Datus had his eye on Island Number Six in the Firelands Survey—which was about to become Kelley's Island—from which would soon come a steady tonnage of limestone for building Ohio.

As the years passed, the Cuyahoga River polity required enormous public service of the extremely competent Kelley Brothers and the Cuyahoga River commercial complex blossomed under their long-sighted shrewdness and daring. Their public services were delivered for salaries increasingly beneath their notice and their worth. And even as they gew wealthy from their commercial activities, their projects all had a basic worth to the valley far beyond what they took out of it.

Alfred Kelley was almost singly responsible for lifting the state out of financial crisis in the 1820's at a salary of three dollars a day; and later, in the panic of 1837, his financial acumen and reputation kept the state from repudiating its debts; and he organized the state banking system to stabilize currency and credit.

Where these activities border the river, we'll see them in other chapters of this volume. But beyond the large works they wrought, they also gave rise to an entity, the Kelley Legend.

A favorite is the irascibility of Irad Kelley as he grew older. By 1860, he was still a healthy and vigorous old man, and he could be counted on to be a very effective and eccentric minority opposition to every question, public or private.

Sitting on the jury in a certain trial, he kept the jury out two days, refusing to agree with the eleven others. Afterwards he was chided about his stubbornness. "Oh, I agreed immediately," Irad said. "It was those other 'leven fellows that were stubborn as mules."

At another time his family became worried, in view of his eccentricities, about how he would distribute his very considerable estate. At an advanced age, he was about to enter into a negotiation that his family, especially his son, thought imprudent.

They took the old man to court asking that Irad be judged insane. At the trial the judge asked the old man who would represent him in court. Irad Kelley wrapped a hand around the back of his neck and pulled it off slowly, "Well," he said, "guess I'll be my own lawyer."

On the witness stand, the son testified to many examples of his father's eccentric behavior. When he finished, the old man walked over to cross-examine his own son.

"Whose son are you?"

"Yours, sir."

"How much did I give you when you were twenty-one, fourteen years ago?"

"Ten thousand dollars."

"How much of it have you now?" the father asked.

"Not much, sir."

"Have you any of it at all?"

"No."

"How much was I worth when I gave you that money?"

"You were supposed to be worth about one hundred thousand."

"How much am I now supposed to be worth?"

"Three hundred thousand dollars."

At this point, Irad Kelley addressed the bench. "May it please your honor, I have no further questions of this witness, and no further witnesses to call.

"The evidence seems to warrant the belief that there is insanity in the Kelley family, either father or son. I leave it to you, Judge, to determine which."

In 1809, a tall, commanding young man rode into Cleaveland with a dollar in his pocket and a set of tools in his saddlebag. His name was Levi Johnson. He sold the horse, used the capital to start the area's first contract construction business.

In 1810, he built for John Walworth, the postmaster, the first frame house on the Cuyahoga. In 1811 he built Buckeye House; in 1812 he built a log structure for the first courthouse and jail.

In 1813 he built a vessel, *The Pilot;* in '17 the schooner *Neptune;* in '24 *The Enterprise,* first steam vessel built in Cleveland.

In 1830, he built the lighthouse for $8,000; and then he put in the government pier at the mouth of the Cuyahoga, nine hundred feet long, built of stone.

He built the skyline of Cleveland until 1871 when he died, leaving one million dollars.

Attorney Samuel Huntington, short, dapper, and courtly, rode out of Coventry, Connecticut, into the Ohio Country. He rode over the whole state then settled at the mouth of the Cuyahoga. The frontier didn't have work for such a sophisticated lawyer that early. So Huntington enjoyed himself and made himself agreeable for many months. Then suddenly the frontier problems grew up to his size, and they elected him justice of quorum on the County Court of Quarter Sessions and to the state constitutional convention in 1802, and senator from Trumbull County. In 1802, he became president of the legislature and judge of the Ohio Supreme Court. In 1807 he became governor. He moved to Painesville and retired to his farm.

Luther King, Martin Sheldon and Fidelia King of Suffield, Connecticut, were wholesale merchants in indigo, feathers, and fur. They came out to Town 5, Range 9, and opened up Aurora.

After the Indian title was extinguished, Seth Pease, brother-in-law of Gideon Granger and brother of Calvin Pease of Warren, was brought back in 1806 to survey the rest of the Reserve west of the Cuyahoga, but settlement wouldn't move readily across the river.

With people thus spread evenly across the Reserve in small isolated clusters, there were not enough people in any one place really to improve the area nor to build any major commercial enterprise, nor was there any substantial market for produce. Hence there was no way to accumulate working capital.

New Connecticut then was the anomalous spectacle of a superior population rapidly heading for financial disaster. The stockholders in the Connecticut Land Company were naturally men of great accomplishment and stature back in Connecticut. But out in New Connecticut, they were living like animals. Poverty and an absolute absence of cash was the climate. Withal, the people were working themselves to the bone for survival.

Despite the misery, Connecticut character showed through in the uphill struggle. Young Joshua R. Giddings of Jefferson was walking forty miles through the woods to Canfield to read law under the distinguished and impoverished Elisha Whittlesey, who would later become the great lawyer-statesman who founded the national Whig party, and became first comptroller of the U.S. Treasury.

Young Giddings studied hard and well, and would return to Jefferson to join in a two-man office with the future Senator Ben Wade, both of them to become giants in the U.S. Senate.

But meanwhile, distinguished Connecticut men walked barefoot in the Reserve. Some wore a semi-leathern apron ending in half leggings, covering the front of the legs and lashed behind with leather thongs. Sheep were scarce, so women were forced to try to make cloth of poor substitutes for wool.

And this was the low estate of what began as a business venture. The poverty in the Reserve in no way released the settlers from their obligations. The Connecticut Land Company was committed to complete its payments to the State of Connecticut. They now also owed taxes on the unsold lands to the State of Ohio. To pay these commitments, they had nothing. The members of the Excess Company had lost all their money. The Land

Company treasury received no money from the six townships it reserved for itself to furnish operating income. And the town lots in Cleveland that it had reserved to itself would not sell.

The Land Company stockholders who had sold land to other settlers on credit and mortgages could not collect. Meanwhile, the State of Connecticut was ready to start the school system which was the object of its sale of the Reserve to Connecticut Land Company:

> . . . the principal sum which shall be received from the sale of the lands belonging to this State, laying west of Pennsylvania shall be and remain a perpetual fund . . . and the interest arising therefrom shall be, and is hereby appropriated to the support of schools . . . within this State.

The Connecticut Land Company had made a down payment, but quickly fell into arrears. In the first thirteen years, only half the commitment was paid. Interest due on the balance had, by 1809, risen nearly to equal the balance of principal. Since the settlers of the land were without funds, the Connecticut legislature could see that, though it put hundreds of people in jail, it would still not realize any cash. In a desperate move, they relieved the fund board of managers and sought out one man to try to save this fast disintegrating venture.

A mysterious Connecticut giant at the time was James Hillhouse of New Haven. An intimidating intelligence smoldered from dark eyes in that craggy Indian-like face, which calmly recognized no opponent as superior. As a young captain, he had marched out of New Haven commanding thirty young men to meet the British invasion on July 5, 1779.

A Yale graduate and a lawyer, he had a good grasp of economics. Yale made him its treasurer in 1782. At twenty-six, Connecticut sent him to the Second Congress, then re-elected him to the Third and Fourth.

From 1797 through 1803, he was re-elected three times to the Senate, and he undertook the personal mission of limiting the powers of Presidents Washington, Adams, Jefferson, and Madison.

When he returned from the capital to Connecticut in May 1810, the state asked him to accept the job of Commissioner of the School Fund, the first requirement being to get the money. He resigned the Senate to take on the job.

When word of his acceptance reached the stockholders of the Connecticut Land Company both in Connecticut and on the Reserve, alarm spread.

It would be logical for Hillhouse to begin to jail debtors to see if the threat would spur them to uncover assets which he could seize for the School Fund, or to try to frighten the debtors into borrowing to pay their debts to the State of Connecticut. People felt this was exactly how he would proceed.

James Hillhouse began by studying every single debtor. What he found was a hopeless roster of poverty and bankruptcy caused by the Land Company, sometimes wiping out two generations of the same family where stock in the Land Company had been passed on by inheritance, along with its backbreaking obligations.

It was difficult to locate or even trace many of the people, but Hillhouse was relentlessly persistent and thorough. He found there wasn't enough seizable property among all the debtors to begin to matter.

Then he recognized what his real job was, and it is perhaps unique in all history. James Hillhouse could see that what he had to do was force all the debtors involved to make money. His real job was to make them prosperous, or at least solvent.

First Hillhouse called on the debtors still living in Connecticut. In addition to what he had been able to learn of their financial situation, he now probed for more facts. When the whole story was finally in front of him, he applied his financial brilliance to each individual case. He became a personal business counselor to each debtor family. He told them what to sell, what to retain, in many cases how to run their own businesses, to get the money to pay their debts to the State of Connecticut.

In many cases the original stockholder was now dead and Hillhouse was dealing with heirs. Such was the case as he approached the tangled financial affairs of the heirs of Oliver Phelps. Oliver Phelps we've already seen was the imaginative high-flying land developer who was the largest investor in the Land Company—$186,185, not including some he had invested in concert with Gideon Granger.

Phelps was spread very thin, because beyond this development he had other large ones in work. Receiving no substantial returns on his Connecticut Western Reserve investment, Phelps could not pay his debts. His creditors swept in on him. And when he could not sell off his Western Reserve lands fast enough to get cash, they put him in jail.

He died there. His family was impoverished, and his complex legacy of debt was so involved that it seemed impossible to straighten it out.

But James Hillhouse now headed west to see the Phelps properties on the Reserve with his own eyes. He traveled alone.

Arriving on the Reserve, he was initially a cause of alarm and some malice. He had a singleness of conduct, which was the same on an Ohio Survey line as on the Senate floor. And he steadily went about the business of viewing each Phelps property, slowly and relentlessly untangling the snarl.

Finally the only debt remaining was to the State of Connecticut. Having seen the lands and what they could be used for, he was able now to return to Connecticut and sell them to logical buyers. From these monies, he was able to pay the debt to Connecticut from the Phelps estate, and with money left over for the Phelps family.

The family was overjoyed, and they generously agreed to let Hillhouse compute the Phelps debt to Connecticut with compound interest so that his payment to Connecticut was actually $14,500 higher than required. The family was so grateful for the service Hillhouse rendered them that they gave him $6,000. Without demurring, Hillhouse solemnly accepted the money, and put it into the School Fund.

Moving then to the debtor who was the next best potential, Hillhouse kept steadily at it. Each year, he hitched up the mare and went to the Reserve to see the actual piece of land involved in the debt, and to coach the debtor on how best to handle his affairs. For fifteen years he labored at this work. The stockholders of the Connecticut Land Company had now multiplied to five hundred as stock was subdivided, largely through inheritance. Hillhouse had not only recovered all monies owing to Connecticut, but a half million besides. He never once resorted to litigation.

Hillhouse brought solvency to the Cuyahoga valley and the entire Western Reserve by 1825. In that year another towering individual would almost singlehandedly move the valley forward into actual prosperity.

No marker on the Western Reserve is memorial to Hillhouse.

8

The Redmen

STIGWANISH (or Stigwamish) walked into Carter's Tavern, paused at the door for his eyes to accustom to the gloom, and looked for Major Carter.

Carter, on his account, looked up to see what caused the lull in the excited voices. Then he smiled. Stigwanish, the Seneca, was a more commanding presence than Judge Samuel Huntington, who worked at it.

A seaman off Captain Thong's boat, in a binge of sentimentality because of the big announcement, walked over and offered the Indian a mug. The Indian shook his head preoccupied, and moved toward the bench where Major Carter talked to Captain Thong. The affronted sailor called to others to witness the Indian's misprizing his generosity. But the locals knew that Stigwanish had greater responsibility than the sailor, and that he had not tasted liquor since he had killed his own child in drink.

Stigwanish did not wait for a pause in the major's conversation, nor allow himself to enjoy Thong's surprise at his excellent English.

He merely said, "I have decided, Major. I go British."

"No, Seneca!"

Carter couldn't leave Captain Thong at the moment; but he knew that if Stigwanish went British, so would all the Senecas, Ottawas, Chippewas, and probably the Delawares.

Stigwanish turned to leave.

"Wait for me, Seneca!"

But he didn't.

On the twenty-eighth of June, 1812, a man who had a hut along the Cuyahoga had to decide what nationality he was. And it was often difficult.

Survival by Englishmen, Frenchmen, Indians, and colonists on

82

the Cuyahoga frontier had not been a matter of nationality. It depended rather on hunting, trapping, growing corn, and procuring ammunition.

But when the rider arrived from Washington to announce the Republic had declared war on the King of England, the scattered handfuls of settlers along the Cuyahoga stared at each other and helped each other decide what they were—British or American.

Major Carter in his log tavern at the mouth of the Cuyahoga was having trouble enough getting settlers to stay here. And he couldn't bear to let anyone leave. He poured another jolt of Monongahela for Captain Thong, master of a Canadian vessel, "We can't let you sail out of here now anyhow, Captain. 'Twould aid the enemy."

Thong drank the drink and the thought. "Major, you've spent time in Canada before, why don't you come up with *me?*"

"No. Besides, I'm head of militia here."

Thong poured one for Carter. "Then I guess you'll want me to pull my hook and clear your harbor today."

"No, Captain. In fact, in duty, I don't think I can let you go home—legal." Carter poured Thong another. "In fact, the way I see it, you call on three American ports and only one British. Doesn't that make you American?"

"Can I use your warehouse?"

"Glad to have your custom, Captain. Can you haul some ammunition in from Erie?"

When Carter went to his warehouse to clear space, Stigwanish was waiting there, as Carter had hoped. While Carter's code was direct and decisions were simple to him, for Stigwanish the decision was complex, because he was a complex man. The white men called him Seneca because he was acknowledged head of the Senecas and one of the finest leaders on the Cuyahoga. Some members of the fragmented Ottawas and Chippewas also acknowledged his leadership. He moved up and down the river, but he had a hut on the west bank near the mouth.

Between the major and Seneca was something quite beyond their official relationship. Each lonely, each unrelaxed in toughness, Seneca and the major paid each other the compliment of insulting candor. Carter told Stigwanish he thought he had more sense than to let his men persuade him to go British. "You should talk more wisdom into your men," he told the Indian.

"I could, Major, if your action matched your talk."

Carter disliked an argument with Seneca. Only Judge Huntington could win a debate with the chief. But it sounded as though Seneca were still open-minded. Carter knew that Seneca still wanted retribution for the profane hanging of the young Indian, John O'mic, by white men. So he proposed, "Ho ma yen de zin, O'mic." Carter always addressed Seneca in his own language. It was part of what was between them.

Seneca addressed the major in English better than the Major's Seneca. "Perhaps, Major. But how could you fix that? O'mic is dead. I told all the Senecas and Ottawas Major Carter promised to bring Darrow and Williams to trial. Now they ask when."

Carter did not look away, but he smarted inside. He told Seneca not to go British and throw away the protection the Indians had earned under the American flag.

"Protection?" Seneca smiled. "Remember the Moravian Indians?"

Carter walked to the edge of the Cuyahoga and stared into it. Suddenly he snapped erect and pointed at Seneca, "But remember the Eries? The British did that! And now you want to join them? They'll leave you nothing. He genno latreta!"

Seneca also stared into the river. The surface was turgid, but beneath it a strong undercurrent pulled.

And between the major and the tall Seneca flowed an angry undercurrent of history that began with the Eries and ended with the hanging of John O'mic.

Both men knew that the Cuyahoga valley was an Indian story, but a sad one. After the annihilation of the Cat Nation of Eries by the Five Nations, the conquerors occupied the Cuyahoga country under no pronounced geographic pattern. Small groups of the conquering tribes settled haggle-straggle up and down the valley. Small bands from other tribes westering through found this river good and stopped to camp, then stayed. After the Eries' last stand, the Indians of the Cuyahoga were migratory. One week you'd find certain clans up at the mouth, another week, down at the head of the Tuscarawas.

They were mostly Ottawas and Senecas with quite a few

Delawares and Mingoes, and a straggle of Oneidas, Cuyingas, Massanges, Shawnees, and Chippewas. This cosmopolitan population was partly assembled by the fact that within the big U of the Cuyahoga, three great Indian trails crossed. One was the Central Trail (these were white men's names) from Old Portage to Fort McIntosh by the way of Big Falls to Fish Creek, where the trail divided and went *up* the Cuyahoga to the source and *down* it to the mouth. Second was the Fort McIntosh, Muskingum, and Sandusky War Trail. The third was the northern trail along the lake shore from Buffalo to Detroit, which became US 20.

Despite the proximity of villages, the Indians got along quite peacefully. Ottawas lived within ax throws of the Senecas. One reason was the stature and wisdom of the Ottawa and Seneca chiefs. Mingoes and Delawares also built very close to each other.

These scattered villages would often be as small as three to six huts. Others would be fifty or a hundred. Every little stream flowing into the Cuyahoga had a village at the confluence. And they were peaceful, despite constant Indian nervousness of the white settlers from Connecticut.

But there were many white settlers who knew how to get along with Indians. Lydia Wetmore of Cuyahoga Falls was not the nervous type, and she understood how lucky the settlers were to have Senecas, Ottawas, and Delawares as neighbors. She understood, too, that diplomacy was required.

But she would have owned to a touch of real concern when spring burned through in the year the youngest of her three boys turned twelve and her eldest sixteen. As she scrubbed their work trousers, she watched out her real glass window at Silver Lake.

The three Seneca girls bathing in Silver Lake were handsome and lively. The sun glinting off their coppery limbs painted the beautiful kind of picture which would haunt any young man's nights. And the trousers Lydia was scrubbing were definitely long pants now.

A boy was a man at sixteen out here, if he was going to be. But Lydia and her husband, William, cofounders of Cuyahoga Falls, felt that serious trouble could break out if settlers' sons coveted Indian daughters in this girl-scarce land.

Three times this spring the Seneca girls had bathed here, splashing and laughing with the light-footed joy of emerging from winter boots. Lydia watched them dry off in the sun, and with a woman's heat lightning awareness, she linked it to the sudden cessation of ax blows from up on the rise where the boys were clearing. The Indian girls dressed, but their short, open-sided summer manteaux were far from Connecticut fashions. She saw that they were headed now not back to their village, but up to her own house to visit, as they often did.

Lydia Wetmore was a woman of understanding. For white settlers to tell Indians to wear Connecticut dress would be clumsy. And Silver Lake, she felt, belonged more to the Indians than to her. Suddenly she reached down a bolt of blue-dyed sacking, scissored off seven feet, folded it, cut an interesting neckline at the fold, and sat down with needle and thread, composing herself as one not in a hurry.

"Come in," she called casually to the knock.

Lydia Wetmore was a favorite with Seneca girls. They smiled with pleasure at sight of the crisp clean sacking. They crowded close, inquiring with soft Seneca exclamations. Lydia Wetmore smiled around a mouthful of pins and nodded them to be patient.

Intently they watched her work, and they argued pleasantly in Seneca about what she was making. She kept them in suspense, until she finally unfurled it with a flourish. Then it all came clear. Lydia nodded to the tallest girl who gasped and snatched the cloth. She put it on right over everything else, and looked down at herself with pleasure.

But the short girl laughed and spread her arms wide, "H-a-a!"

Mrs. Wetmore laughed, too. She cut off a narrow band from the bolt, wrapped it around the tall girl's waist and tied a bow.

The short girl folded her arms and cocked her head, "Ah-h!"

And she stared involuntarily at the bolt of cloth. Mrs. Wetmore unrolled the bolt and handed her the scissors. Then she threaded three iron needles.

The Seneca girls ran across the trail to their Silver Lake village. They had not been gone long when their smiling mothers suddenly appeared at Mrs. Wetmore's door. One held out a blue sacking waist sash and nodded with aggressive geniality.

Inside the hut, Mrs. Wetmore held up the diminished bolt

against the nodding mother. There was a problem of girth. But she told them to get hides and pelts and come to meet her at the trader's cabin. A negotiation was made for yard goods.

After that, the Seneca women met in increasing numbers every Sabbath in the Wetmore cabin. She taught them how to keep the stitches very small. They kept coming.

There were a few other whites, men like Major Carter and Kingsbury, who understood the tenderness of the Indian's pride and took pains to protect it. But the sad part of the Indian story on the Cuyahoga was that while the Indians had arrived at a resigned, peaceful attitude toward living with the white encroachment, the white population still contained a few of the old-style Indian killers like Simon Girty, Captain Brady, Captain Delawn Mills, of Portage County, Jonathan Williams of Deerfield.

How were the other Indian settlements located along the Cuyahoga? They were not grouped neatly by Indian nationality. The large Eastern Indian nations which had broken up left migrant bands of different tribes. The remnants of southern Ohio nations were withdrawing north. So we find pockets of tribes here and there along the Cuyahoga. Old Cuyahoga Town, north of Akron was a sizable village. Big Falls had two villages as did Silver Lake at Cuyahoga Falls. There were believed to be a thousand Indians in these two villages.

On Turkeyfoot Lake, Chief Wam-te-kek had a large Delaware village. Captain Pipe, King of New Portage, had a large village in Coventry where Louis Young's famous roadhouse was. At Apple Orchard in Medina County, Chief Beaver Hat had a village of Chippewas on Chippewa Lake.

On the upper waters, near Streetsboro, Chief Big Son, brother of Stigwamish, had a village of Senecas before he moved. Prominent in its leadership were his two sons John Hanur and John Mohawk and his three sons-in-law, George Wilson, Nickshaw, and Wobmong.

Traces of many villages have been found along the Indian trail which ran across the northern border of Windham township in Portage County to the Seneca village near Streetsboro on the Cuyahoga.

Bath had a Mingo village which considered Logan its chief.

A half mile north of Boston on the west bank was a large village called Ponty's Camp. These were Ottawas who looked to Pontiac and Ogontz. These Indians in Boston were believed to be fairly good farmers. Mature apple trees were found here by the first white settlers. The valley had some little-known, but sophisticated English-speaking chiefs. Net-a-wat-wees of the Delawares was a chief of high stature here and was included in every major treaty meeting. Ogontz of the Ottawas was a plain chief, but a man of great responsibility. He was educated by the French in Canada and became a prominent churchman.

Polemic Hopacan, better known as Captain Pipe, was less educated. Tough, wily, and predatory, he was important to the Indian communities in making gentlemen out of some of the whites.

The valley tends to overclaim the two great chiefs, Pontiac and Logan. They spent little time on the Cuyahoga, but they did leave faint marks on it.

Pontiac, tiger of the Northwest, spent much time in early manhood at Ponty's Camp on the Cuyahoga. On Lewis Evans's map of middle British colonies, it is called "Tawas."

Pontiac later became chief of vengeance for his race and was little seen on the Cuyahoga. But his son, Blackbird, the Ottawa chief, was educated with money paid by Mr. Bissel of Twinsburg, Ohio, and was seen a lot in the villages on the Cuyahoga before he became busy as Indian diplomat, scholar, and author.

Blackhawk, born prior to 1772, was reared on the Cuyahoga, but moved to larger Indian affairs in the West. Captured at the end of the Black Hawk War, he was being brought to Washington through Cleveland. There he asked permission to visit his mother's grave on the Cuyahoga, which was granted.

Mingotown on the Cuyahoga considered Logan its chief, though he was seldom there. He was an Indian of national importance and one of the best Indian friends of the white man, up until Colonel Cresap murdered all Logan's relatives. When Logan turned on the white man, he started the second bloodiest war in the Ohio country. And when it ended, Logan made his famous speech under the Logan Elm which shamed Lord Dunmore's staff and nearly every thoughtful white man who has ever read it since.

Wabmong is the object of some funny stories by casual historians who have him cavorting around like a chicken thief, unaware that he was heading five hundred Senecas, and personally prevented the massacre of the white population of Stow Township at the outset of the War of 1812, when the Indians in the Cuyahoga valley had to decide between the Americans and the British.

Wabmong's village of five hundred Senecas was just south of Silver Lake. Like Stigwamish, this chief had complex loyalites and elected to move his Indians under the British flag. But his people had been bribed by the British to wipe out the village of Stow upon departure. Wabmong learned of it and advanced the removal date by a surprise announcement. He moved them out in a single night.

In the evening gloom beside the mouth of the Cuyahoga, Carter and Seneca discussed these things. Seneca said, "And we learn the Moravians are still wandering from river to river, looking for ground they can hold."

Carter had heard that already, "But you're not in need of that."

"No. I need promises that will hold. Like your word Williams and Darrow would be brought to trial."

The failure to bring two white men to trial would prove to be crucial in Seneca's thinking. In 1807 a David Diver in Canfield was shot by an Indian. Two men from Canfield, Darrow and Williams, set out to track down the murderer.

In midwinter, an Indian, close friend to Seneca, was shot. His name was Nickshaw or Nicksau, and he was rather well known along the Cuyahoga, being impressive in appearance.

The Indians suspected Darrow and Williams of killing Nickshaw in the belief that he had murdered David Diver. Darrow and Williams claimed self-defense. Meanwhile it became strongly possible that the man who killed Diver was an Indian named John Mohawk. Seneca said to Major Carter, "That makes your Darrow and Williams murderers. And the killing of Nickshaw was an unnecessary murder."

"But Darrow and Williams claim self-defense."

"I do not believe they are true. Come with me and bury Nickshaw. You'll see."

Carter and Seneca went up onto the escarpment together.

Nickshaw lay in the snow. The wound was in the back of his head. He had fallen face down. There were no scuffle marks in the snow, and no new snow on top of Nickshaw.

Carter said, "You're right. There was no fight. No self-defense."

General Elijah Wadsworth of Canfield wrote to Judge Samuel Huntington at the mouth of the Cuyahoga:

Dear Sir: Since I last wrote you, we have information from your quarter that Nickshaw was killed instead of John Mohawk. If this be true, and as Mohawk was the one shot Mr. Diver, ought not Mohawk be demanded of their chief, Ogontz, and delivered up for trial?

Your   serv't

Elijah Wadsworth

To General Wadsworth, Canfield:

Dear Sir:

As the deceased was not one of Ogontz's nation, he said he would not like to lead in obtaining redress, but would be satisfied with whatever Seneca agreed to.

Seneca said he wanted the same measure of justice dealt out to Indians as white men. He said he was not content to see all the exertions of our civil authority used against those who had shot the white man while we were asleep as to the murder of an innocent Indian. He concluded by saying that he would be satisfied if both the Indian and white aggressors could have a fair and equal trial. And only then.

I gave him assurances that the law would be put in force equally against both, and persuaded him to remain peaceful until court should meet at Warren. My expectation was, and still is, that the Court of Common Pleas would issue a bench warrant for the apprehension of Darrow and Williams.

But it is said that the magistrates of Hudson have been deterred by threats from securing the offenders. I hope for the honor of the country that the majority of the people there do not countenance such atrocities, and that some of the civil authorities will have firmness enough to put the law in force.

But Mr. Allen Gaylord told me that the first man to arrest Darrow or Williams will be shot, and the constables do not dare issue a warrant against them, and that if Seneca wants war they were ready for it.

Major Carter agrees with me that the best way to give the Indians satisfaction in this is to do them justice.

On the same day I saw Seneca again, who said he had been threatened by some Hudson [Ohio] people. But he told me he did not wish to start war, and would deliver over John Mohawk for trial voluntarily, but only when Darrow and Williams were secured for trial.

He and Major Carter agree. They went up to the place where Nickshaw was killed and buried him. There was no appearance on the snow of a fight or scuffle and no club near. Nickshaw appears to have been shot in the back as he was running, and fell dead in his tracks.

Seneca observed, "The Indians might lie, and the white men might lie, but the snow could not lie." He is well convinced it was "an unnecessary murder" . . . under this conviction justice demands and our own interests require that he should be gratified.

In case it should be necessary to force the delivery of John Mohawk under the treaty, the regular course is to get affidavits to the facts, transmit to the governor and request him to make the demand, using militia.

But Major Carter and I believe this unnecessary. . . . We have no doubt that Seneca will deliver John Mohawk when we can assure him that Darrow and Williams are arrested for trial.

Meanwhile, I think you can assure your friends that for the present none of the Seneca nation among us will harm your citizens of their property.

> I am sir, respectfully
>
> Sam'l Huntington

"But you never delivered John Mohawk," Carter said to Seneca.

"I will as soon as I see you arrest Darrow and Williams."

"Why not before?"

"Distrust."

"When I make you a promise, I keep it."

"But your people don't."

"Where not?"

"The execution of John O'mic."

"O'mic was guilty of murder, Seneca. You saw the trial."

"Yes. But you promised us dignity. Dignity is very important to a conquered people. You made a feast of it."

There was no question in Carter's mind that the trial had been fair. John O'mic, a fine-looking young Indian, had been one of three Indians who had murdered a family of three whites and stolen their property. Two Indians escaped.

Yet it seemed to Carter that Samuel Huntington or Sheriff Baldwin or Alfred Kelley or some of those being paid for law execution in 1812 could assume the responsibility for the prisoner. But they felt the Indians might mobilize to free O'mic, and no one had the respect of the Indians as Major Carter did. So O'mic was in chains in Carter's house.

O'mic asked Carter to explain how it would be tomorrow on execution day. Carter didn't feel he should have inherited that job either, but he explained it forthrightly.

"Will you go up on the platform with me, Major."

"They have other men supposed to do that, John."

"But will you do it?"

"Yes, John."

"Don't tie my arms or put a blindfold. I'll show those white faces how an Indian dies."

Major Carter poured the Indian some whisky and sat with him the night.

The next day on the way to the execution, young O'mic sat on his coffin on a wagon.

An eyewitness account by the Honorable Elisha Whittlesey describes the scene in Cleveland:

He was a fine looking young Indian and watched everything that occurred with much anxiety. The gallows was erected in the Public Square in front of where the old courthouse was erected.

After the religious services were over, Major Jones attempted to form a hollow square of militia so the prisoner would be well guarded. He rode back and forth with drawn sword, epaulets and scabbard flying, but he didn't know what order to give.

Carter said to Sheriff Baldwin, "Get that damn fool off that horse and out of the way."

Arriving at the gallows, Mr. Carter and the sheriff and O'mic ascended the platform by a ladder.

A rope was put around the prisoner's neck with a loop in the end. Another was let down through a hole in the top piece, on which was a hook attached to the rope around the neck. The rope with the hook was brought over to one of the posts and fastened near the ground.

As the sheriff brought down the cap, O'mic was the most terrified being I have ever seen. Seizing the cap with his right hand . . . he stepped to one of the posts and put his arm around it. The sheriff approached him to loose his hold, and for a moment, it was a question if O'mic would throw him to the ground.

O'mic asked for Major Carter. [Again] Carter ascended the platform and a negotiation in regular diplomatic style was had. It was in the native tongue, as I understood at the time. Mr. Carter appealed to O'mic to display his courage, narrating what he had said about showing the white faces how an Indian could die. . . . Finally O'mic . . . said that if Major Carter would get him a pint of whisky he would consent to die.

Carter sent to his tavern for a full glass tumbler of the fine Monongahela. . . . O'mic drank the whisky in as little time as it took him to pour it out of the glass.

Mr. Carter came down, and the sheriff again drew down the cap and the same scene of terror was reenacted. Again he asked for Mr. Carter.

Mr. Carter ascended the platform, and O'mic gave him the honor of an Indian pledge that he would no longer resist the sentence of the court if he could have another half pint of whisky.

Carter sent for the whisky and stood with O'mic. When the whisky came, he held it to John O'mic's mouth while he drank. The sheriff tied the Indian's arms back and tied the rope to prevent the prisoner from going to the side post again, avoiding the trapdoor.

Humanity at its worst—people who had known O'mic and his father—stood and watched.

The execution took place. To quote Elisha Whittlesey again:

At that moment a terrific storm appeared suddenly and came up from north north-west with great rapidity, to avoid which, and it being doubtful the neck was broken . . . the rope was drawn down with the design of raising the body . . . so that it would fall several feet and thereby dislocate the neck. The body was put into the coffin and the coffin into the grave.

The storm came on heavy and all scampered away but O'mic.

The real disgrace occurred later that night. A doctor and a

group of medical students barely waited for dusk when they converged on the grave, dug up the body and carried it to a dissecting table.

Although through many decades the raising of bodies for study by medical students has seemed a fit subject for jokes among thick-skinned, thin-souled doctors, this particular grave robbery was to cost the Cuyahoga communities.

"So I'm leaving, Major, and taking them all with me, Ogontz, Big Son, Mohawk, Pipe . . . the Ottawas, Senecas, Chippewas, Andastes."

Carter nodded.

Seneca put out his hand, "But, Major, if you ever want to join us, you could be . . . you could be . . . a Seneca."

While the local militia companies were arming to fight the British, the chiefs on the Cuyahoga marshaled all their men and marched them off to join the British. Not one remained.

After the war, five came back to the Cuyahoga valley. Four of them were shot by Captain Delawn Mills's men. After that, a handful came back for a short time. But by 1817, it was hard to find an Indian in the Cuyahoga valley. And today, if you stand looking at the massive signal tree on the Goudy farm on Peck Road in Cuyahoga Falls when the wind is blowing through its branches . . . it sounds like a hundred-voice *a cappella* choir in a mighty Amen.

9

Decision at Station Hope

As HE RODE into Cleveland along the Lake Erie escarpment, mornings, Ashbel Walworth was used to having the wind sting his right ear, but not talk into it.

So the morning the wind started talking, Walworth turned his horse slaunchwise down the cliff to the Cuyahoga to look. He found himself gawking down at a strange confrontation.

On the east bank facing west a well-dressed Southerner sat a fine horse. On the west bank facing east a large and ancient-looking Negro sat on a fallen tree.

Between them, on the Negro's side of the river but closer to the water, Major Lorenzo Carter stood broadbased and feather-edged to both of them. Cradling a long gun like some forest judiciary, Carter turned his head from the Negro to the Southerner and back as each spoke. Not a benevolent-looking referee, he seemed superior to both and eager to be shut of this.

Of course most people spoke politely when Major Carter was around. Still Walworth was struck by the mildness in the Southern voice, "Ben, think now, hasn't Mr. Young used you well and treated you as well as any on his place?"

Carter watched the Negro think. After awhile the Negro said, "Yes, that's true."

"And now with your crippled up foot, wouldn't you do yourself better in hot country . . . I mean physically."

After a long pause, Ben said, "I guess that part's mighty right. But I knowed that 'fore I came away here."

"Mr. Young wants you to come back, and says you'll have your own cabin," the Southerner told him.

The Negro said to Carter, "Could that be ja s'pose, Major?"

What men most feared and admired about Carter was direct

fairness. He said, "I can't judge that. You got to decide for yourself."

The Negro grasped his forehead as if to squeeze out a decision. Ashbel Walworth had tied his horse and found himself edging closer, eager to hear the runaway's decision.

Carter said, "I would suggest you remember you're talking to a hired slave catcher. He gets a fee to bring you back."

When the gentleman from Kentucky had first ridden in, inquiring for "a slave named Ben," he found his way naturally to the Major's cabin, the capitol west of Conneaut.

The Kentuckian was very polite. "Ben ran away from home Mr. Carter. 'N ah heard up the river that he's here in your town. Do you know where, sir?"

Spitted on Major Carter's stare the visitor felt constrained to explain, "I'm sent for Ben by Mr. Young. You know how the law goes."

Lorenzo Carter was all the law they had here at the Cuyahoga's mouth. Cleveland was still just a scraggle of cabins astride a mud road a rod wide and a foot deep. It was the Republic's only toehold on the Great Lakes Country. But Carter already acted as if it were the seat of a new civilization, "We haven't made our laws here yet. I haven't had time."

"But I trust you do honor the *federal* laws," the Southerner had said.

"Can't say. I haven't had time to read 'em yet."

The Kentuckian was politely persistent. He hoped the Major wouldn't let sentiment color his actions in a matter of property.

"Sentiment? I don't even see Ben enough to have a sentiment about him. He keeps to the woods. I don't personally care an echo off the mountain. In fact with the cold comin' on, he'd be better off in the South."

"Then I'll just go get him. You'll tell me where?"

"Nope. He's in my town," snapped the Major.

"But Ben's no good to you."

"Not to you either. His toes froze on the cliff one day. And the rheumatism has twisted up his legs so he can't walk."

The Kentuckian cleared his throat. "But he's still our property. I'm responsible to get him back. And you are subject to a five hundred dollar fine for interfering in recovery of property."

When Carter had no good answer, he didn't try. He shrugged. But you could tell he wouldn't move.

"All right," the Kentuckian replied amiably. "If he doesn't want to go back with me, he can stay where he is. But just let me see him face to face."

The Major eyed the Kentuckian curiously for a moment. "To-morrow morning," he said slowly, "be on the east bank near the foot of Huron Road there. Ben'll be on the west bank. You'll get your chance to see your slave, but the river stays between the two of you. You can talk across the water."

The Kentuckian was there early the next morning, but not early enough to see Ben hobble out of the cabin and down to the ferry that Carter used to transport hunters and supplies to the west bank. The Major was already on the opposite shore, the grimy green of his buckskins blending into the trees.

The Kentuckian's voice sounded like a patient father, "Ben did you have good quarters on Mr. Young's place?"

Ben stumped slowly out of the woods. The poor black walked gingerly on his crippled feet and even at the distance, the Kentuckian could see that his legs were twisted like ropes of tobacco.

Ben held onto a tree, eyes on the ground. "Yes, sir," he said.

"Mr. Young ever whip you, Ben?"

"No, sir."

"The land was better to you, too, wasn't it, Ben?"

Carter studied Ben. The land here had been hard on him.

Early last spring Ben had been a passenger in the canoe of a Mr. Hunter who was paddling his wife, daughter and a small Negro boy from Michigan to Cleveland. They had just passed the mouth of Rocky River a few miles west of the mouth of the Cuyahoga, when a storm wailed in out of Canada and slammed the canoe against the American cliffs that front the lake.

The children died first, and finally only Ben was left. French traders discovered him still clinging to the frozen tree and brought him to Major Carter's at the mouth of the Cuyahoga.

Runaway slaves were just beginning to find their way to the shores of Lake Erie, guided by no more than the North Star. The long valleys of the Blue Ridge and Cumberland mountains formed a natural trough to the Ohio. And then it was an easy path up the Tuscarawas, across The Portage and up the twisty Cuyahoga to Lake Erie.

All through the summer, Carter nursed Ben back to a kind of health. By fall, Ben was barely able to totter his big bulk around the cabin and to a practical man like Carter who would pitch a hound dog out of the house if it didn't earn its keep, it went against the grain. From the trail of rumors the Kentuckian had followed down the river, it was obvious that the Major was anxious to be rid of "poor Ben." In fact he had even made the statement, "Niggers are no good up here." Ben knew that.

The Kentuckian called across the river, "And the people were better to you down South, too, weren't they, Ben?"

Ben looked at Carter. Carter looked sternly away.

"Yes and no," Ben said.

"Got to be one way or the other!"

"No. Turns out it don't, Mister."

Carter looked across to see what the slave catcher would make of that. He couldn't tell. The Southerner was thoughtful. Then he said, "Why'd you run away, Ben?"

"Guess the freedom talk got into me."

Carter studied him. Freedom! Remember Carter . . . remember back in Vermont when you had a farm, friends, and civilization to keep you company? What made you want to blaze a trail through a thousand miles of woods to chop a cabin out of the forest and fight malaria and disease and hunger on a frontier river with no doctor within a hundred miles?

Freedom! That's what you wanted. That's all the black man wanted. A man would walk the shoes right off his feet, and the feet right off his legs for that. Carter took a new look at Ben.

Carter did not at that time know that Ben was the first of an endless line who would be marching north, in spite of laws and fines, to reach *this* port on the lake.

The Kentuckian fired his final question. "How about it, Ben? You want to stay here or come on back home with me?"

Walworth inched closer to hear the reply.

Freedom or slavery? Ben was on his feet now. He didn't look like a man who had made a decision. He looked more like a hound dog that had been called off the rabbit chase. He paced up and down the shore.

Several times the Southerner was about to add one more argument. Carter thought it was almost wickedly canny judgment that he each time withheld. He had Ben rocking back and forth on the knife edge of a decision already. Anything he added would probably lose him a $2,000 property.

Now he called across the Cuyahoga, "Ben! If you decide against going back, you don't have to worry about retalia—about further pursuit. Mr. Young said to tell Ben he's a good man and I forgive him gettin' enticed away. But tell him he can come home if he wants."

Carter crimped his lips in recognition of the Kentuckian's telling stroke. He squinted to see if he could detect a smile on the Southerner's face. He couldn't.

Ben looked over at Carter as if to ask advice, but did not. Then he lowered his head and trudged slowly toward the ferry raft Carter kept tied up for crossing the river.

Walworth watched the Major paddle the little craft back across in silence while Ben stared at the approaching east bank. The Kentuckian was already at the landing as the boat scraped ashore. Ben climbed out painfully and stood before him. The Kentuckian smiled and put his hand on the big black's shoulder.

"Good, Ben."

The Major shook his head and strode up the riverbank to his cabin. Ben was already becoming one less thing the Major had to do.

But some in the settlement didn't forget Ben so easily. No doubt the Major told the settlers in the tavern what the slave had decided, and he probably let it go at that. But even though more than a century separates us from that day in 1806, perhaps the Major did not forget that easily. There is a sequel to the story.

Next day, Ben and his captor made their way up the Old Carter Road through Cleveland Mills. Ben was riding and the Kentuckian walked alongside, chatting amiably. Suddenly two men leaped out of the woods. Their rifles stared at the Kentuckian like two unblinking eyes. The Kentuckian stared back.

"Ben, you damned fool!" shouted one of the riflemen. "Jump off of that horse and take to the woods."

Ben jumped. His twisted legs carried him like a scurrying crab into the woods. His "liberators" disappeared after him.

The Kentuckian never protested or tried to find Ben again. The account of Ben's history recorded by Ashbel Walworth tells us that only three people knew about Ben's "escape." They were described as "two hangers-on" at the Major's tavern named John Thompson and James Greer. The third person was Lorenzo Carter.

Perhaps it would never have been known that Thompson and Greer had set Ben free again. Their motives are still obscured by a veil of years. But their part in the adventure came to light that winter.

A son of Major Spafford and a young brother of Nathan Perry were out hunting in the West Bank wilderness one day and became lost. After tramping about aimlessly for some hours, they stumbled upon a horse's track which led them to a rude hut hidden away in the forest. There was only one person living there—Ben.

Ben was the first Negro resident of the Cuyahoga.

Eventually the twisty Cuyahoga became a main road to freedom. Slaves from all over the South found their way along its banks, later following the towpath of the canal that led them to the lake and Canada.

And all along the way the fugitives impressed strong men like Lorenzo Carter to help them in their journey—men who came to call themselves station masters and conductors on the road to freedom.

Later when the network of roads to freedom were established with such cunning and secrecy that they became very efficient from station to station, the network became known as the Underground Railroad.

And the station that operated at the mouth end of the twisty Cuyahoga was named Station Hope.

10

The General

IF YOU should ever find yourself driving over Portage Road, City of Akron, County of Summit, State of Ohio, pull over out of the rush of today. Get out, put your feet right on that road, and walk into the sixteenth century. It is worth a half hour of your life, and it will jar you a little.

Over the rumble of fast traffic on brick you'll see the trees still meet over the street, nodding smugly of old events. The road you will be walking over is almost surely the oldest main artery in America. It appeared on the earliest European maps of North America. It's still the same length, and it still bears the same name that it has carried in every language from Erie to Iroquois to Delaware to French, Spanish and only recently, English— Portage Path.

For centuries when the continent lay sleeping as far as white men knew, there was a steady flow of traffic over the Portage Path. Who knows what maps and compasses primitive men use? But they had found, perhaps by centuries of trial and error, the gateway for the water route between the Gulf of Mexico and the Great Lakes.

When the continent was solid trees, you could hardly travel from the lakes to the gulf by land. But Indian tribes found they could come by water up the Mississippi to the Ohio River, then up the Tuscarawas which gave them an easy route up the formidable slope of the Continental Divide that splits the continent laterally, water off one slope flowing to the Gulf, off the other to the St. Lawrence.

Now if upon reaching the head of the Tuscarawas, an Indian walked overland to the north only eight miles, he came to the Little Cuyahoga which flows north. If he put his canoe back in and followed the current, he plunged down three hundred feet in thirty miles to Lake Erie, which would take him down to the St. Lawrence.

The main key to this two thousand-mile trip was this short eight-mile portage; and the white man found that generations of Indians had beaten a groove about nine inches deep, one man wide, and eight miles long.

This Portage Path became, in 1785, the Western Boundary of the United States. Forty years later, the white man took it over and for the same reason the Indians had used it. He wanted to move his boats from the Great Lakes to the great Gulf by water. But these were big boats eighty feet long and thirty tons heavy, and there were hundreds of them.

Where he needed to lift his canalboats three hundred feet, practically straight up from Lake Erie to the Portage, they had to build thirty-nine locks. To service the canal horses, feed the passengers and unload the boats during the six hours of locking up the escarpment, a city grew at the high place, what was known as the Summit.

The Summit would have been nothing but a lock tender and tavern keep to the canal if it hadn't been for the Cuyahoga tributary, the Little Cuyahoga, mightiest creek in America.

Lost in a gigantic gorge forty sizes too big for it, like the uncomfortable kid whose mother buys coats with "growing room," the Little Cuyahoga is undignified.

In some places it chatters down over stairsteps of shale. In other places it is a turgid swale of stained bubbles, carry-off from a chemical city. In many places, it bubbles literally *under* Akron today, fighting for a look at the sun between factories, only visible now and then blinking under a street bridge just before hurtling down into a culvert, emerging later in a gush only to duck under another plant. Kids mistake it in places for a big storm sewer.

Yet, without any qualification whatsoever, this little creek literally built Akron. The land, before it was Akron, had not the first thing a city needs, and its growth defied the laws of economic gravity. Akron was started by four men who wanted both navigation and hydraulic water so badly that they hand-made it.

Not traditional frontiersmen, these four were of the last of the great colonial leader breed, giant patriots of the all-'round type who did some farming, law, science, politics, and a lot of nation building. They were Dr. Eliakim Crosby, Judge Leicester King, Senator Alfred Kelley, and General Simon Perkins.

Now when a man is put to a lot of extra trouble over a low-paying project it sticks in his memory—and even in his affection.

Perkins as a young surveyor back before the War of 1812 had had a lot of grief surveying for a client a thousand torn-up acres between the head of the Tuscarawas and the loop of the Little Cuyahoga. Therefore, years later, when Perkins saw a notice that this tough thousand acres was going for taxes, he paid $4.03 and was certified to the land; and then he forgot it for eighteen years. It was to become one of the all-time bargains of history.

By 1825, Simon Perkins, a handsome, rugged forty-six, was living in Warren. He heard that land surveyors were driving stakes through his thousand acres over by the Little Cuyahoga. He mounted and rode fifty-two miles west of Warren. It had to be the canal fellows surveying, so he tried to figure how high a price he could charge the canal, for Perkins was above all a financial man. He was in on the founding of several businesses, including the famous Western Reserve Bank.

Upon arrival, though, at the Little Cuyahoga, he made a surprising move. Two men had cabins near the big bend in the Little Cuyahoga, Paul Williams and Major Miner Spicer. They'd come together in 1810. Perkins found them both and traded reports of what had become of the men of the 7th Ohio Volunteer Infantry; then Perkins suggested that instead of charging the State of Ohio for their land, they all three *donate* it for the canal.

Williams and Spicer understood the move, and instantly donated a wide strip. But to complete the strip, a parcel was needed from a Charles Brown, a carpenter from Connecticut. He answered, "I'm not a moneyed man, General. I need to sell, and sell dear."

"Then The Canal will never buy it." Like a few other ambitious men, Perkins was beginning to speak of The Canal in capital letters.

"They've *got* to come through here, so they've *got* to buy it."

"No. They can go to the west, come upstream alongside the Maumee and down the Miami. Miss us completely."

Brown chewed the inside of his cheek.

Perkins said, "If you'd give up a strip, The Canal will turn your remaining land into gold."

"That could be a long time off."

"Not long after slack water goes through."

"If you believe that," Brown said, "why don't you buy my land and give part to The Canal?"

"Well, it will be long enough," Perkins said, "that I couldn't lay out cash, but I could trade you. I own forty-five acres in the Little Cuyahoga valley and a hundred farther out and three hundred over in Trumbull County."

Brown picked up a handful of clay and balled it. "I'll take the forty-five close in," he said.

Perkins figured that the spot where the Pittsburgh-Columbus stage crossed the right of way of The Canal, which climbed up the escarpment from the Cuyahoga and down Portage Path, would become a kind of center of things. Being a surveyor, he measured out a township, with an area in the center for a business district surrounded by three hundred cabin lots.

He did the work alone, because looking at that heavily timbered, fully gouged ridge, few others got the picture of tomorrow.

When he took the platte to Ravenna, county seat of Portage County, the clerk said, "To file townsite papers, General, you have to have a name for the place."

Perkins took off his great fur mitts and studied the ceiling. Educated in the tradition of the great colonials, Perkins had studied Greek. As he stood envisioning the highest place on the escarpment in his thousand acres, a place known to Indians and settlers as "the summit," a place for which he now had high plans, a lofty Greek word came to him meaning *high place*. He reached for the quill, and he wrote . . . *Akron*.

But in 1825, Akron was only a name on a platte in the Portage County clerk's office. Yet word drifted out that on the Portage Path, at The Summit, land had been measured off for sale for a village. Those who wanted work on the rumored canal inquired how to get there.

The general took it that far. And it might have stayed that way if it hadn't been for the doctor and the judge. But before they could do much good, a thirty-three-year-old man had to come along, named Kelley, Alfred Kelley.

11

Kelley's Canal

THE *village* of Akron was built by the Cuyahoga and General Perkins; the *town*, by the Cuyahoga and Dr. Crosby. But the *city* of Akron—quite another matter—was built by the Cuyahoga and the toughest little giant who ever rode down this valley in the sleet and hail—"Mister Kelley."

The Mister was because—well—with his linen soaking wet from rain and sweat, standing calf-deep in canal mud, he was a Mister—that's all.

Lonesome from a soaring intellect, dyspeptic from a gnawing canker of duty, Kelley was driven, and he drove the valley to the largest engineering earthwork in the then history of the world— the Ohio and Erie Canal.

The fact is that building the Cuyahoga or Akron or Cleveland were way beneath Kelley's sights. He was out to save the whole frontier from financial disaster. On his way to that it just happens he left in his wake a score of major cities.

A whip-figured man with the winkless eyes of a fighter, Kelley's was not a comfortable presence. His forehead was broad above a high-boned face. The mouth was a thin-lipped slash, and the eyes blazed blue impatience.

He was out of pace and patience with the slow land. It was not ideal equipment for the eight hundred miles of human hurdles and digging that lay ahead of him.

In dealing with his sixty-two legislative colleagues, his heavy sense of destiny, unrelieved by any flash of humor, threw away the fatherly indulgence he could have had as the youngest senator in the state's history.

The feathers he really ruffled were on legislators whose counties would be bypassed completely by the canal. Kelley expected them to rise above sectionalism and vote for the good of

DAILY LINE OF OHIO CANAL PACKETS

Between Cleveland & Portsmouth

DISTANCE 309 MILES IN 80 HOURS.

A packet of this Line leaves Cleveland every day at
4 o'clock P.M. and Portmouth every day at 9 o'clock
A.M.

T. INGRAHAM, Cleveland
OTIS & CURTISS, do. } AGENTS
G. J. LEET, Portsmouth

NEIL, Moore & Co.'s Line of Stages leaves Cleveland daily for
Columbus via Wooster and Hebron.

Cleveland Directory 1837

ma

The

Muskingum River
Elev. 700'

Slackwater Navigation
91 miles to Marietta
& Ohio River

Walhonding River

DRESDEN
ROSCOE
ADAMS MILL
COSHOCTON

Muskingum River

Tuscarawas River

TABLE OF DISTANCES	from Cleveland	from Dresden
CLEVELAND LOCK 42	O MILES	149
BOSTON	19	130
PENINSULA	21	128
LOCK 1 AKRON	35	114
BARBERTON	42	107
WOLF CREEK LOCK	44	105
CLINTON	50	99
CANAL FULTON	54	95
MASSILLON	63	86
NAVARRE	68	81
BOLIVAR	77	72
ZOAR	81	68
CANAL DOVER	91	58
NEW PHILADELPHIA	94	55
NEW CASTLE	97	52
TRENTON	101	48
EASTPORT	105	44
PORT WASHINGTON	109	40
NEWCOMERSTOWN	116	33
COSHOCTON	132	17
ADAMS MILL	143	6
DRESDEN	149	0

NEWCOMERSTOWN
PORT WASHINGTON
CANAL DOVER
NEW PHILADELPHIA
ZOAR
Zoar Dam
Sugar Creek Slackwater
Milton Dam

the region, all the while insisting the canal should parallel the
Cuyahoga—where his own personal real estate lay, and his
brothers'.

Kelley's brisk manner caused other men to slow down to a
drawl. "Mr. Kelley, this hard times extends all the way from the
Maumee River to the Muskingum. Why will digging a ditch from
Cleveland to Cincinnati lift that whole patch?"

"Because the sun doesn't rise out of the Muskingum, Senator
Beardsely, nor at the Maumee. The canal will take our produce
out where prices are up."

"They're not up much in Erie or Louisville."

"I was thinking of New York and New Orleans."

Kelley worked for the canal like a man afraid for his life.
Actually he was afraid for the people.

Kelley reminded men that the state was only an ax throw from
bankruptcy. The bank notes of not one regional bank would pass
at face value. Some were discounted 75 per cent. Things were so
bad that by 1819 trade stopped, land sales stopped, immigration
stopped.

Alfred Kelley and Governor Ethan Allen Brown knew what
was the matter. There was good money in the East, but it would
not flow west.

The trouble was you couldn't get a barrel of, say, Ohio flour to
New York overland without paying a dollar a hundredweight
drayage every hundred miles to push it across the Appalachian
barrier. That put a barrel of Ohio flour on the New York dock for
about eleven dollars—and there she'd sit. Of course you could ship
it down the Ohio River to New Orleans. But the problem was
getting it to Cincinnati from upstate, so it could make the trip.

Now if there were a north-south canal through Ohio from Lake
Erie to the Ohio River, that barrel of flour could travel from just
about any place in Ohio, up to Lake Erie and across New York
State's proposed Erie Canal and down to New York City for a
dollar seventy a barrel, shipping. It could sell for anything over
$5.20.

Eastern dollars would then flow west.

On the floor of the legislature the anticanal men brought everyone back to what they called *reality*. "With only $133,000 in
the state treasury, Mr. Brown and Mr. Kelley talk of spending

five million. The taxable value of all the land in the state is only fifteen!"

As legislator and as governor and as U.S. Senator, Governor Brown personally labored eight years to pass the canal bill, using all the considerable skill at his command, "Alfred, the word *canal* has become a fighting word. Let us change the designation to the *Internal Improvements Bill*. It's hard to be against *Improvements*."

But many were, "Let us not be confused. This new bill is for the same old canal. This impoverished state is supposed to build a canal longer than the wealthy state of New York is building, and with twice as many locks."

Alfred Kelley inherited the leadership on the canal drive as it passed down from Thomas Jefferson to Governor Worthington to Thomas Morrow to Governor Ethan Allen Brown. But Brown went on to the U.S. Senate. As the new leader of the canal movement, Kelley came up against the leaders of a hundred local revolts. If the canal plans left out a town, that town set out to kill the canal by passing resolutions to declare they would not pay taxes if any part were to be used to pay the interest on money borrowed to dig a canal.

They sent copies to New York newspapers in paid space, because Governor Brown was at that very time in New York trying to borrow construction money from John Jacob Astor and other financial firms. These notices showed the financiers that the governor did not have his state behind him on this project.

Kelley was not a strong speechmaker. He couldn't stump these towns, but he sought out the leaders.

General Simon Perkins was a natural leader in Warren, and he was thrust to the head of the Trumbull County anticanal movement. The canal was not planned to go through Trumbull County.

Kelley knew from previous land transactions that Perkins was land wise. He would know that the canal would make his Cuyahoga-Tuscarawas land valuable. Yet he fought that route.

So Perkins was sincere in believing the canal should route itself through the larger communities, like Warren.

"Let's say that were true, General, have you considered the shape and cost of a canal that would go through Warren, Columbus, Chillicothe, Circleville, Dayton, and Cincinnati? As a former surveyor, I think you can picture that."

Perkins admitted that no other route was so right for water supply, drainage, and directness, "But the people don't know, Mr. Kelley. It's going to seem more logical to them to run this canal north-south right through the exact center of the state."

"True. And that would put it even farther from Trumbull County, wouldn't it?"

Perkins smiled. "But we think in the legislature we can out-weigh those central Ohio men and pull it over our way."

Kelley knew this to be possible. But he said that if he had his way, the canal would go down the Cuyahoga, and he intended to make it a full-time cause. "So even if we don't go through your county, Trumbull County may well want permission from the canal to make some interesting improvement, leading to Warren."

Perkins said, "I'll think it over."

All Kelley usually needed was for men to *think*. When Perkins came out in favor of the Cuyahoga route, he was bitterly attacked by the anticanal camp. "He's as selfish a man as exists," said the Sandusky *Clarion*, "which will account for the liberality of this weathercock."

The canal bill needed friends from wherever. There was an-other stubborn, unsocial, dedicated man in the legislature who wasn't doing very well, Nathaniel Guilford. For as long as men had been trying to pass a canal bill, Guilford had been trying to pass a school bill for public education. He had inherited it from Caleb Atwater and Ephraim Cutler.

Kelley studied the record of voting on the previous canal bills and the previous education bills. Then he went to Guilford, "I notice that in the counties where education is weak, the canal is strong, and where you're strong, we're weak."

Guilford, after many years and many deals, was not enthusi-astic. He addressed himself to his ale. But Kelley went on, "I believe we could get all our procanal legislators to vote for your school bill, if you could get the education people to vote for the canal."

Now Nathaniel Guilford put down his mug.

Fighting localism all the way, Kelley had to bend. In fact, to run the canal past the most votes, they split the canal in two: one from Cleveland south to Portsmouth; one from Toledo south to Cincinnati.

Even so, the canal bill went through an ordeal of committees. Sandusky and other irate areas continued to fight it bitterly and effectively. Nevertheless, on February 4, 1825, the canal bill passed the Ohio legislature.

The bill was so poorly seated that Kelley rushed the state into beginning construction before the law could be modified or hog-tied by enemies of the canal who now set out to elect an anticanal legislature.

Kelley was under fire because the very first section of the canal to be built was in his own area—the thirty-eight-mile stretch from Cleveland to the summit (Akron)—so that shipments to New York could begin early from a large part of Ohio, bringing revenue to settlers and townsmen and toll revenues to the state, which would be evidence to Eastern banks that the balance of the canal construction money would be well lent.

Micajah Williams suggested, "It might be well if you would be at pains to inform widely, particularly in the south and west towns of Ohio, why we have begun the canal in your part of the state. I am told Daniel Heaton on the Mahoning River and James Kilbourne on the Sandusky are saying that Canal Commission members are favoring their own regions."

"I agree with the usefulness of your thought," replied Kelley, "but as the false rumor will be apt to travel like a bird while any correction will travel like an ox, the latter will never overtake the former. It would do best to get the canal dug fast and bury the false rumor in dollars."

But for the human hurdles Kelley had to cross, it wasn't necessary to look to his outright opponents in southern and western counties, nor to the fifty million cubic yards of mud to be moved at ten cents a yard, nor the eight hundred miles of timber four feet across at the stumps, nor to the three hundred feet of lift up from Lake Erie to Akron.

Look right beside Kelley at the man appointed to be the other active commissioner, Micajah Williams.

Kelley was full of duty. And Williams was full of frolic. At thirty-six, Kelley was a precocious young man. At twenty-eight,

Williams was even more so, and ambitious and able in a different way. Politically they were opposite. While Kelley was for Adams and helped organize the Whig Party, Williams helped organize the Jacksonians.

Williams wanted to build an organization, delegate to it, and make it function. Kelley wanted to see everything himself, in person.

But in the face of laying eight hundred miles of slack water through a nearly unbroken forest, they ground each other against the enormity of the thing.

After the legislators and money men, Kelley's biggest human hurdles were the contractors.

He organized a very sound and elaborate bid-evaluation system. And as soon as the news was out, professional contractors from New York's Erie Canal began moving onto the scene. To Kelley's surprise, many of the best ones weren't bidding. They were hiring on as foremen to local men who hastily organized contracting companies.

This disturbed Kelley. He called in Ephraim Johnson, a long-time successful contractor off the Erie. "I was surprised you didn't bid on any sections, Mr. Johnson."

"Too early yet, Mr. Kelley."

"Early?"

"Well, Mr. Kelley"—the contractor was a man of thirty-five with a face weathered for fifty—"You've got bids from local contractors in there ten-fifteen per cent under your own estimates for various sections. Right?"

"Yes."

"Then my kind won't get any work until half of those men go out of business."

The professional canal contractor was a special breed who came on from the Erie, the Chesapeake and Ohio, the National Road, the Connecticut canals. They knew more about canal building than Kelley. Tough, cynical and extremely able men, they knew what their first competition would be, and that these local contractors would hire local farmers to do the digging. So the professionals knew that while initially they would probably have to hire out as foremen, when hard weather sent the farmers home, then the professionals would take over.

They would bring in the sad-faced, glad-voiced sinewy Irish

who could push dirt fourteen hours a day on thirty cents, slum-gullion, whisky, and the durable hope that in three years they would have "worked off the dead horse"—paid off the contractor who had paid their passage from Ireland.

These were the tough, determined, great Gaels of Ireland whom the gods made mad. Contractors who knew how to keep them mad enough to dig—but not mad enough to quit—had a special secret no local contractor would match.

They could take a strip of wilderness full of ague and shoulder-smashing timber and rain and cold and slate and clay, and, come hell or high water, they could cut through it a ditch twenty-four feet wide, four feet deep, and as straight as an Irishman's wrath.

They could leave a graveyard every ten miles, and know that was the cost, and say an Irish prayer and get the ditch moving again before the sod was placed.

Kelley needed this.

"Then, too, Mr. Kelley," said the contractor. "My bid will be higher than your locals because, beyond paying each of my men twelve dollars a month, I'll be paying a dollar a day to men who will work in water."

The professional contractor calculated the rise in wages and materials which he knew would begin when the job got moving. He also planned on smallpox, cholera, and canal fever in his bidding.

"And we won't know how to bid, Mr. Commissioner, 'til we see how these resident engineers of yours work. If they're good engineers who know how to judge a canal lock by more than how the face stone is dressed, and if they carry enough weight with you to get a foolish specification changed—"

"Sir! Our specifications have been carefully drawn."

"Uh-huh. But you've got some Jesus clauses in there."

"Jesus clauses?"

"Specifications that would need Jesus himself."

Johnson pointed out a few other things that were too tough about Kelley's contracts: holding the fall to one inch per mile, holding to hammer-dressed lock facings, insisting on clearing two rods wide on each side and allowing only $250 a mile for timber clearing, insisting on ninety-foot oak timbers in dam construction.

There was a long list of grievances against Kelley's tough specifications and rules. The amateur contractors accepted all these
docilely. The professionals fought them. So the local contractors
won most bids. Their enthusiasm and conscientiousness got the
work off to a big start in July, 1825.

Five thousand men attacked the forest and the earth along the
Cuyahoga through Cleveland, Independence, Northfield, Boston,
Peninsula, Ira, Cuyahoga Falls, Akron. And they did good
work.

But in the second summer, the rains came and the heat. It
dropped Western farmers on their faces in the mud by platoons.
Smallpox ran down the right-of-way. For every one buried, three
went home.

Now the professional contractors came, and the great, flat-
muscled, stone-faced Irish. They chopped forty-one giant steps
into the rising shale-clay escarpment from Lake Erie to The
Summit, which became forty-one locks with massive oak plank
gates on iron hinges.

Sullen . . . silent . . . strong, and organized, they dropped the
trees and grooved the land; fifty barrows running behind a leader
from the canal bed to the spoil bank and back from dawn to
dusk, relentlessly.

"Holy Mither!" Irish foremen fractured the air, "ye roll them
barrows like my granny's granny on her way t'church! Call your-
silves Irish! Arragh! A disgrace to the race!"

But even the toughest Irishmen were amazed at a tougher one,
Alfred Kelley. In all weather he was out on the canal, night and
day at three dollars per diem. Contractors tested him by building
some parts of the towpath with a cover of clay over piled trash
timbers. It saved them from burning the timber and hauling fill.
Kelley carried a four-foot iron rod as stiff as his spine. Before
accepting a section for payment, he'd walk the towpath and jab
the rod into it every so often. Sometimes the rod would go in too
easily.

"A shovel please, Mr. Johnson."

"Never mind digging. We buried some timber scrap in there to
fill that cut. But it's big trunked stuff. It'll hold."

"It'll settle in five years, Mr. Johnson."

"By then you'll need to resurface anyway."

"The contract says stone fill and clay surface, Mr. Johnson."

"Look, I've got to get paid to meet payroll."

"As soon as you rip out and fill this with stone and clay, Mr. Johnson."

"It'll take two weeks!"

"I'll come and re-inspect the moment you're ready. Day or night."

"Mr. Kelley, I'm in a hurry to get my money!"

"We don't have time to hurry, Mr. Johnson."

Some contractors couldn't stand up under Kelley's stern inspections and his driving timetable. They absconded with funds, leaving their Irishmen stranded without pay.

Kelley instituted the system by which contractors had to prove they'd paid their men. Kelley held contractors so brutally to the letter of their bids that they turned to confiscating materials: stone, timber, lime, from adjacent lands.

Always inspecting, Kelley broke his robust health, but he rode anyway, through the mud and rain and heat, always attired as if for the senate floor.

Kelley missed the birth of one son as he married the bitch

public, and reduced his legal marriage to an affair of lonely letter writing . . . "even you my wife much as you wish to see me would not have me leave so important a work at which I have been so long engaged when apparently so near consumation . . . besides you know it would be inconsistent with our character for . . ." (January 21, 1825).

But the work owned Kelley.

Simon Perkins, who had come over to Kelley's side at first reluctantly, now demanded a piece of him. He wrote him asking him to rest after a severe illness, ". . . because I do not see how your substitute is to be found elsewhere if you should get sick again."

But he did get sick, again and again, in contractor huts, in inns in Akron, in settler cabins along the route. Doctors were sent to find him.

Micajah Williams wrote Kelley, "to preserve yourself for the balance of the work you must depend upon your resident engineers and spare yourself the long hours in saddle and on the work site."

Kelley lost a son. And by now even those who had hated his stringent rules and laughed at his dedication would not release him.

In anticipation of the opening of the Akron-Cleveland part of the canal, boxes and barrels and bulk shipments of goods were piling up beside the locks at Akron. So the public would not let Kelley break off with it and return to his family.

In fact, upon the death of Kelley's young son, Micajah Williams wrote: "You will not fail to remember that your friends and your country yet have a right to expect your energies and intelligence to be exerted in their behalf." The letter then went right on with canal matters.

As the contractors worked their way north from the Portage Summit and simultaneously south from the mouth of the Cuyahoga, the first step was grubbing and clearing to a width twenty feet beyond either side of the excavation, stumps to be no higher than twelve inches.

Excavating south from Cleveland, the men were constantly digging under water. Work animals were useless on long stretches where they could get no footing.

The arduous swamp work was killing, yet little worse than the laborious lock-building by which the canal climbed up the escarpment to Akron. In late autumn, men and animals slipped on the steep frozen face of the ridge. Falling shale slid down from the higher locks to the crews carving out the lower locks.

Lock 1 at the top (Exchange Street, Akron) was at the 968-foot elevation. From there north the locks butted together down twenty-one steps to the beginning of the Portage Path. The canal ran level for a short distance to Lock 23 at the junction of the Cuyahoga and the Little Cuyahoga, then it stepped down three locks to Number 26, Mud Catcher, at Ira, Lock 27 at Everett, 28 and 29 at Peninsula, Johnnycake Lock and Pancake Lock. At Peninsula, the canal crossed to the east side of the Cuyahoga by aqueduct. In the next few miles to the north, the canal walked down many locks. Number 32 at Boston was difficult. Thirty-six at Brecksville was a hard one, built in conjunction with two aqueduct crossings, including the long one across Tinker's Creek.

By 1827, the trail of the Irish across northern Ohio could be followed by the marks they put on the land: from Irishtown in Akron through two Irish cemeteries to the north, and three Irish settlements, on up to St. Mary's-of-the-Flats at the Cuyahoga's mouth.

They dug a reservoir hole at the summit that you could lose a town in. But most of all, they left a thirty-nine-mile straight cut on the earth that would hold slack water and float a billion dollar commerce.

On July 4, 1827, Kelley trudged down the bank of the Cuyahoga to board the grand opening canalboat, the *Allen Trimble*, which would run south to meet the northbound *State of Ohio*.

Wracked from illness, his face was drained of expression. People stepped out of his path and turned and hushed.

"That's him. It's Mr. Kelley."

He recognized a face here and there and nodded. He paused beside Ephraim Johnson, "Are you lowering the miter sill on the first lock so the boats can enter the river when the lake level is low?"

Johnson removed a cigar from sun-cracked lips and smiled. "Godalmighty, Mr. Kelley. The men can't work right through the ceremonies!"

"Then we'll hurry the ceremony. How you going to do it with six foot of water standing on the sill?"

"We rigged a clam bucket on a chain."

"You're a good canal builder, Mr. Johnson."

"You ain't the worst yourself, Mr. Kelley."

The ceremony was that the first vessel to float on the canal, the *State of Ohio*, built by the Wheeler brothers in Akron, came

floating down to Cleveland bearing a distinguished load of Ohio statesmen to band music.

But the important event that day was the *second* boat which floated into Cleveland after the band music had stopped. It carried wheat in on July 4, 1827.

No one seems to know the name of that vessel. But overnight, on July 5, 1827, wheat that had sold for twenty-five cents a bushel jumped to seventy-five cents.

Northbound on the canal floated flour out of Akron, wheat, pork, whisky, flax, ginseng, coal, potash, walnut timber. Southbound over the canal, headed for the hinterland at the canal head, floated iron, brass, glass, plaster, iron nails, tools, books, millstones . . . and settlers. Instantly, the moment the water filled the canal.

Henry Newberry dug some coal out of the Cuyahoga bank at Tallmadge, loaded it into a canalboat, hauled it to Cleveland. He wagoned it house to house, but nobody wanted the dirty, black stuff, so he gave away a free sample.

Then John Ballard saw it burn pale orange hot in a blacksmith shop. That year he built an iron foundry on the Cuyahoga where Henry Newberry's coal could float right up alongside. He told Newberry to pile the coal beside the kidney stone iron ore.

Today, side by side, piles of red and black still line the Cuyahoga banks. But the signs overhead say Republic Steel and Jones & Laughlin; and fifty coal companies have their seat at the Cuyahoga mouth.

It began with Alfred Kelley.

12

The River's the Doctor

WHEN THE staircase of locks had been built from Akron down to the world, boats began to walk back up loaded with wonders that were *not* of the Western forest: real glass for windows out of Pittsburgh via Portsmouth and the canal; plaster dust for cabin chinking out of Buffalo via Cleveland and the canal; whale oil lamps, china plates. And converging on Lock 1 from the Akron hinterland for transshipment to the world came bulk from the land, outbound via the mouth of the Cuyahoga.

The land beside the locks at Akron became stevedore, warehouse, terminal, and tavern to the canal, and Akron thought itself doing very well. But Dr. Eliakim Crosby didn't.

He began telling Akron they were missing the chance of a lifetime. "A town has got to *make* something to ship *out*. Can't just be a place people go *through*."

But Akron had no outstanding farm land, no minerals. Timber, yes, but the whole Northwest Territory had timber.

What *did* they have?

Dr. Crosby finally found something. But it would require tremendous amounts of work, a ton of money, and, most of all, some long-sighted men. Crosby sent messages over to Trumbull County to General Simon Perkins and Judge Leicester King to meet him in Akron a week from Sabbath.

They arrived with the superiority of busy men being imposed upon. But Crosby being Crosby, you couldn't afford at least not to hear him out.

The doctor took them out to Lock 1 on the canal just south of where the Little Cuyahoga joins the Cuyahoga. The men could look down on heavily cargoed canalboats crawling both north and south. It gave Judge King an idea, which irritated Dr. Crosby at the moment. King was overjowled and had never become a part of these woods. He was still Connecticut. He said, "Look at that traffic! If we only had *another* canal now from here to Pittsburgh, Akron would become—"

But Crosby interrupted. "I want you to look down there at the Little Cuyahoga."

"I don't think you heard me," King said, "a canal from Pittsburgh would make Akron the hub of a three-way slack-water commerce."

"So we would sell a little more hay to canal mules and ale and warehousing to canalers," Crosby snapped. "We need factories like the water-powered mills at home along the Connecticut River."

King, remembering the broad Connecticut, looked at the skinny Little Cuyahoga and he smiled. "Take forty days and forty nights of rain to make water power from that trickle of sweat, Dr. Crosby."

Perkins laughed. But Judge King, though young, was a handsome, commanding presence, and his benign smile had a worse effect on Dr. Crosby than Perkins's forthright guffaw.

The blunt-faced doctor snapped, "*That* river isn't going to furnish the power!"

Perkins elbowed King, "The doctor is going to *make* a river, Judge. Don't you know about Crosby?"

"I was forgetting." King nodded gravely.

"If I could have a moment of your attention," Crosby said, "unless you rode all the way over here to admire your own wit." He took a map from his saddlebag, squared it with the land, and said, "We don't have any large river. But look what we could do. The land rises so gradually between here and Middleburg that you don't notice there's a vertical difference of almost a hundred foot.

"Now suppose we tapped the Little Cuyahoga right here"—the doctor's finger stabbed the map at a point of high ground (near Case Avenue)—"and built a millrace to divert water over here, then run it down the face of this valley to Lock Five on the canal. Between these two points, with a drop like that, the water would run twenty mills. Put twenty dams and a millwheel at each dam, twenty factories."

The doctor looked up at General Perkins and Judge King.

"By God," Perkins breathed, "he *does* want to build a river."

"Amen," King said.

They made a three-way handshake.

Studying the requirements, they found the sheer digging to cut a river down the steep sides of the valley was enormous. The job of acquiring the land from the owners along the route of the proposed new river would be in itself a major project. They would not have the governmental right of eminent domain. And if owners figured out the purpose, land prices would shoot up, particularly if it was suspected that King, Crosby, and Perkins were involved.

It would take a wagonload of borrowed money. But King and Perkins had a lot to gain in improved valuation.

Crosby would build the millrace, Perkins would lay out another town at the junction. Judge King drew the delicate job, buying a strip of land for the millrace without kiting the price.

Some very careful regional writers record that Judge King asked Crosby to "Mark the line for the millrace at night."

"The trees are too thick to work at night."

"Full of the moon is due in a week."

"Under that cover of oak the moon won't light the work enough for running a straight line," Crosby said.

"Then run it crooked, Doctor, and just straighten it daytimes."

"People will still see our survey blazes."

"Don't use blazes. Put out hunting traps with a stake to mark the traps."

Word was passed to the lock keepers to warn people there were 'coon and fox traps set in the valley. They should be careful.

Judge King went over to Ravenna Courthouse to study the deeds to the land. And he went to the tavern beside Lock 1 to study the owners. With whom would he be dealing in buying the right-of-way? He hoped he wouldn't find any absentee owners living back in Connecticut. It would be costly to acquire such titles. He found only three of those, but he found one name that alerted him—Charles Brown.

King went to Perkins, "You traded a lot on Little Cuyahoga to a Charles Brown to get him away from the canal right-of-way?"

"Aye."

"Well, he's now standing right across the right-of-way of progress again."

Perkins shook his head as he remembered the deal he had made with Brown. "How could it happen?"

"It had to happen. Men who have a good land sense are always choosing the same pieces of ground. That's what fills the courts."

If they asked Brown to move *again,* he'd know that *again* there was a good reason. Brown had now had a chance to see that Perkins had been overwhelmingly right about the canal. It had succeeded; it *had* raised land values.

"And if *I* go to see him about moving again," King said, "won't he spread the word that something big's afoot?"

"I guess so," Perkins said.

"Maybe if *you* went to see him, he'd just think you wanted your own land back very badly."

Perkins fretted several days about how to move Brown again without running up land prices. Regional scholar Hugh Allen records the opening of the conversation this way.

Perkins said, "You made a good trade with me before, Mr. Brown; I think you're satisfied."

"I am," Brown's replies were guardedly respectful.

"Now I want it back."

"Why, Gen'ral?"

"Need a piece close to town. Always liked that piece."

"Last time you asked me to move, the big canal worked out like you said."

Perkins barely nodded.

"Somethin' else big comin'?"

Perkins went right on, "I'm offering you fifty-six acres for your forty-five. Let's ride out and look at it."

"I'll look," Brown said.

Brown liked what he saw.

But meanwhile Judge King ran afoul of a tough burr, the husband of Mehitabel Barston, who said, "Unusual for a big man like you to come to me, Judge King, for such a small part of my land."

Then after a verbal skirmish, Barston thought awhile. "Judge King, I'll sell. But you got to take the whole tract to get that stony hillside."

"What price?"

"Fourteen thousand dollars."

King's jowl joggled. "Don't think I can raise it."

"Well, there seems to be some activity around here in land, Judge. How long you expect me to hold it?"

"Give me a five-day option at fourteen thousand."

They wrote up the option, ending it at midnight on the fifth day. It took Judge King four and a half days to raise the money, and a half day to get papers to prove it and the evening to ride back to Barston's.

But Barston didn't appear. Midnight chimed on Barston's Connecticut pendulum clock.

Judge King pulled out his pocket clock. Barston's clock was accurate. He rose and paced the kitchen. Suddenly a door from the shed opened and Barston walked in, "Judge, your option has expired. I have changed my mind about the price."

"The transaction is completed," King stated. "This land stands jointly in your name and your wife's. Five minutes before midnight, I counted out cash and paper for fourteen thousand dollars and made a legal tender. You can talk to a lawyer if you want, but you've sold your land."

Barston did consult a lawyer. He *had* sold his land.

Leicester King worked quickly. Curiosity rose about his purchases, so he did not buy in a straight line, but bought first on one end of the line, then the other, avoiding the middle. As speculation became more acute, he even bought a few parcels far away from the river so that they destroyed any pattern or shape which might be becoming apparent.

He did his work so well that not until he had finished did the sellers of the land get together and discover the pieces they had sold fitted together in a strip that paralleled the Little Cuyahoga and obviously were part of a major plan.

When that plan became known, it started the biggest drinking laugh that had been available at the Summit. "Crosby's going to build a river!"

When the digging of the "Crosby Creek" began, the men sweating up on the ridge behind shovels looked down at the canal. They could see themselves being pointed out by the canal captains as local curiosities. On hot quiet days, laughter would float up to them. They knew the laugh was spreading to every lockside tavern between there and Portsmouth and Cleveland.

Cutting the millrace along the ridge, sometimes through solid rock, chewed up men and money faster than channel. Crosby, Perkins, and King had to find new loans.

It took two years. But when they were finished, Little Cuyahoga waters plunged downhill laden with kinetic power enough to turn twenty large wheels. The millrace flowed down along Main Street to Mill Street, then turned into the canal. Immediately the building of what came to be known as Old Stone Mill began. It turned its wheel in 1832. That date could be called the real birth date of Akron.

The mills which now grew up along "Crosby's Cascade" forced people to take a new look at Eliakim Crosby. People who used to call him "Doc" when he was a doctor, called him "Doctor Crosby" now that he had stopped practicing medicine. He was the surgeon who amputated a slice of river, grafted it to a town, and brought into the world a city.

It remained for General Perkins to complete the town platte around the split-off waters of the Little Cuyahoga. He platted Howard Street, paralleling the canal as the main street, named it Howard for Dr. Crosby's son-in-law who started the first store at the corner of Market. The store was built by Seth Iredell, the Quaker, and first mayor.

The new town became North Akron, a mile from the "old" Akron. They were divided by a gore-shaped tract—and a thousand acres of jealousy which would in its own way later rock mid-America. But we must stick to the river.

The water power from the Little Cuy's left hand, grabbed later by a stubborn Dutchman, made Akron the flour and cereal capital of the world, starting with Old Stone Mill.

But Crosby, Perkins, Kelley, King, and the Cuyahoga had ahead even greater destiny for Akron, and a bigger fight.

Judge King started it. He began a campaign in the legislatures of both Ohio and Pennsylvania for another canal to link Akron and Pittsburgh. Then he went out to raise the money.

13

The Luck of

Jedediah Brownhead, Esq.

"TAKE THE PISTOL, LANT." Frost nudged an old-fashioned brass single barrel across the desk at his sharp-jawed friend. "One of those blacklegs is going to start shooting. Then what'll you do?"

"Same as last time." Lane squint-smiled with his one good eye. "Run."

Sam'l Lane was not a man to accept a fight on just any terms unless it was worth it; and along the upper Cuyahoga in the 1830s, a fight could be for keeps. Specifically, he saw no gain in a physical fight. Unfortunately, his character, principles, and devil-take manner stirred up enemies in his wake like dry leaves after a fast horse. The Cuyahoga valley echoed with the damning of Sam'l Lane.

The damners wanted action, not debate. And Sam'l Lane's only weapon was his pen. He became the first biographer of the Cuyahoga.

Scarce nineteen years old when he came to Akron in 1834, Lane was already a well-traveled man. Therefore, the finely at-tired strangers who inhabited the canal resorts did not impress his worldly eye as they did the local settlers. He'd seen them before in every big town from his home in Connecticut to New Orleans, which pumped these blacklegs up the Mississippi river arteries. To Sam'l Lane, the ruffle shirts, plug hats, kid gloves, and be-jeweled fingers were the plumage of gamblers, counterfeiters, and thieves.

Four years in canal-bustling Akron grew Lane's first fringe of chin whiskers and his first head of real anger. While still prac-ticing his trade of sign and house painter, he took up the pen to write a little semiweekly newspaper that voiced his opinions of blackleg activity and life in general.

While Lane's pen flushed out coveys of blacklegs, it was a poor defense against their bullets, bludgeons, and bare knuckles.

"Dammit, Lant, you were lucky to get off with only one buttoned-up eye!" exploded Frost. "You're tweaking the nose of every gambler, saloonkeeper, counterfeiter b'hoy, thief, pickpocket, and . . ."

". . . con man," added Lane.

"And to top it off," bellowed Frost, "you even dig at law-abiding citizens."

"Now, Henry," Lane rasped in the harsh Connecticut dialect that characterized his articles in the *Buzzard*. "Uncle Jed sez that a real jolly, nothin'-tu-du-with-polyticks, anti-blackleg, respectable paper will du well here, an' that's jist what I'm goin' tu print."

"Lant, that phony accent and the false name, Jedediah Brownhead, Esquire, won't protect you. They know who writes it. Half the town calls you 'Jed' already."

This time Frost picked up the heavy little cannon and held it out to his friend. "Careful. It's loaded."

Lane squinted down the sights, lining them up through the window at a stem-legged stranger across the street who was ushering an awkward giant of a farmer into the saloon.

"Bang!" he said. "There goes another blackleg, compliments of Sam'l Lane." A smile crinkled the wide mouth. With the fringe of whiskers framing the smooth-shaven upper lip, the mouth and jutting cone of a nose, Sam'l Lane came closer to being the clownish Jedediah Brownhead, Esq., than the sophisticated editor of Akron's much talked about newspaper. Lane gently laid the pistol on the desk.

"Henry," he drawled, "I was raised to the occupashun of teechin' the young idear how to shute. But seein' as how that's rather poor bizness in this secshun, I've concluded to try my hand at editerin' awhile."

Frost sat as stone faced as the blacklegs did when they read Lane's humor.

In booming Akron, blacklegs made no attempts to front their professions, or purpose. It was every man for himself, and while all communities had their reform groups, the general attitude toward transients, upon whom the blacklegs preyed, was that "he who gets fleeced should have kept his coat buttoned."

The traffic through Akron was heavy. Inland farmers from as

far south as the big bend in the canal at Newark shipped north to Akron. They accompanied their farm produce that far north, where it was transferred to boats bound for the mouth of the Cuyahoga. The farmers stayed in Akron to make purchases of goods imported from New York via Cleveland. Very often these men had with them nearly their full savings. Sometimes they brought with them their land payment money.

Now these were lonely men who had licked a hundred acres of beech trees and supported with their bare hands life amid raw nature. For some, it had been several years since they had been among strangers or seen a woman wearing new cloth and bracelets. The big U turn on the Cuyahoga was a bright new world to them, and they were not expecting it to be peopled by predatory blacklegs. They fell easy prey to the friendly smile and the handsomely clothed people.

When the witty pen of Jedediah Brownhead, Esq., went after them in his strictly reform paper *The Buzzard,* it made good reading. And when people read, they sometimes acted. So with half the state's blacklegs concentrated right here in the new canal city like gaudy green horseflies on slow-melting sugar, a man could stir up a lot of trouble with hardly tossing a name.

Along with their dazzling display of high fashion finery, the blacklegs presented an elegant friendliness which bored travelers on the canal packets found overpoweringly attractive. Boston and Peninsula were already favorite haunts during the blackleg working hours. There the boats began the laborious stair-step through the locks to the summit.

To eat, the passengers often had to disembark and cook their own meals over open fires. This, along with the practice most canalboats had of carrying their spare horses on board, led many passengers to accept the hospitality of the well-dressed strangers, ride with them into Akron for a friendly glass or two to wait until their boat caught up with them on the summit . . . *"And perhaps a hand of cards or two."*

This was part of what Sam Lane was determined to clean up. This was what moved the pen of Jedediah Brownhead, Esq., and kept the brickbats flying at Lane's head. Plain, hardheaded luck kept them from doing damage.

"Sum folks may think, perhaps, that I've got a curious name for my paper," Jed quipped in one issue of the *Buzzard.* "You see, a buzzard is a kind of hawk, an' my Buzzard is near of kin tu the turkey buzzard that I've hern tell on way down South where it's a fine tu kill 'em, cause, you see, they remove all the filth and carin from the streets. Now, you see, I calkulate to make my paper prodigous handy in this way. If there's enny thing wrong goin on, I calkulate to tell on't, an expose, an endevor to remove new-sances and so forth from the city."

The *Buzzard*'s sweeping forages on blacklegs were extremely successful. But Lane had many close squeaks. Pelting with rotten eggs was common. Once he was cowhided for his commentary on a local drunkard and cohort of the blacklegs; but the whip wielder was relatively easy to outrun. She was the drunkard's wife.

The buttoned-up eye Lane now displayed to his friend Henry Frost was still tender from the fist of a notorious Negro pugilist and dancer named John Kelley who had attempted to obtain possession of a hall for a "distreputable exhibition" and had been severely criticized by the *Buzzard*. Having been knocked to the ground on this occasion, Lane had been saved from a lethal stomping by his own agility at pivoting on his back while keeping his feet toward his attacker—and the timely intervention of by-standers.

Lane was constantly being lured by invitations into dark alleys, secluded back rooms, and lonely woods by irate blacklegs. It wasn't common sense that saved him.

This was why Henry Frost now pushed the pistol toward Lane, more insistently.

"Lant, you've proved you don't show the white feather. But you've also proved wit and words aren't going to help. Take the pistol."

Lane stared at the miniature cannon, fingering his beard.

"I was a barkeep once," he said. "Only way I could earn a living." His right hand reached for the dull gleaming pistol. "The meanest of all occupations," he continued, "is that which requires a man to dole out whisky at three cents a glass when he knows perhaps a whole family is suffering for the bread which should have been bought with the coppers."

Lane was idly checking the primer. Suddenly he leaned for-ward, roughly clattering the pistol to the desktop. "Say," he exclaimed. "That'd make a good temperance item. 'Man's most miserable occupation.'" He reached for his pen.

Henry Frost started for the door. "Promise me you'll carry the pistol?"

The scratching of his pen on paper drowned out Lane's soft answer. "Like the barkeep, Henry, a man's got to live."

Only a few days later, with the brass pistol pulling at the skirt pocket of his overcoat, Sam'l Lane called at the Hall Hotel, on business with the landlord's brother. There were no threats to his person this day—no rotten eggs, no horsewhips, no fist-swinging pugilists.

Just Dwight Spooner.

Through drink-puffed eyes, Spooner watched the editor bustle through the taproom. "Bartender," he growled. Bottle clinked on glass. The liquid disappeared in a gulp. Dwight Spooner rubbed the stubble on his face and waited.

Half a dozen lounging blacklegs caught the look, ordered another round and waited with him.

Lane didn't keep them waiting long. As he picked his way through the taproom toward the door, Spooner's hulk rose and blotted out the sun. A fist like a hand of bananas knotted around Lane's collar and he was yanked into mid-air by a yard of beef. Sam's hand instinctively flew to his hat, keeping it squared on his head. The other dipped into the skirt pocket.

A well-manicured hand, trimmed with starched cuff, fell on his elbow, a hand decorated brightly with several razor-sharp diamonds that can slash a man's face. A voice hissed in Lane's ear, "Don't pull the pistol, Jed, or it's the end of you."

Lane managed to roll his eyes enough to make out the town's most notorious blackleg. He could also see Spooner's other fist suspended like a ham hung for smoking.

"Landlord!" choked Lane, quietly withdrawing an empty hand from the pistol pocket. "Give me protection!"

The landlord smiled, pushed open the front door and turned to Lane who still dangled limply from Spooner's grip. "If you are going to fight, gentlemen, do it outside."

Lane was dragged out.

"Go ahead, Spooner—mash the polecat!"

Lane's right hand sneaked into the skirt pocket again.

Spooner's eyes glistened. "How 'bout it Jed Brownhead," he taunted, "shall I strike you?"

Lane's hand came out of the pocket, the pistol cocked.

"Shall I mash yer face for you?"

The pistol was against Spooner's belt buckle.

"You can do as you please about it, Dwight," Lane gasped as calmly as he could. "But you may feel bad about it afterwards. Real bad."

Another hand linked into the cocked hammer of Spooner's fist. "Now hold on, Dwight," drawled a friendly voice. "You could get into serious trouble mashin' up a prominent citizen like J. Brownhead, Esquire, here."

Spooner's fist wavered. A howl went up from the blacklegs.

Another friendly voice drifted into Lane's now pounding eardrums. "Lay off, Dwight. There's nothing to gain by mashing *our friend.*" The emphasis was threatening. Spooner's fist dropped a little and his eyes circled the ring of bystanders. The circle was complete—blacklegs on one side, friends of Jed on the other.

The clamp that bunched Lane's collar slowly relaxed and, slowly, the pistol was uncocked and slipped into the skirt pocket again. Apparently no one had even seen it.

But Sam'l Lane had only half an hour to recuperate from big Dwight Spooner. He returned to his office, taking care to place the pistol on a convenient shelf above the editorial table.

Dwight Spooner was herded into the tavern by the blacklegs. There he filled up with more corn courage and a few proddings.

Jedediah Brownhead looked up from his editorial as the stumbling thumps scuffed up the stairs to his office. He laid the pen down and took the pistol from its shelf just as the door banged open.

Spooner swung on the doorframe like a side of beef, eyes glittering, "Lane! You gonna buzzard me any more?"

The pistol cocked. Spooner saw it this time.

"Get out of my office, Spooner, or I'll buzzard you so you'll stay buzzarded!"

Spooner got. Lane stood at the office window, watching the giant disappear down the mud street.

He chuckled. So, Sam'l Lane—the pen can start a fight, but it takes a pistol to finish it. You might even run for sheriff one day and put some of these pen-scratched principles into action.

Lane looked hard at the pistol. No need to keep it primed now that danger's over. With his pen, he pried the wadding from the barrel and shook the charge onto the desk. Out tumbled four large shot, three slugs of lead, and a pile of powder which even to an unpracticed eye was a large mouthful for any pistol, not to mention this one with its old-fashioned brass barrel.

Sam'l Lane shuddered. In his great concern, Henry Frost had tried to double the protection for his friend. But if the trigger had been pulled, it would have blown Lane off the earth.

Sam'l Lane had been carrying a bomb.

If the experience of very nearly blowing himself from the lives of the blacklegs was any lesson to Sam'l Lane, he never showed it by future caution. His long and varied career was a continual oscillation between the pistol and the pen. He served as editor of several publications alternately with terms as sheriff, probate judge, and finally mayor of Akron.

The same bravado characterized both his pen and his pistols. But he never actually fired the pistol. He just used it to protect his pen . . . and this was what people remembered.

In later years, Lane helped Akron's *Beacon-Journal* make a name for itself that continues today; and he wrote perhaps the most detailed book on the embattled Cuyahoga—to which all subsequent regional books are indebted, including this one.

14

The Biggest Financial Man

on the Cuyahoga

THE MOST BELOVED, most exciting money man on the entire Cuyahoga shore from 1800 to present writing was James Brown at Boston.

While many doers of good works are scored as cowards, Mr. Brown in his vast larceny was a symbol of unbelievable gallantry. Heroically molded, he stood straight as a promise, six foot two, unbooted. Feature by feature, the face was not carefully handsome, but it had slashing good looks under blue-black hair, and it was lighted by a born-lucky smile.

Even his most effective enemy, Sam'l A. Lane, sheriff of Akron, conveyed well on two thousand "Reward" posters that Brown's frame was commanding, and that his deep-set eyes were touched with heat; and he described Brown's voice as genial and his manner even courtly.

Clothes hung on him as on a tailor's dummy. His drinking was correct and his marriage to Lucy Watrous Mather was the acme of social distinction.

Brown's friends, who were many, often complimented Lane on the accuracy of the written descriptions of him on the *Reward* posters and on the pages of Akron's reform newspaper.

As editor of *The Buzzard,* Lane had flushed out of the Cuyahoga valley scores of corrupt and fraudulent men. As sheriff he jailed them. But with neither portfolio could he make a case stick against the towering prestige of James Brown. While in the same breath sincerely complimenting Lane on his descriptive prose, the people said of course they had no information leading to the conviction of Mr. Brown; and, if they did, they would certainly have no part in the downfall of such a fine man. "In fact, you ought to write a book about him."

Being both experts of the world, Lane and Brown recognized each other as formidable. It was not lost on Brown that Lane was one of those wiry enduring men who never tire. Lane's humor he knew was not the jolly unguarded type. He laughed a split second too late.

Lane himself admired Brown, but he was committed to arresting and convicting him.

"I'm going to tell them in print what you're doing."

"Why? They already know."

"But see what they say when I print it all."

"They'll say I'm doing more good printing money than you're doing printing *The Buzzard*."

When *The Buzzard* came out it carried a complete story on James Brown.

James Brown built a house on the west bank of the Cuyahoga. In 1825, he built on the same land a storehouse, laying in twelve hundred dollars' worth of merchandise and keeping tavern in the same building.

Many men in the commerce of coal, iron, whiskey, hogs and brass awaited the opening of The Ohio Canal in 1827 to ship their cargoes, [wrote Lane] but none waited so eagerly as James Brown who was planning to ship money—in bulk.

Haven't Brown's neighbors noted that the colleagues he has assembled are very well dressed and well spoken for the operation of a mere store and tavern?

Have any wondered how it is that Mr. Brown needs such impressive help in the running of a store which stocks under $2,000 in merchandise?

For your own protection, you should note the stature of the men who have taken up storekeeping in the little neighboring town of Boston. They are William G. Taylor of Cleveland; Abraham S. Holmes, Col. William Ashley of Boston; William Latta of Bath; Jonathan De Courcey and Thomas Johnson of Norton; Joshua King and Joe Keeler of Portage.

James Brown has a very able brother, Dan, who is very like him, except more handsome but less statesmanlike in crime.

These men—are counterfeiters; and on a vast and damaging scale.

The next morning, Mr. Lane's editorial office was a pile of broken glass and wood. While he was inspecting the debris a courier came up to give him "the compliments of Mr. Brown and will you meet him at Hall's Tavern?"

Lane rode to Pittsburgh instead for a bag of type, leaving a workman to clean up *The Buzzard* office. When he returned in four days, the press was upright and cleaned. It was not damaged.

The courier repeated the invitation. Lane went to Hall's Tavern. Brown greeted him from the center of a table of men without rising, but *with* courtesy, proffering a draft of Cuyahoga neck oil.

Lane accepted, but insisted on paying with his own coin.

"Fine, Mr. Lane. But the proprietor finds *my* money very acceptable," Brown spread U.S. bank notes on the table.

"I don't. You wanted to talk to me."

"To tell you your paper spoke to my disadvantage, Mr. Lane, and I incline to get mad."

"So do I, Mr. Brown." Lane always had his eye on history's clock. "And you're going to jail, if it takes forty years."

"I'll take longer, Mr. Lane."

It was extremely difficult, however, because whenever Lane caused Brown to be arrested, a crowd gathered around and accompanied the genial Brown to the jail to see that he got out on bail without delay.

When Brown's cases came to trial, they were arranged for bad weather, when possible, to prevent overcrowding. The crowds came not only to see Brown, but also because such distinguished and colorful attorneys handled his defense.

Jim Brown was eager to have his brother, Dan, come in with him on a full-time basis. But Dan was then in the business of droving horses east to Pittsburgh—other people's horses. Jim argued with him that horses were a long roundabout way to make money. "Why go through those middle steps when we can make money direct?"

A special condition of the times made the counterfeiting business especially workable and especially direct. It was an era when forty different kinds of wildcat currency were abroad in the West, the bank notes issued by local banks. These currencies were all different colors, denominations, and conditions of discount. Much of it would not pass at 25 per cent of face value, and the actual value fluctuated day to day, even hour by hour.

Many a settler, just paid for pork he had canalled to the Cincinnati market, heard that the four hundred dollars he had received was in a tender fast falling in value. While he scurried around the waterfront trying to convert it to a coinage more stable, the four hundred dollars had turned to one hundred dollars in his hands— or to ashes. Such settlers never knew that their own frenzied effort to convert actually cut the value of their money in that immediate vicinity.

But the point is that if a counterfeit dealer was available in such moments of panic, he could easily exchange his counterfeit for legitimate currency. Of course he must make sure that the real money was worth more than his counterfeit, before trading.

Brown saw his biggest opportunity in the one currency which stood up very well any place, United States bank notes, issued by the Philadelphia branch. Naturally, these became nearly as scarce as hard money; and hardly any of them flowed west.

It was this money shortage which Mr. Brown proposed to relieve. He was determined to run a strictly quality operation. He acquired some very fine plates hardly to be distinguished from U.S. bank notes. He had good engravers and printers with him. However, to make the notes in commercial quantities, some expensive printing equipment was needed which required the sudden raising of capital. Brown always insisted on paying his bills in good money.

Now the way Brown raised good money when he needed it made him legend up and down the Cuyahoga.

Two assets particularly permitted him to *do* what other men only dreamed: a personal effrontery and an uncommonly powerful black horse named "Old John," procured for him by Dan.

Brown caused to be forged a bank draft on the Bank of Pittsburgh. Being scrupulous in financial affairs, he also had it marked "certified."

He then took five horses from his shed on the bank of the Cuyahoga and rode east at night with the string toward Pittsburgh. He dropped Old John off first at a stable in Warren. The other horses he dropped off at about thirty-mile intervals, telling each hostler to feed it well, but leave the saddle *on.* The last horse, he rode into the Pittsburgh area.

Resting during the day, he sauntered casually into a bank late in the afternoon, and with the easy boredom of a man of large affairs he placed forged credentials before the banker along with the certified bank draft.

"It's a large one," the banker said. "But should be no trouble on that bank, sir. What currency you want it?"

"U.S. bank notes, if convenient. Small denominations."

"There'll be a twenty dollar charge as we'll have to send an armed man when we collect from this bank."

Brown unrolled some bills. "Very well."

When the draft was cashed, Brown thanked the banker, and strolled casually out the door. But once the door shut behind him, casualness stripped off him like a sweater. He ran down the steps, jammed the bills into his saddlebag, untied the mare, and jumped on. His heel raked the mare's flank as he headed her west through the cut in the Allegheny escarpment.

At Aliquippa he leaped off, threw the lines of the lathered mare to the hostler. "Get me the Virginia Red!"

The change-over was under five minutes, and he was westing toward the Cuyahoga. When he reached Warren, he was exhausted, but the giant Old John pounded the trail west. Dawn was lighting the sky when Brown crossed the Cuyahoga. He went into his shed long enough to get water for Old John and himself and to change his clothes and grab an ax.

He went back outside with the ax, over to his boundary line where he began splitting wood loudly under his neighbor's window.

The neighbor's wife came out and Brown asked her, "What time is it?"

"I don't know."

"Since my clock is broken, would you go into your house and look?"

She came back out, "Half after seven, Jim."

When the extradition officers came from Pennsylvania, they talked to Brown's neighbor's wife who said, "It's impossible; I remember talking to him at half after seven the next morning."

The Pennsylvania constable mounted his horse and flapped on his hat. "It's not him then. No horse could do it from Pittsburgh in one night."

When Brown's own press was operating, it turned out good quality U.S. bank notes.

Now you must understand the scope of Brown's thinking. It was no part of his idea to go around personally handing off bogus money at the retail level. Nor would he permit his agents to do so. Instead he marketed the bills in volume, *as counterfeit,* to dealers at 20 per cent of face value. The men who bought from Brown and from Brown's men knew what they were buying. They almost never saw Brown, the head of "Moneyshop Hill" who seldom so much as touched a bogus bill. In his own pocket, he liked to carry genuine U.S. bank notes.

Brown's shipments of queer went aboard canalboats northbound for New York State, southbound for New Orleans. Cargoes were substantial. He would, with some regularity, ship quantities of as much as one and a half million dollars.

Besides U.S. bank notes, Brown printed a considerable number of mortgages on property in Eastern cities, and he printed some bonds of Western states which he sold in the East.

A major part of his management ability was acquiring the plates. In addition to commissioning the finest engravings, he would sometimes steal the original plates in daring maneuvers in which he was very lucky.

Lane printed in *The Buzzard:* "How is it that small packages come in over the canal for Brown's store in Boston, but only large shipments go out?"

Brown would personally set the pattern for opening a new territory. When he did, few could emulate his boldness or brilliance. To open the money market in lower Canada, he rode out of the Cuyahoga valley on Old John before the thaw one spring. He established several dealers, but Canadian law officers picked up his scent, and by the time he reached the middle of the north shore of Lake Erie, they were in full pursuit.

Brown's escape from them and from Canada was the subject of admiring talk up and down the Cuyahoga valley for decades. The Canadians were so close behind that time was counted in heartbeats. He was heading west along Lake Erie, but he suddenly reversed and headed Old John east over thawing Canada soil for the east end of Lake Erie where it narrows. Soon he arrived at the place where he saw the spring ice break-up was beginning at the edge of open water.

He rode still eastward along the shore, picking the exact spot where he judged the ice to be thawed to just between slush and ice. Then he rode south across the breaking ice. Old John's hooves sucked slush, and once broke through. Brown whip-slapped him on.

Canadian officers were still testing the ice at various points when Brown crossed the U.S. border in midlake. By the time they found sufficiently firm ice for crossing, Old John and Brown were clattering up onto the United States shore near Silver Creek.

Brown's Canadian outlets over the years dispensed several million *Made-in-Boston, Ohio,* dollars—U.S. bank notes of high quality, but not legally negotiable.

One of the greatest threats to Jim Brown was the dangerous admiration of his own colleagues who yielded sometimes to the temptation to brag of their leader to their drinking companions.

Except for this, he might not even have been arrested for his perfect execution of the Boston, Massachusetts, "transaction." He had had forged a very large draft on a bank there. He proceeded then from Boston, Ohio, to Boston, Massachusetts, and negotiated the draft. Then he used the same trick as in the Pittsburgh "transaction": a prearranged relay of horses to race back to Boston on the Cuyahoga. He made sure to be seen there immediately, sauntering casually down the road as church let out.

His own colleagues were so amazed that word of the feat seeped out and spread. Sam'l A. Lane sent the lead back to Massachusetts. Brown was extradited by Massachusetts authorities, taken to trial in Boston. However, the court ruled, that "With the fastest mode of travel known, no living man could have performed the journey in the time intervening between perpetration of the crime here and Mr. Brown's thoroughly proved presence in Boston, Ohio."

Thereafter, Ohio sheriffs riding after James Brown could put no heart into their work.

But Sam'l A. Lane pressed relentlessly. He had been able to convict many of Brown's *customers,* but Brown himself had a towering immunity to conviction. Such crowds of admirers gathered 'round him at trials now that even judges were affected and leaned toward acquittal.

One judge summed up: "Even the prosecution concedes that Mr. Brown did not personally misrepresent to anyone that the bills were real. In fact, he aggressively stated to the purchasers that they were *not* real. The man who passes a spurious bill off as *real* is guilty. But a man who announces it is *not* real has not passed a counterfeit bill because his statement has stripped it of its counterfeit quality."

Arrested and tried often, Brown still stood so high in the estimation of citizens of the Cuyahoga valley that in April, 1834, they elected him Justice of the Peace of Boston. He administered this office with such authority and conscientious attention to detail that he was twice re-elected.

While he held office, it was known to all that he headed the Cuyahoga valley money syndicate. Many were in fact grateful to him for freeing the money-tight economy, not inspecting their cash too carefully. If it passed from hand to hand, what mattered?

In 1837, Samuel A. Lane, through *The Buzzard,* started a new editorial drive against Brown. He avoided butting head on into Brown's towering, born-lucky popularity by addressing his newspaper campaign not directly against Brown, but against counterfeiting in general.

The campaign was so forceful that it incited the law of three counties to go on a rampage. With a concentration like that, they were bound to apprehend dealers who bought counterfeit bills from Brown and who were inept in passing the money. Arresting the dealers led the officers to Brown's own confederates, some of whom bought freedom by giving information about Brown. They were reluctant, but they did it.

Brown was therefore arrested and brought to trial approximately a dozen times in the next two years. "Going to Mr. Brown's trials" became a thing to do.

The state often had to ask for a continuance in order to assemble witnesses, letting Brown free on ten to twenty thousand dollar bonds. In five such cases, when the new trial date was set, the many witnesses were suddenly unavailable, missing, or relocated.

Many of Brown's colleagues and customers were put in the penitentiary during this drive, but "Old Jim" as he was now called, remained chief of bogus banking in the West.

In the early 1840s he moved farther upriver and was elected Justice of the Peace at Northampton in October 1845.

But in 1846, Brown's distinguished defense attorney, Judge Rufus P. Spalding, lost an examination on a charge that Brown counterfeited coin. Judge McClure on the bench bound him over to U.S. District Court in Columbus, letting him wait at home on $20,000 bail.

The trial in Columbus, August 1, 1846, was presided over by Justice John McLean, the later admired Ohio Supreme Court Justice and U.S. Postmaster General. Brown's defense attorneys were Hon. Rufus P. Spalding and Hon. Noah M. Swayne (later U.S. Supreme Court).

Nevertheless the case went against Brown, and his sentence was ten years in prison.

The three barns which burned down in the following week had only one thing in common. They all belonged to witnesses against Brown.

In prison, Brown's great spirit shrank like a caged eagle. Yet his commanding presence even here won him the respect of the officers and prisoners. Within a few months, he was made file leader of the first platoon in the lockstep march of the prisoners between dining hall and shops.

Sheriff Lane who had worked hard for Brown's arrest and conviction went to visit the prison. It shocked him to see how gaunt and unsmiling the giant had become.

Mr. Brown was later given special charge of the prison hospital. While he held that responsibility, cholera broke out. Brown was a bulwark of strength, in constant motion day and night nursing sick prisoners. The prison officials credited him with personally saving scores of lives.

His work was so dramatic that prison officers assisted Brown's only daughter, Laura, in forwarding a request for a pardon for Brown. President Zachary Taylor granted the pardon and Mr. Brown walked free July 22, 1849, after two years and eleven months in jail.

But once out of jail, Brown's property was dissipated and Lane had jailed and scattered most of his gang. He was forced to a lower level of operations. Going downhill, Brown was finally arrested and convicted on a lowly charge of passing a counterfeit bill.

In the years following, he was in and out of jail on counterfeiting charges.

While serving one three-year term, he had a visitor, Sam'l A. Lane, ex-sheriff and ex-editor of *The Buzzard.*

Brown did not rise. "It's too early for the buzzards. I'm not dead yet."

Awkwardly, Lane explained his mission was to open negotiations for the publication of Brown's biography to be written by Lane with Brown's help, the profits to be equally divided.

Brown's handsome, shaggy head went back in laughter. The black hair was salted with gray, but still thick. The voice was grainy and vibrant, "I'm your whole life, aren't I, Lane?"

Lane walked to the gate and signaled for the guard.

"Lane!" Brown had risen. "I'll let you write my story on one condition. You spent your life getting me *in* here. Now if you want to write my story, get me pardoned."

They stared at each other many seconds.

Finally Lane turned and trudged out of the cell.

15

Oilbow on the Cuyahoga

SELDOM CAN the surge growth of a city be traced to one cause and one day. But in the case of Cleveland, real growth began in the hour that the *State of Ohio* tied up Cleveland in 1827, having dropped down from the Akron summit.

The frontier period ended abruptly with the canal opening. Now came that flood of goods pouring down the Cuyahoga valley on the canal, fed by Cuyahoga water. These shipments brought cash to the West, which started a stream of imports from the East. This commerce gave rise to a row of commission houses lining the east bank of the Cuyahoga, men who learned the sources of all products.

Construction of houses drew heavy imports from the East. A few ironmongers were getting started, using the red kidney ore found on the surface along the Cuyahoga. Coal came down the Cuyahoga valley by canal from Massillon.

A good shipping trade developed between the mouth of the Cuyahoga and Buffalo. The commission houses on the east bank of the Cuyahoga stretched farther south from the mouth as long slender warehouses grew there.

And by the time of the Civil War, the Cuyahoga stage was set for a vast national commerce.

When you break partners with a man in a close-out showdown, you suddenly realize from then on you'll have to fight the very same strengths you once wanted on your side. But by ten o'clock on the morning of February 4, 1865, the three Clark brothers hadn't taken the breakup that seriously.

All six of the men in the showdown that morning on the east bank of the Cuyahoga near the mouth of Kingsbury Run did understand that the outcome today would tell whether the three

Clark brothers and their lawyer had more nerve than the young partner they were trying to dismiss.

It was also understood that the whole of the Andrews & Clark Company should go to the high bidder. However, *none* of them understood that the outcome would affect the lives of millions of people over the next hundred years, and turn the banks of this river shiny black.

Maurice Clark knew the young partner best. They had been very close friends. That's why it jarred Clark now as he stared across the table into the coldest blue eyes on the river. What had attracted Clark in the first place was the young man's unbelievable calmness in the face of business panic, and his humorless sense of destiny.

Even now, as the business was about to break up, the young partner sat facing them as calm as ice, just as if alone he was an even match for the three Clark brothers and their lawyer.

Maurice snapped, "John, the Clark Brothers bid five hundred dollars for the business."

"Rockfeller's bid will be one thousand dollars, Maurice." The young man's expressionless bid echoed so fast it looked as if he'd go all the way to ten thousand dollars.

Clark knew he'd have trouble panicking his young partner because of the spartan discipline under which John D. Rockefeller had been raised.

When he was a boy his red-haired, blue-eyed mother praised him highly for diving into the river to save a drowning boy; then she immediately whipped him for being on the ice himself without permission. It would take a lot to shock him after that.

Maurice Clark jumped the bid suddenly. "Five thousand dollars!"

The young partner didn't even hesitate. "Fifty-five hundred," he said.

At an early age the young man developed a canny way with a dollar. His father spread it all over town that "I trade with the boys and skin 'em, and I just beat 'em at it every time I can. I want to make 'em sharp."

So John probably knew the true value of the business. Maurice Clark figured the bidding might as well get up there. "Ten thousand dollars is the Clarks' bid."

"*Ten thousand five hundred,*" came the echo.

However, if John had to *borrow* to pay, he'd probably drop out next round. As a boy the young partner had lent out fifty dollars from his turkey-raising money to a farmer for a year at interest. At the end of the year he got his fifty, but in addition interest— $3.75.

He saw how easily that $3.75 came compared to worked-for money he had just received for three days of potato digging at 37½¢. He wrote in his diary, "The impression is gaining ground with me that it is a good thing to let my money be my servant, not make *myself* a slave to money." The young man liked to *get* interest, not *give* it.

"*Eleven thousand . . . cash!*" said Clark.

"*Eleven thousand five hundred,*" said Rockefeller.

Another unnerving thing about bidding against this calm young man, he could lose all but the last hand, and still win. He had that shot-with-luck bearing. His sister had said, "When it's raining porridge, you'll find John's dish right side up."

"*Twelve thousand,*" bid Maurice Clark.

"*Twelve thousand five hundred,*" said John Rockefeller.

The Clark brothers stared at their partner, gauging his stubbornness.

They knew of his famous stubborn job hunt. When he graduated from high school, John went to Folsom's Commercial College for three months to learn "bookkeeping and business ethics."

Then he laid siege to Cleveland for a job. The sixteen-year-old boy made a list of all the *large* companies in Cleveland. He wanted training that would lead to his own business. He started right down his list—canals, banks, wholesale merchants.

He got all the way to the bottom of his list. No job. So he started at the top of the list again, making a second round of calls. Some of the employers who recognized this as a second call became very unpleasant. They were shocked at his reaction. It was as if he hadn't even heard them. Just thanked them, and walked out.

When he hit the bottom of the list for the second time, without a job, his family and friends stepped in. They told him to try smaller places of business. John thanked them and started at the top of his list, third time. He said that he was not the least discouraged, "Because I'm every day at my business, the business of looking for work. I put in my full time on it."

Halfway down his list on the third go-'round he walked into Hewitt & Tuttle, commission merchants on Merwin Street on the Cuyahoga River. Mr. Hewitt offered him the job of bookkeeper-clerk in Hewitt & Tuttle on the morning of September 26, 1855. Salary was not mentioned.

That same afternoon John Rockefeller hung his hat on a peg beside the high desk which contained the ledger, the letter press, and the blotter on which he was to record every transaction. He put his foot on the rung of the high chair like a man who had finally got the toehold he was looking for, and he swung onto the seat like a man taking charge.

He never did ask the salary.

As Maurice Clark studied his partner, he knew that a man who'll go without work until he gets the job he wants, won't shake out of this bidding at thirteen thousand dollars.

And a man who has so little regard for money that he doesn't even ask the salary is hard to bid against.

Clark took a deep breath and announced, "The Clarks bid fifteen thousand dollars."

"Fifteen thousand five hundred," echoed the partner.

The position at Hewitt & Tuttle relieved the young clerk's family, but it worried a friend of his that he still didn't know his salary. It even worried Mr. Tuttle, the other partner in Hewitt & Tuttle.

"Young man, if you ever have occasion to procure goods for this firm, always inquire the price before buying."

"Yes, sir."

"Now your salary is three dollars and fifty cents a week. Why didn't you ask before?"

"I cared very little about that. My real pay will be learning business."

Tuttle stared at the young man. "I'll write your first week's check. How do you spell Rockefeller? Everybody'll have trouble with that one."

Many have, including Maurice Clark. But along the Cuyahoga there was little trouble with it, and principally because of Mr. Tuttle and Mr. Hewitt. They were so pleased with the ultrapre-cise, ultracareful work of young J. D. Rockefeller that they talked him up in the trade. He was raised to twenty-five dollars a month, then five hundred a year. But his real pay was much greater. Hewitt & Tuttle was a commission merchant firm and a whole university of business education, if you knew what the ledgers were saying.

What they said to the young bookkeeper was that bushels of corn located downstate in country counties were worth fifty cents. But floated north to the forty-four thousand people of Cleveland, they were worth a dollar and a quarter each. But *how* you moved them was important, in what kind of containers or vehicles. It was also important to be able to store them—to wait for favorable market prices.

He learned the value of an item is *where* it is located. He learned that the science of *moving* the item to where it is worth more is an art. You can use up the margin or preserve part of it.

Shortly Rockefeller was given great freedom and authority to arrange complex transactions involving transshipment of goods over various carriers—canals to the Cuyahoga to dock, to railroads or lake vessels or wagons.

In 1858 he was raised to six hundred a year.

That year he took some of his own money and bought eighty barrels of pork on his own account and resold them at a profit. Then he bought some flour and hams and resold.

Isaac Hewitt noted the young man's innovations and adopted some of them.

Rockefeller asked for eight hundred dollars a year. Hewitt would like to have paid it, but felt he couldn't. He offered seven hundred dollars.

In the auction, Maurice Clark, who remembered how recently Rockefeller had been earning seven hundred dollars a year, knew that his next bid would seem like a lot of money to the young man.

"Twenty thousand dollars!"

"Twenty thousand five hundred dollars," said John.

Clark of course, knew that John Rockefeller had been accustomed to big financial responsibilities. His mother had looked to him since late boyhood as the head of the household. There were two brothers and a sister to support.

The father, William Avery Rockefeller, was an excellent businessman in early life, but the opposite of his son John. A handsome black-haired giant, he had a smile like the sun coming out, and charm to burn. However, he unfortunately had over-charmed Anne Vanderbeak, a part-time housemaid, who explained it to the sheriff. William Rockefeller was indicted. And from then on, he took longer and longer trips away from home; his business, on the fringe of medicine, became vague, mysterious and slightly suspect.

Mrs. Rockfeller therefore leaned on John D. At fifteen, the lad was a man in money matters. At twenty-six, he probably couldn't be frightened off at the twenty-five-thousand-dollar level.

Maurice Clark looked a query at his two brothers and his lawyer. The brothers nodded. Clark said, "Thirty thousand dollars!"

The six men in the room focused on John Rockefeller who stared out the window at the Cuyahoga. Without looking away from it, he said, "Thirty thousand five hundred dollars."

Clark now figured Rockefeller was up to where he'd have to borrow not only from friendly banks, but some from more hostile money sellers.

Yet he remembered Rockefeller had an almost swaggering nerve when it came to borrowing money. Clark, of all people, had reason to know that.

In 1859, when John had been turned down for a raise to eight hundred dollars a year, or fifteen dollars and thirty cents a week, he felt it was time to "go for himself."

Along the river were several other commission merchant and produce shipping firms. In one of them was another ambitious clerk, Maurice B. Clark, highly capable, and highly discontented with his pay. Clark and Rockefeller had talked a lot about forming a partnership as commission merchants in grain, hay, meats, miscellaneous goods.

Now was the time. They figured they needed four thousand dollars to start, two thousand dollars apiece.

Clark, the senior of the two, had saved two thousand dollars; Rockefeller only nine hundred dollars. Clark said, "Well, let's start with that. And you can owe eleven hundred dollars into the pot."

"No. We should be even. I'll borrow."

"How can a bank lend you money on a business that isn't even working yet?"

Well, they couldn't. But John Rockefeller went to his father,

"You told me you'd have one thousand dollars for me when I turned twenty-one, sir."

"Aye. But you're a long way from that."

"Only sixteen months, sir."

"And you want the money sooner?"

"Yes, sir. Tomorrow, sir."

Rockefeller senior stood up. *"Tomorrow!"*

"Yes, sir. But I mean to pay you interest on it for the sixteen months before I'm twenty-one."

The Senior relaxed and said, "Very commendable. Six and one-half per cent."

"Five and a half, sir."

Rockefeller senior smiled broadly and sat down, "Very good. You're ready."

Two days later John Rockefeller, with money in hand, said to his friend, "Maurice, I'm ready."

The Clark & Rockefeller Company opened its doors on the Cuyahoga at 62 River Street. Rockefeller was young, but working on rented money matures a man fast.

In the auction, Maurice Clark knew that now at twenty-six, after all they'd learned together, John wouldn't hesitate to borrow a large portion of thirty thousand dollars. The bid must be much higher. He took a breath. "Forty thousand dollars, John."

Young Rockefeller had already developed a habit of laying both hands side by side over his face, as if staring into the future. When the hands came down, he said, "Forty thousand five hundred, Maurice."

"You realize, John, the bidding has gone past the point of faith in the company. We're up to where you need tremendous confidence in the industry."

"Yes."

However, Maurice Clark, of all people, should know the confidence John Rockefeller had in the industry.

The firm of Clark & Rockefeller started off so strong that in their first year they sold four hundred fifty thousand dollars worth of other peoples' hay, wheat, pork, stone, and coal. Shipped it up the Cuyahoga or the canal or out over the five railroads along the river. Took out a net profit of four thousand four hundred dollars.

Clark did most of the searching for new shipments to handle. Rockefeller ran the office, arranged the transports and the loans from banks to buy merchandise for resale. The partners already had their eyes on the extra warehouse space available along the river at Nos. 39-45 River Street, and some space on the dock.

This prosperity was based on the buying, selling, forwarding of good solid, age-old commodities. But in the matter of *confidence*, the firm was about to take a sudden change that required confidence in the new and untried.

One morning at dawn in 1860, John Rockefeller looked out his office window on the east bank of the Cuyahoga to the black west shore as river commerce awakened.

The sun behind him ignited the bottoms of the clouds, then the tops of the trees. The waters remained dark except that suddenly a shaft of sun sliced between two warehouses to ignite a cross-current strip of the turgid surface of the Cuyahoga.

But this morning the river did not burn iron red, nor coal black. It shimmered iridescent, a sparkling scum of rainbow that would color the economic history of America.

It caused John Rockefeller to call his partner. They stared at it.

"Aye, John, petroleum."

"It comes out of the ground crude at fifty cents the barrel, I hear, Maurice, and sells for eighty cents the *gallon*, refined."

"But there's so many in it, the spread is dropping fast."

"Well, are they careful businessmen, Maurice, like us? Or aren't they careless, that so much of their profit floats by our window this morning and out to sea?"

Clark explained that he'd been approached by a fine young chemist from England, Sam Andrews, who had experience in illuminants. Although Andrews had no money, he wanted to get into the petroleum refining business. "I discouraged him, John. I told him that you and I didn't have two-hundred fifty dollars we could spare out of our business."

"Perhaps we ought to listen to him, Maurice."

In 1863 Clark and Rockefeller put up half the capital to establish a small petroleum refinery on the south bank of Kingsbury Run where it emptied into the Cuyahoga. It was three acres located right on the track of the Atlantic & Great Western Railroad. The rest of the capital came from Clark's two brothers, James and Richard. Sam Andrews was in charge of production.

The company was named Andrews, Clark & Company.

In the auction, Clark bid forty-five thousand dollars. There were three Clarks drawing a living from the company. They could bid pretty high to retain the jobs of three men.

"Forty-five thousand five hundred," Rockefeller said.

Refining was simple. Crude was strained into a tank and flowed to a still to be boiled. The first distillate was gasoline, practically a waste product. Next benzol or naphtha; next kerosene, which is what you were after for lighting and cooking.

Except for the time John Rockefeller took to ride his horse up past the Spelman house, hoping for a glimpse of Laura Celestia Spelman, he spent his days and nights on the Cuyahoga shore tending two thriving businesses.

Rockefeller believed that when a business has natural buoyance, *that's* the time to help it grow. Put money in it.

He began borrowing money to expand the petroleum facility. Even started another small one upriver a few miles, as part of Clark & Andrews, called The Standard Works. It meant Maurice Clark had to co-sign the bank loan notes.

Then Rockefeller suggested to Clark, "Let's hire a plumber by the month instead of by the job."

It meant a steady expense, but it worked out all right. Then Rockefeller pushed again. He said, "Maurice, let's buy our own pipes and joints in quantity. Not from the jobber."

They saved half the plumbing costs. But it meant Rockefeller had to ask Maurice to co-sign with him another bank loan note.

Maurice was nervous about borrowing. But Rockefeller was beginning to realize he could make better use of the money than the banks could.

Next it was the barrels.

"Let's stick to the business we're in," Maurice said.

"We're in the barrel business. All our oil goes out in barrels."

"But we'd have to borrow."

"For the difference between ninety cents and two dollars and fifty cents, we can pay the highest interest in town."

"How much must we borrow to build a cooperage?"

"It hardly matters *if* we're going to *stay* in petroleum."

Maurice Clark co-signed the increasing loan notes with increasing reluctance.

Rockefeller meanwhile was crosswise daily with Clark's brother. Big Jim Clark did the buying of crude for the company; and he fretted under Rockefeller's tight bookkeeping. Jim Clark was tough and profane. Their feud broke out in the open.

Clark bid, "Forty-seven thousand."
"Forty-seven thousand five hundred," said Rockefeller.

About the time that Maurice Clark became openly worried and Jim Clark became resentful, Rockefeller saw that in buying timber for their barrels, they were paying top dollar.

"We need our own timber tract, Maurice."

Maurice signed another note reluctantly.

Soon after that John pointed out, "In hauling green timber to the cooperage, we're paying freight on a lot of sap. We need to build a kiln on the timber tract."

Maurice exploded, "We've been asking too many loans to extend this oil business! Why we've borrowed over *a hundred thousand dollars!*"

"We should borrow whenever we can safely extend the business that way."

Maurice threatened to break up the business right then and there. Rockefeller smoothed it over. He privately concluded, however, that if any of the Clarks ever again suggested breaking up the company, he would not smooth it over. So that he would know how to handle the problem if it ever came up, he reviewed his personal credit around town. He found, to his surprise, that he could muster $50,000 in loans.

In the bidding, Jim Clark tapped Richard Clark on the arm. Richard Clark consulted some papers in a notebook from his chest pocket. He snapped the book shut, and nodded to Maurice. Maurice took a deep breath and exhaled, "Fifty thousand dollars."

The figure silenced the room. A half a hundred thousand dollars was a figure to command great respect.

John Rockefeller had a wife, a baby, a sister, and a mother to support, and a pair of brothers to help get started after the war. At $50,000, you stop to consider these things. Besides he needed time to raise funds for the Erie Street Church, and he wanted to keep 10 per cent of his own income free for his charities.

But, after all, the refinery was earning well. It was big as refineries went along the Cuyahoga. And even without the Clarks, Rockefeller would still have Sam Andrews' excellent engineering ability.

"Fifty thousand, five hundred," said John Rockefeller.

A week after Maurice Clark threatened to break up the company, John Rockefeller challenged Jim Clark on a couple of items of his travel to Titusville and the oil regions in Pennsylvania to buy the crude oil for the refinery. John wanted a better accounting for Jim's expenses and for the oil he bought, too.

Jim Clark vulgarly abused Rockefeller, and scathingly referred to him as "the Sunday School Superintendent." It was true that Rockefeller *was* a Sunday School Superintendent. But he knew he was not being complimented on it.

He endured a profane blast suggesting that it was time to get the Sunday School element out of the business. Then he said quietly, "Jim, I better tell you not to try to scare me with a bluff you don't mean."

"I mean every word I said!"

"Do you speak for your two brothers?"

"Yes!"

"Good. Remember this conversation, Jim."

In the years ahead, Jim Clark would remember it many times. John Rockefeller walked out of the refinery.

The next morning the three Clark brothers were stunned to see a notice of dissolution in *The Cleveland Leader,* signed by Rockefeller. After the initial surprise, they rallied quickly, realizing there were three of them, and in a buy-out showdown they should be able to raise more money. They asked Andrews where he stood.

He stood with Rockefeller, but he couldn't command important dollars.

The Clarks needed to shake Rockefeller out of the bidding quickly now as they approached their own top limit.

"Sixty thousand," Clark said.

There was a pause, and then a quiet voice, "Sixty thousand, five hundred."

None of these men had expected numbers like this. The attorney was stunned.

Jim Clark said, "Rockefeller, don't bid a number you can't raise in cash dollars."

"Anything I bid, I'll pay."

"There are three of us to go bond on hired money," Jim Clark said. "We can run this up as high as we want."

Rockefeller said, "I told you once not to bluff with me, Jim, unless you want to live with it."

"We're not bluffing! Sixty-five thousand dollars."

Richard and Maurice Clark sucked in air and looked at Jim Clark, then at Rockefeller.

Rockefeller said, "Sixty-five thousand, five hundred dollars."

Jim Clark snarled, "Seventy!"

"Seventy thousand, five hundred."

"Seventy-two thousand!" said Jim Clark.

Maurice Clark cut in, "John, we're up beyond faith in the company and faith in the industry."

"Yes, Maurice. We're up to faith in ourselves." Rockefeller looked out the window into the Cuyahoga's slow current, as if measuring himself in the reflection, and he said, "Seventy-two thousand five hundred dollars is my bid."

"The business is yours!" Maurice Clark stood up.

The next day's *Cleveland Leader* carried an advertisement for carbon oil, benzene, and lubricating oils from the new firm of Rockefeller & Andrews.

That same issue of the *Cleveland Leader* was exciting if you worked along the shores of the Cuyahoga. It explained that there were now fifty refineries, large and small, on the Cuyahoga. They represented an invested capital of three million dollars, and they were putting out about six thousand barrels of refined oil per day. Two thirds of it was shipped to New York and other ports for export.

And on one refinery there was a new sign: The Rockefeller & Andrews Company. Shortly after that there was another sign at the head of Kingsbury Run:

THE STANDARD WORKS
Owners:
J. D. Rockefeller
Samuel Andrews
William Rockefeller

Just about that moment, the Gilded Age began—and it seemed to run on iron and oil, which turned the Cuyahoga iron red with an iridescent scum of oilbow colors.

There were some in carriages going over the bridge who looked down at the red and the rainbow and said it was a shame to dirty the river that way. But those who were right down in the waters in boats and barges and scows thought the red and the rainbow were the sweetest colors a river ever had.

And a young man named J. D. Rockefeller was just on the point of becoming a legend among the bankers of Cleveland—in fact, of the world.

16

The Quaker's Oats

THE MAN WHO made the Cuyahoga one of the most influential rivers in the United States was a short, tough, strait-laced German, Ferdinand Schumacher.

But before he arrived some preparations had been made. While Cleveland evolved with the opening of the canal, Akron sprang into being. And it grew not in a gently rising curve, but in sharp steps like the stairway of land locks to its summit. Most of these steps up resulted from the canal's reaching new major shipping towns on its way south and finally cutting through into the Ohio River in 1830. Akron's population jumped to 910.

The completion of Dr. Eliakim Crosby's Cascade Millrace using the waters of the Little Cuyahoga was the next big step up.

Then as each of five grinding mills was built at each of five dams one above the other, climbing the side of the Little Cuyahoga valley, Akron grew to 2336 people.

In 1840 the city took an extra large step up. Leicester King had always wanted to connect Akron to Pittsburgh by canal. General Perkins and Dr. Eliakim Crosby helped on this one, too, but King spearheaded the politics and financing.

King had ten years of saddle time invested before Ohio agreed to make available one dollar for every two dollars raised by private investment. Pennsylvania voted $50,000 to the long canal from Pittsburgh to Newcastle to Youngstown, Warren, Ravenna, Akron. King needed eight hundred and forty thousand dollars; so again he took to the saddle, riding thousands of miles on the byways along the right-of-way, raising funds.

Despite the financial panic of 1837, King was successful, and the Pennsylvania and Ohio Canal came into Akron in 1840, using for its last leg the runoff spillway of Dr. Crosby's millrace. That connected it to the Ohio and Lake Erie and from the moment of that connection another major phase of Akron's growth began as the city became terminal, tavern, warehouser, and stevedore to a three-way water-borne commerce.

Now within the city other industries grew, particularly clay products, farm machinery, wool, leather goods, and boat building.

But the Little Cuyahoga was about to make Akron into the nation's headquarters for one of mankind's basic staples—with the help of an unsmiling little German storekeeper.

While Ferdinand Schumaker was becoming Akron's largest industrialist, the young pioneers who furnished the waterway foundations for his industry had become old men.

General Perkins was the first to die, in 1844.

Dr. Crosby, encouraged by the success of Cascade Millrace, set out to build an even greater one at Cuyahoga Falls. But he ran into trouble with financing, then he ran into harder digging than he anticipated, then he ran into the financial panic of 1837. With his fortune and his health smashed by the project, he moved West in 1853 and died in 1854.

Judge King built a fortune and died in 1856.

The general, the doctor, and the judge left their names on streets, schools, and the pages of history.

Dr. Crosby had been right when he said Akron would not grow into a really great city just by being a warehouse and a tavern for the passing canal traffic. He said they had to *make* something to ship out. And they couldn't do that until they had power for manufacturing. To furnish that power they built Cascade Millrace, a controlled sluice split off from the Little Cuyahoga on such a course that it came down the escarpment over a series of dams to turn five enormous water wheels. At these damsites five mills grew up: The Aetna, a distillery; the Center Mill, north of Market; the Cascade, near the bottom of the hill; Perkins Mill, wool; and the City Mill.

These weren't little village mills where you took your grain to be ground while you waited. The Little Cuyahoga's waters ground the grain, fifty barrels a day, then went over the spillways into the canal and floated the flour north to Cleveland, south to Cincinnati. That made Akron a very large flour center. But that was about to seem small.

Even at twenty-nine, Ferdinand Schumacher wore an older man's beard, squared off severely below the chin, heavy on the sides but with the smooth ecclesiastical upper lip. Above it sat a Quaker's shovel hat which shadowed a stern face set against relaxation, tobacco, and liquor.

In 1851 he came from Hanover, Germany, to Akron, and there he started a small grocery on Howard Street.

The only reason that is important to the Cuyahoga is that Ferdinand did not like to see his customers buying such deluxe and fancy foods. He thought it was a little sinful. Back in Germany in the grocery business, he used to sell a lot of oats, good solid grain that grew good solid people, and cost very little. America ought to be eating it. So he put in a stock.

Now Akron was not a town accustomed to eating oats at the table. So the oats did not sell. But Schumacher was a stubborn man. For three years, he worried about people not eating oats; and in 1854, he invented a chopper to make tiny cubes of oats. He packed them in one-ounce jars.

Akron people took a liking to these little cubes of oats, bought a lot of them. In five years, Schumacher built a small factory near Market and Howard. It was referred to as the German Mill. He did so well that in five years he needed a second plant. The railroad had arrived. Since he had one plant on the canal, he built the new one in the triangle formed by Main, Market and Exchange Streets.

In the next ten years, Schumacher's business grew like wild oats. When you consider that Akron left the oat strictly for the horse until Schumacher chopped it into blocks, the growth was dramatic.

The oat is something to which you must apply quite a lot of ingenuity to make it marketable. Now in 1876, the stubborn Dutchman found a way to precook the oats and run them between rollers so that they flaked off—rolled oats. I can't go ashore far enough to show you all the excitement this caused. But even from the banks of the Little Cuyahoga's Cascade Millrace, you could see that the whole United States liked Mr. Schumacher's rolled oats.

More Schumacher plants went up alongside the Cascade and the canal—and now alongside the railroad. Schumacher mills occupied an entire city block, and turned Akron's skyline into towering elevators for grain storage.

The eight-story Jumbo Mill was the biggest enterprise in Akron. Ferdinand Schumacher had become far and away the nation's greatest miller. In addition to making rolled oats, he also made flour; and he marketed all the way from Boston to San Francisco.

He was not a leader in the sense of drawing men to him or organizing them or stirring them. He *was* a leader in the sense

that men said, "Look what Schumacher's doing; let's get some of that, too."

Following Ferdinand Schumacher's success, many others in and beyond Akron went into the rolled oat business and into the flour business. It had been a mill town ever since Dr. Crosby built the Cascade. But by 1880, there were ten large mills along the Cascade and Little Cuyahoga, and eleven smaller ones.

Strangely enough, the big trouble that started now was because of a wise Scotchman in Canada who was looking down upon the American milling picture from north of the Great Lakes. It seemed to him that American flour mills were too far from their best source of grain. He thereupon built a large mill in Cedar Rapids, Iowa, in the heart of the wheat and corn country. He made flour.

The instant that happened, nearly every mill along the Little

Cuyahoga switched instantly from flour to oatmeal, Schumacher's special domain.

Cummins & Allen, owning two mills, built a third right under Ferdinand Schumacher's nose beside Old Stone Mill.

Crowell & Andrews over in Ravenna had bought up the Old Quaker Mill there. They were two powerful young Clevelanders with a lot of nerve and drive. They built this mill up so that it made a strong challenge to Schumacher's mill.

When Schumacher reached the age of sixty-four, he faced a very rugged test. Just as Crowell & Andrews were hitting him hardest in the market place, a fire in the night hit his mills.

For a deeply religious man like Ferdinand Schumacher who looked for the hand of God in nearly every action about him, this was a double blow. The fire caused dust explosions, instantly followed by implosions. And by morning, the mightiest mills in America were ruins.

While smoke still curled up from standing blackened posts, word spread through the crowd which was almost all of Akron, "Well over half a million damages."

"He'll never make it back."

"Who? Schumacher? He'll be rebuilt in six months."

"Nope. No insurance. He says death, storms and fire are God's punishing us. To insure against Him is blasphemy."

Ferdinand Schumacher was crushed. But he didn't whine. The only sign to the town was that hour after hour Schumacher's small figure paced the blackened site of his mills.

He would stop and retrieve a trinket here and there.

This made the population nervous, because in this town, no matter what business you were in, you were in the milling business. If you weren't *in* the mill, you were serving or selling to those who were.

Seeing its largest employer wiped out set Akron scurrying to put him back on his feet. But Schumacher was a hard man to help.

The men from the brewery walked over into the charred ruins. When they found him, they pointed out to him that the huge piles of grain on the surface were only water damaged. "We can use that. We'll pay cash. It could bring you enough to start construction."

The little purist pulled himself up. "I'll not have part in corrupting youth with alcohol."

Albert Allen of Cummins & Allen, the stiffest competition, walked over onto the burnt acreage, "If you say the word, we'll supply your customers until you can rebuild. We'll ship it in your bags. Hold your trade for you. Be glad to do it."

"I should think ye would," Schumacher said, "you have a vine new mill and no business. I have business and no mill."

The town worried, Schumacher's brutal abruptness was driving off all those who would help them save the business of Akron. They watched him walking along the banks of the Little Cuyahoga, then along the canal with his hands clasped behind his back, thinking.

One morning the gate guard at Cummins & Allen sent a runner to the outer office saying unless he was losing his mind he had just admitted Ferdinand Schumacher through the gates though the man would not give his name. He had brushed right by.

The outer office told the inner office, and Albert Allen had all cigars and cuspidors removed from his office.

The man with the spade-cut beard who walked in snapped, "You were good enough to offer your assistance."

"Yes." After his recent rebuff, Allen answered in lean language.

"I accept your offer," said Schumacher, "but different. I have thought this over very long. When Alex Cummins died last year, he made you sole executor of his estate, without bond. That means he thought you an honest man; he ought to know. I understand you increased the value of his estate substantially, so you be also a good business head. I'm proposing to you—your company and mine should merge."

Allen could have been surprised, or he could have been reluctant. But he said nothing.

"P'raps you're wondering," continued the great miller, "what is to gain you should merge with a company with burned down mills."

The old man now took paper from Allen's desk and a pencil from his vest, "Here is your plant along this canal. You must cart your grain four blocks up and down the rise to gain the rails. Here is *my* loading platform alongside the railroad tracks.

"I believe we could lay pipe under the road—with a blower here—und blast our grain from the cars direct to your mill."

Allen studied the sketch and fingered his chin.

"Appraisers can value the two properties," Schumacher said. "We let that set shares."

Within the month, Schumacher Milling Company was incorporated for $2,000,000.

Work began on a great trench and three large pipes, ten inches, eight, and seven.

To the amazement of Akron, it worked just fine.

Akron went back to work.

Many today who can find the Little Cuyahoga cutting in and out underneath Akron don't know that the pipes are still at work under there, blowing grain between the Quaker Oats elevators on the hilltop and the mills down over the canal.

Now the oatmeal business appeared to do so well for Ferdinand Schumacher that twenty-one vigorous competitors had crowded in by 1886 to glorify the oat—and to chop the price. The weaker companies kept cutting the price to survive. Chaos set in.

To stem the falling prices, an enormous association of oatmeal millers formed. All but one company joined. Schumacher, the stubborn, stayed out.

The association had problems. The marginal members quietly accepted a shaved price now and then. Buyers knew that you could approach certain association members with a price deal. The association failed in a year.

Another was formed; this one levied severe fines on any member company which cut prices. But what this did was hold prices protectively high to allow twenty new nonmember companies to form and sneak in under the association price to undersell them *all*.

H. P. Crowell stepped forward. He was one of the young industry leaders who had begun with Andrews in Warren and moved to the Little Cuyahoga. He called a meeting of the industry and he made a blunt proposal. How can the public favor the miller who uses the best grain and the best processes when it's sold in bulk? If we put it in a package with a name on it, the customer could tell the good from the bad.

He proposed the formation of a big new company which would intensively advertise a brand name. "And I'm sorry, Ferdinand, but it shouldn't be *Schumacher*."

Seven out of the twenty-one companies were willing, and they merged to become American Cereal Company.

Ferdinand Schumacher thus became president of the largest cereal company in the world, without even liking the idea.

He didn't believe in Crowell's ads and his fancy package. "I built the biggest business in the whole country without advertising. Und this foolishness in putting oatmeal in fancy boxes is a waste. Let them scoob it out of the barrel like before. Cheaper, too."

The name they put on the package was picked by Crowell, Quaker Oats.

Schumacher tried to continue as before, supervising every detail of the business himself, including reading all the company's mail, personally. Not only that, he answered it all in person.

They had to move the offices to Chicago to be central to their western plants and Akron. When the Dutchman left the Little Cuyahoga, he walked out of our story. But not until he had fulfilled Dr. Crosby's prophecy that if the waters of the Little Cuyahoga were made to furnish power, it would make Akron great.

17

Giants on the Little Cuyahoga

ONE EXPECTS the mighty and overpowering rivers to influence the destiny of the people on their banks. Indeed rivers of barely controllable brute strength like the Ohio, the Colorado, the Columbia, are so totally imposing they force conclusions upon their shores and their men.

But the short winding Cuyahoga is exciting for the opposite reason. It makes the men loom large because they took in hand her small breadth and currents and through man-made works amplified the Cuyahoga's power and reach and navigability.

The tremendous national flour and cereal industry headquartered in Akron and made possible by the millrace which Dr. Crosby split off from the Little Cuyahoga vastly exceeded the expectations of Crosby and his colleagues. Yet Cuyahoga waters were about to start another chain of events which would make Akron the center for an enormous international saga.

When C. A. Barnes, owner of an Akron hat store, returned to visit his home town of Jamestown, New York, he met there a frail young doctor who had ceased practicing medicine and was carrying around an idea too large for most men to see.

Benjamin Franklin Goodrich had started to practice medicine so young that people had no confidence, so he wandered into other vocations, at one point real estate. In this business, he came into possession of a failing Hudson River rubber plant which he could not sell. He felt his only way out was to operate it.

He was not able to halt the failure; but he became deeply involved in the mysterious personality of the witch, rubber. Soft and resilient when given its freedom, if captured in a mold only a little smaller than itself, rubber would crack iron to get out. Sometimes sticky, it could also be hard and glassy.

But Benjamin Franklin Goodrich could make it do his will

rather predictably; and he could think of a thousand uses for it. He knew the process had to be different from that dictated by the equipment in his old shop on the Hudson. He needed big money and a lot of water to cool hot rubber.

Goodrich had married a Jamestown girl, and he was there looking for capital when C. A. Barnes came home to Jamestown from Akron. Goodrich was still not the confident type of man one pictures raising substantial capital. Yet when he discussed rubber all could see he had a mind with an upstairs in it. Listeners could picture him in the laboratory, if not behind the ledgers.

C. A. Barnes heard him. Barnes too was a quiet man, but in his work of fitting hats to the leading heads in Akron, he had come to know the soul and mind of his adopted town with a strange sureness.

From the back of a small drawing room Barnes watched Goodrich conclude an impromptu but earnest presentation of the potential in a rubber factory. Though Goodrich's earnestness had captured the concentration of the man, his forthright statement that he was seeking capital started men edging away.

Barnes caught Goodrich's eye and beckoned. Natively courteous, Goodrich required several minutes to disengage himself. But when he finally did, Barnes said to him, "Akron. Akron, Ohio, is the place you want. It has water from the canal and the Cuyahoga River."

"I have water on the Hudson. What's needed is—"

"Men who need a business that needs water. Akron people built water channels to encourage manufacturers."

Goodrich stared with the natural suspicion of the oft disappointed. Barnes continued as if he spoke for all Akron "Write down these names: Colonel Perkins; George Crouse; Schumacher; Seiberling; David King; Buchtel."

Goodrich's face was puzzled. Barnes went right on. "Those men will understand, and if they believe you, they'll find the money."

Goodrich made a trip to Akron.

Perkins and Crouse listened first. Colonel Perkins, son of General Perkins, then traveled to New York to look at Goodrich's rubber shop to see if there was some machinery there and to see what he could learn of the rubber business.

When he came back to Akron, he called a meeting at the Empire House near Lock 1. Perkins looked around the taproom

mentally taking attendance: Miller and Buchtel from farm machinery were there; Schumacher, Cummins, Hower, Allen from
rolled oats and flour; Christy, a banker; David King, son of the
Judge; and J. Parke Alexander, a professional town builder. The
action men of Akron had come.

It was a formidable and an able court. Perkins said to young
Goodrich, "Tell them your mind, Ben."

Ben Goodrich rose. He explained the vast and varied market he
saw for rubber. "I plan to start with fire hose. Leather hose leaks
or breaks just when you need it most. Then I'd go to other lines.
I'll bring some of my machines from New York; and I'll give it all
my time. Everything else has got to come from somewhere."

The most able of men can get their feet through their collars
when confronted by a showdown meeting like this one. Goodrich's earnest, but modest delivery, coupled with his too varied
biography, caused a silence in the room as Akron studied him.

But one of the leather men—a square-shaped block, George
Crouse—stood and faced the group. In a slow, deep voice that
vibrated windows, he said, "This young man has something
Akron needs. We've got to keep him here. I subscribe one thousand dollars now."

Perkins said, "Put me down for one thousand."

In a half hour, there were notes for $13,500 on the table. It was
a pivotal moment at Akron. In view of what happened, of course,
this was pin money, but it came from some men who had never
seen a piece of rubber.

Goodrich needed more. So the fund raising continued, and he
took in as partner his brother-in-law from Jamestown, Harvey
Tew.

For availability of water and transportation, he located his
plant near Lock 1 on the canal. The canal swaled out here to
form two wide basins with sluice gates to release more water.
Goodrich's new neighbors on that site were mostly houses except
for Mr. Ohio Columbus Barber who was building a new match
factory there.

So beside the waters of the Ohio Canal inherited from the
Cuyahoga rose Goodrich's two-story brick factory, 50′ x 100′. It
would change the economy of the Midwest. But at this moment,
it housed a rusty jumble of iron which wilted the enthusiasm of
the backers.

As they watched, however, they saw the slender, balding young man, with large intense eyes and a wind-catching mustache, move with new poise and purpose. They figuratively exhaled. What the doctor lacked in committee he made up for in motion.

When the first shipment of Brazil Para rubber came up (at $1.17 a pound), Akron went down to Lock 1 to poke it, smell it, taste it, and shrug. "Too supple to build much on."

B.F. GOODRICH PLANT
1880

And when the stench of vulcanizing sulphur floated down the canal and the Cuyahoga, noses turned up. When the silver coins turned black in cash drawers along the canal from Goodrich's sulphur, the shrugs became a nose punch and a thumb in the direction of Lock 1.

But one day coils of fat black snakes were stacked in front of Goodrich, Tew & Company—fire hose. The shrugs changed meaning. "Who knows? Stranger things have happened."

The young company had no sales force. It had to write letters to city governments to sell fire hose. City governments didn't buy much through the mail. So Goodrich, Tew & Company made rubber machinery belting, fruit jar rings, valves for pumps, and tips for billiard cues.

It took in $50,000 in its first year. That was remarkable; but what bothered Goodrich, he needed more money. For five years there were no profits. Backers who had lent money became nervous, muttered about getting their money back. Harvey Tew was losing faith.

Ben Goodrich finally said, "Harvey, it looks like a buy-or-sell matter. You want to buy me out or sell to me?"

Tew thought a while. "I'll sell."

The settlement figure was $12,500 for Tew's one-quarter interest in what became the B. F. Goodrich Company.

Tew's withdrawal naturally drew unfavorable attention. The other subscribers now pressed Goodrich. He talked to Colonel Perkins about the future of the industry and how close the company was to profits. "But I need *more* money to get into more product lines."

Perkins came away convinced all over again. He raised enough dollars to pay off all the nervous subscribers. Before paying them, Perkins offered each man the option of converting his loan to stock. Almost all took the cash.

Even with Perkins's help, another money crisis struck in 1878. Perkins couldn't help this time. So George Crouse stepped in and countersigned company loan applications up to $45,000. Crouse and Perkins were now stockholders.

The former subscribers, now very much relieved to be out of it with a whole skin, could afford to be cordial again. But the grins froze in 1880. B. F. Goodrich sales reached $319,000. Profit was $69,000, and the company paid a 10 per cent dividend. This meant that Dr. Goodrich was able to draw $4,000 over and above his $2,000 salary. Colonel Perkins and George Crouse also drew their first returns in eleven years.

While most of the world considers such a return slavery, a man starting his own business feels blessed. On the strength of it, Dr. Goodrich built another building beside the first. It cost $9,000.

After another eight years of rather slow, smoldering growth came the brush fire bonanza. A veterinarian in Scotland, Dr. Dunlop, wound a piece of rubber tubing around the front and back wheels of his boy's bicycle to take up the shock of cobble-stones.

The pneumatic tire had arrived.

Everything that rolled could now roll faster. It was the second birth of transportation. Production of all vehicles increased—and the demand for tires. On the Little Cuyahoga stood Ben Goodrich, ready.

Bunyanesque parade: Ohio Columbus Barber, Frank Seiberling,
    Well, you know the rest of the story.
    The waters of the Ohio Canal and the Little Cuyahoga were
    They needed soft wheels. Akron was ready.
about to spawn a giant industry, because here and there across the country now the air was rent by an occasional series of explosions and blue smoke as a succession of angry black beetles began blatting over the roads, scaring horses.

There came now to the banks of the Little Cuyahoga a

Arthur Marks, Stahdelman, Litchfield, O'Neil, Harvey Firestone —tire builders.

But men along the Cuyahoga should pause and tell their children of Eliakim Crosby and C. A. Barnes. Because of them, three quarters of America's rubber products are made in Akron on the Little Cuyahoga.

18

The Iron Men

THE CUYAHOGA VALLEY is iron country. It all began way upstream south of the big U-turn in the river in the mind of "Crazy
Dan" Heaton.

He was Crazy Dan Heaton because he was always flying in the
face of what many called practicality; never crazier than when he
announced that he could make iron in the Ohio woods and save
the wracking trip to Pittsburgh, which was the westernmost point
at which a man could buy bar iron.

But Dan Heaton had found rocks in the bottom of Yellow
Creek, kidney-shaped rocks flecked with gray, the kind that he
and his brother James had not seen since they left Winchester,
Virginia, about the year 1800. The Heaton brothers had been
ironmasters and they knew iron ore when they saw it.

These good-sized boulders weren't more than 5 per cent iron,
and a modern ironmaster wouldn't give them furnace room; but
to men a hundred hard miles from iron bolts, axheads, and plow
blades, they looked good in 1803.

Dan and his brother acquired land and mineral rights on both
sides of Yellow Creek in the Western Reserve in what is now
Struthers, Ohio. That's a long way from the Cuyahoga, and yet
you will see in a way it's the main current of the Cuyahoga
story.

The brothers built their furnace with stone walls twenty feet
high. To get a blast, they pumped water into a long wooden
trough, compressed the air in the box, then forced it into the
furnace.

Cast-iron plates an inch thick could be carted west to the
Portage and floated down the Cuyahoga at $180 a ton, perhaps
the first sign of civilization in the Western Reserve.

Cuyahoga Steam Furnace started up in 1835 on the west bank

of the river opposite Cleveland. They built cannon. Whittaker
and Wells followed these by the river in 1839. Geauga Furnace
opened near Painesville. Elyria and Dover had furnaces. Coal
began to come down the Cuyahoga so that furnace men didn't
need to burn up acres of timber to get charcoal for the furnaces.

The area grew an appetite for iron—for gun barrels, bolts,
screws, axheads, chain, singletree attachments, tools, wheel tires.
They had, by now, quite a few men trained to make iron. But it
was harder and harder to find the rocks. Where would the ore
come from?

Answering that question created an iron community peopled
by Cleveland Cliffs, Pickands-Mather, Oglebay Norton, Hanna
Mining, the Columbia Fleet, Republic Steel, J&L Steel, and others along the Cuyahoga River.

In one sense all the stories go back to a pile of iron and rock
slabs at a fork in the road outside the city of Nagoma, Michigan,
on which is a plaque which reads in part: ". . . to mark the first
discovery of iron ore in the Lake Superior region. The exact spot
is 300 feet northeasterly from this monument to an iron post. The
ore was found under the roots of a fallen pine tree in June 1845
by Margi-Lassa Gesick, a chief of the Chippewa tribe of Indians.
The land was secured by a mining permit and the property sub-
sequently developed by the Jackson Mining Company, organized
July 23, 1845."

United States Deputy Surveyor William A. Burt and his company were surveying this unexplored territory for the United
States government. Strangely enough it becomes important that
the day was cloudy. Burt was having trouble with his magnetic
compass needle which suddenly started jumping all around.

It is a revealing moment in history, because what chiefly interested Burt was not the cause of the failure of the magnetic compass, but the fact of it. He was himself the inventor of the solar
compass, and he was now confronted with proof of the importance of his invention in the surveying of these lands where the
magnetic compass would not hold true.

On one page of his field notes is an observation by the young
and brilliant head of the survey and exploration party, Douglass
Houghton, "Spathos and magnetite iron ores may abound on this
T-line."

On the morning of the nineteenth of September, 1844, Burt's field notes show that at one point one of the magnetic compass-men yelled, "Come and see a variation that will beat them all!"

The survey party was astounded to see the north end of the needle swinging a few degrees to the south of west. Burt said, "Boys, look around and see what you can find!" The party scattered and returned in a few moments carrying iron ore. This was on Teal Lake.

Young Douglass Houghton died on the survey, killed in a storm on Lake Superior when his boat upset. His work was carried on by William Burt, who wrote a full and complete record of the survey.

The most exciting thing for Burt continued to be the justification for his solar compass, but the excitement caused by his published reports was something completely different. Since the reports and maps were made in full detail, they revealed to the nation when coupled with the reports published by Jacob Houghton, brother of Douglass, the rich iron deposits of the Michigan country. Immediately thousands of permits were filed requesting permission to explore and exploit.

From that moment, the race was on. Many men came into the Michigan iron country and began prospecting, mining, building furnaces.

In Cleveland, a group of men had founded the Dead River and Ohio Mining Company. They hired a distinguished Ohio scientist, Dr. J. Lang Castles, to go up to Michigan and have a look. He had been head of the Western Reserve Medical School, head of a chemical laboratory, and had one of the few microscopes in the West. Up on the south shore of Superior at the Carp River, he was staggered to find a hill of red dirt a thousand feet high and a mile long. He named it Cleveland Mountain, secured the permit, and rushed back to Cleveland to explain that Cleveland Mountain contained enough iron to make a railroad all the way to the Pacific Coast.

W. A. Adair and ten associates listened, formed the Cleveland Iron Mining Company, and issued stock. What was to become extremely important was that one of the stockholders was a young attorney who had just moved to Cleveland, Samuel L. Mather.

A few of the men went up to look at the hill of ore. They found themselves in a forbidding land, so they returned to Cleveland and turned in their stock for cash. Then the company sent Tower Jackson up to Marquette in 1852 as its first resident mining agent. What he found there would have sent most men home. Those furnaces which were already established were rapidly going out of business. The climate and the lack of fuel made ironmaking impractical. It was necessary to get the ore down to Cleveland, but transportation was impossible. Jackson wrote back to Cleveland demanding the wherewithal to make a plank road like Euclid Avenue to bring the ore from Cleveland Mountain to where it could be floated downlakes into Cleveland.

Building that road is a whole story in itself as the carts careened out of control and killed the mules; but in 1855, Jackson managed to ship downlakes 1,449 tons of ore.

The job of getting this ore downlakes and around the falls at Sault Ste. Marie was unbelievable. So it's an important part of the Cuyahoga story that Charles T. Harvey, a twenty-four-year-old salesman for the Fairbanks Scale Company, was at the Sault trying to recover from typhoid fever. He observed men struggling to transfer iron ore from decks of vessels onto wagons to be hauled around the falls of St. Mary to be loaded into other vessels below the Sault and sailed south to Cleveland. Young Harvey could see what was needed—a canal at the Sault. He decided he was the man to do it. Two years and two thousand heartbreaks later, on June 18, 1855, Charles Harvey personally opened the sluice gate to let a vessel through from Lake Superior to Lake Huron. Two months later, the two-masted brig *Columbia* passed down through the lock carrying the first shipment of iron ore, 120 tons consigned to the Cleveland Iron Mining Company at the Crawford & Price wharf on the Cuyahoga River. The brig *Columbia* was later to give its name to a great fleet of boats on the lakes.

When that vessel tied up, the Cuyahoga River became the center of an industrial revolution in the United States.

But only a few men could see it. Samuel L. Mather was one of them. He was the young attorney in whose office the company was formed. Having attended Wesleyan University in Middletown, Connecticut, he was sent out to Ohio to look out for the Mather real estate holdings in the Western Reserve, and he was swept up in the iron fever which formed the Cleveland Iron

Mining Company. While the fever extinguished in a flurry of depression as the stockholders sold out their stock, Samuel L. Mather held his.

Then the panic of 1857 shut down the iron mills in Pittsburgh, Youngstown, Cleveland, and spread disaster all the way up to the Michigan iron range. The company needed $50,000 more cash to keep its Michigan range in action. Mather went to New York and Boston bankers to borrow. The answer was "No."

That's when Sam Mather invented "iron money." Unable to get real money, he came up with a system of issuing small drafts on nicely printed stock against the treasure of the Cleveland Iron Mining Company. These notes were sent up to Cleveland Mountain where they were used to pay miners, teamsters, cooks, and hardware stores where the company bought supplies. Due to the confidence in the Cleveland Iron Mining Company, these notes circulated freely and were in no hurry to float back to Cleveland to be turned in for cash. This delay was enough to let Mather and the company officers sell more stock.

In this manner, the company inched its way up until the demand for iron increased in 1861. The Civil War needed cannon, rifles, rails. Now came the ships.

Captain Alva Bradley, then of Vermilion, Ohio, built a fleet of schooners and brigs to carry the ore. It was an eight-hundred-mile trip that demanded the utmost seasmanship, but the unloading on the Cuyahoga was perhaps the most challenging dock operation in history.

Captain Bradley, one of the earliest in this type of navigation, continued to increase his fleet. In 1858, he launched the *London*. Soon after that the *Exchange*, and then the *Wagstaff*, which carried iron ore for a quarter of a century. In the year 1873, he launched six new ships, and at that point he began to build steamships. In 1867, the Cleveland Iron Mining Company bought a half interest in the *George Sherman* for $14,000, capacity 550 tons of ore.

In 1869 came the big leap forward when Captain Peck built the *R. J. Hackett*. In 1872, when Cleveland Iron Mining Company was bringing down nearly a million tons of ore, the company bought into the Cleveland Transportation Company, a fleet of steam vessels and schooners especially built for iron: The *Geneva;* the *Vienna;* the *Sparta;* the *Havana;* the *Genoa;* the

Verona; the *Helena;* the *Sumatra.* These vessels each carried a
thousand tons per trip to Cuyahoga docks.

To this point, the Cuyahoga's merchant navy was wooden sail,
but now iron vessels began to enter the trade. The first iron
freighter built specifically for this business, and not a converted
passenger vessel, was the *Onoko* built in Cleveland in 1882. She
was 287 feet long.

In 1888, the directors of the Cleveland Iron Mining Company
commissioned two steel vessels, $400,000 each, capacity of 2,600
tons. These giants dropped the cost of transportation from about
$3.00 a ton to $1.22. That year, Cleveland Iron Mining Company
brought down 5,000,000 tons.

Now the locks and channels and harbors were getting too small
for the vessels. The Poe lock opened in 1896; it was 800 feet long,
100 feet wide and 22 feet deep. Cleveland Iron Mining Company
now built a 426-foot steel ship, the *Cadillac,* with an 18-foot draft
and a capacity of 6,000 tons. Along came the *Choctaw,* the
Andaste, the *Centurian,* the *Presque Isle,* and the *Angeline* at 455
feet. And now the ships were too big for the unloading equipment and the stage was set for a new race of mechanical men on
the Cuyahoga shore.

In 1890, Sam Mather, who had guided the Cleveland Iron
Mining Company, died. His son, William Gwinn Mather, was
vice president of the company, which in 1891 merged with the
Iron Cliffs Company to become Cleveland-Cliffs Iron Company.
William Gwinn Mather became president of the combined opera-
tion and remained so for forty-two years.

But it's time to flash back to another beginning. The most
exciting year in the history of the Cuyahoga was 1883. By then a
plethora of iron companies, working out of the Iron Trades Building at the mouth of the river, had founded such a complex of
mines and vessel companies that they had run out of people. One
man might be sales agent for one company, mine supervisor for
another, vessel coordinator for another. Iron had become a Cuyahoga way of life. Families grew up in it, married into other families who were in it, and compounded the complexity of this
burgeoning business.

Many wished to straighten matters out so that a man could be
clearer about whom he was buying from, whom he was selling to,
whom he was competing with, and who were his partners. But

there was little time for that because of the industry-shaking events which crowded in with more urgency than the desire for organization. The congress had just passed tariff legislation protecting the iron industry, thus attracting more men into the building of furnaces. The Bessemer process was just showing men new uses for lower grade ores; power drills were coming into use so that less attractive deposits could suddenly be worked. Cornish pumps were being installed in the pits and, as the shafts sought deeper levels, new hoisting machines were coming in. A new and longer lock was opened at the Sault, the 300-foot *Onoko* had been built with a capacity of 3,000 tons, promising even greater speeds and capacities. Explorers were moving beyond the Marquette Range into the area north of Lake Superior, opening up the Vermilion Range. The Steel Age was dawning.

Many men saw that to push into this new era some clearer organization was needed in the industry. Samuel L. Mather was in the process of merging to form Cleveland-Cliffs; Hewitt and Tuttle was consolidating into Tuttle, Olgebay and Company, the partnership of M. A. Hanna and Company was forming from the Rhodes and Carter Iron Ore and Pig Iron Agency; but to most, action was more interesting than organization.

The young son of Samuel L. Mather, and brother of William Gwinn Mather, was a shy and thoughtful man who saw that a ton of finished steel was the result of such a puzzle of separate and individual coal, ore, furnace, dock and vessel companies that there was a strong need for an integrated company efficiently coordinating installations all the way from Lake Superior mines to Cuyahoga mills to the Allegheny coal fields. He was working for the Cleveland Iron Mining Company, having served a long apprenticeship in the mines of Michigan. There he had formed an especially strong attachment to two dramatic men: Colonel James Pickands, a Civil War hero now turned mine supply merchant, and a hard-driving iron agent affiliated with a dozen companies, J. C. Morse. These two were men of action, but they had a tremendous respect for the quiet thoughtfulness of young Sam Mather. Morse and Pickands were brothers-in-law, for they had come home from the ranges to Cleveland to marry two Outhwaite sisters and take them back to the iron country.

The three men conducted their dreaming by mail; and then one morning a modest advertisement appeared in the *Cleveland*

Leader: "Announcing the formation of Pickands-Mather & Company, dealers in pig iron and iron ore." They had two rooms in the Grand Arcade in Cleveland, with an option on more space, and they had an office boy named Henry Dalton, with a jovial smile, who loved to sell. In 1884, this infant firm brought down 1,022 tons of ore. Two years later, they brought down a quarter of a million tons. And then, as they carried out Sam Mather's

plan, Pickands-Mather & Company grew from three men and an office boy to thousands of employees working from the Mesabi Range in Minnesota across vessel fleets, blast furnaces, steel mills, reaching far east into the Allegheny coal country, with the Cuyahoga valley being the nerve center.

That Cuyahoga valley leadership continues today. For example, on the shores of the Cuyahoga, Joe Slater brought about one of the technological breakthroughs in the thousand-year history of iron and steel.

In 1943, the United States government begged for more blast

furnaces for the war effort. Now the blast furnace, one of the half dozen basic inventions of all time, had remained very much like the furnace Dan Heaton built in Struthers, Ohio. It had grown, of course, so that by 1943, it stood 100 feet high, 28 feet across; and it could cast 1,400 tons of pig iron a day. But Joe Slater, chairman of Republic Steel's blast furnace committee, wanted to get more iron out of a furnace.

A Mr. Julian Avery, who had never seen a blast furnace, but had a large inquiring mind, had suggested to Joe Slater that the air blast whipped through a blast furnace so fast that not all the valuable oxygen would consume in the chemical reaction inside. He wondered: If you put a throttle valve on the top of the furnace to tame this blast and create a back pressure, could not the chemical reaction be carried out more completely?

While it sounded rather simple to Mr. Avery, furnace men were not keen about any procedure which would turn their smokestack into an explosive pressure cooker. A blast furnace is an awesome monster to tamper with. Its stack contains a tumult of gas, coke, and metal at 2,500 degrees; and the whole is aggravated by a turbo-driven hurricane coming in at the rate of 85 cubic feet of air per second.

But Joe Slater, a patriotic man, was under the pressure of war. He wanted to try putting in the *entire* hundred thousand cubic feet of air needed to make a ton of iron, or what he called, "A hundred of wind a minute." If you could hold it in there without blowing your stack, that should give you 20 per cent more steel. If it didn't work, "there'd be a hell of a mess on the cast house floor."

On the morning of July 7, 1944, Joe Slater and Walter Montgomery, his furnace foreman, pumped in a hundred of wind, holding it in with a pressure top. A long working day later, the pressure top had not blown, and Joe Slater was making more iron from one furnace than anyone in all history. The company president, Charles White, asked Joe if he thought the furnace would take it on a regular basis. Joe Slater replied, "If I can run two weeks, I can run two months. If I can run two months, I can run forever."

Slater tortured his furnace with pressures no other furnace had endured. He found he could also reduce the coke use by 13 per cent, and lower the entire cost a dollar a ton. The furnace could use poorer coke and leaner ore. He died on the job shortly after, but he made the Cuyahoga valley put out more steel for the war.

Meanwhile, Cuyahoga vessels drained the Michigan and Minnesota mines so deep that they were down to lean ore, and ore that was costly to recover. The steel industry in the center of the United States was suffering from competition of richer ores nearer the surface in many countries. That's when the men at the mouth of the Cuyahoga made their next big moves: opening a vast new Labrador iron ore country and benefiting low-grade domestic ores with the development of taconite.

The drama of the iron men continues.

19

Peck's Big Boats

STRANGELY ENOUGH at mid-century, mid-America needed a special kind of hero—a ship. The design of that vessel was trying to be born in a lot of men's minds.

While the iron men from the mouth of the Cuyahoga were opening up the Michigan iron ranges with nerve and muscle, Mark Hanna and others were opening up the coal fields south of the Cuyahoga and floating coal down the canal to feed the iron-masters' furnaces.

But it took a whole navy of three-masted schooners to bring down a little iron, and a cavalry of mules to unload it.

A ship was needed unlike any other. It must be narrow enough to clear the locks, but big enough to bring downlakes acres of the Michigan Peninsula and Minnesota. The ship needed to be deep draft for iron ore capacity, but shallow enough for Cuyahoga navigation. It needed quarters for a large crew—quarters that would take up no space. It needed so many conflicting character-istics that marine architects couldn't design her.

At the age of twenty-five, Eli Peck built his first ship. She was graceful, shiply, and shapely. In 1847, he built one with a grace-ful name, *Jenny Lind;* but she was a slightly ugly boat in front, scowlike.

"What's Peck up to?" people asked of the shipwrights as they watched it build over the months.

Peck was sneaking up on the design for the most unusual mer-chant fleet in world history.

Even among shipping and boating people of the world, few know that hundreds of miles from salt water, the mouth of the Cuyahoga headquarters the nation's most unusual and massive merchant navy in a single trade. This is the Great Lakes bulk fleet—iron ore, coal, limestone, some salt, cement and cereals. Its enormous vessels have decks designed for fast unloading of bulk cargoes, hulls designed against the tantrums of the inland seas, drafted for the shallow channels and rivers. They are also designed to the special appetites and chemistry of blast furnaces.

When strangers get their first close-up of these long, low floating monsters beating the waters between the Cuyahoga and Duluth, they often pull off the highway and stare. At first they think they're looking at two vessels passing each other, or, on hazy days, at an island with a house on each end. Waiting for one at a drawbridge is a ghostly experience. They don't move, they loom at you, strangely silent. And as you wait, the ship never stops going by.

Beating the water between the Cuyahoga and Duluth for about thirty turn-arounds a year, these great ships do the basic hauling for the Midwest's steelmaking complex. To sea coast ship lovers, they don't have the wave-splitting grace; but when you get to know them, these bluff-bowed boxes become truly beautiful.

How they happened is very much the story of Eli Peck, who was as blunt-bowed and relentless as his most famous ship.

At the age of twenty-five, Captain Peck had built his first ship. He set up his own yard in among already existing shipyards, drydocks, and related establishments near what is now West 58th Street in Cleveland. It was in 1847 that his *Jenny Lind*, a 200-ton-capacity schooner, slid off the ways and into the Cuyahoga; and people began to ask, "What's Peck up to?"

The *Lind's* hull was closer in form to a barge than his other ships. The blunted bow and squared cross section carried much more cargo than the usual boat of the same size.

The cargo she carried was best described as "miscellaneous," neither bulk nor package freight, but bricks, textiles, machinery and milling supplies, and groceries. A real need for the big bulker had not yet shown itself by 1847.

But in the year that the Soo opened, Eli Peck and Irvine U. Masters entered into a partnership that bore their names. Peck & Masters was small among the Cuyahoga shipyards which turned out 84,000 tons of shipping, 500 vessels, between 1849 and 1869. Peck & Masters built 50. But it tells you something about them to note that these 50 added up to 27,000 tons, roughly a third of all construction.

Mr. Masters was not a seafaring man; he was a financial partner with other interests, in 1863 being elected mayor of Cleveland. But this capital gave Peck the freedom to carry out his design concepts which built the kind of shipyard they wrote about in the paper:

> It will be seen that nearly all the vessels, whether sail or steam, built by Mr. Peck, were of the first class, being mainly barques and large propellers. They will be recognized by those familiar with lake commerce as models in size, beauty and strength, whilst several have made unusually quick trips.

While conventional boats by conventional builders hovered around the 150-ton capacity mark, Peck combined size and design to produce such boats as: *Desota*, 570 tons, barque (1855); *Evergreen City*, 610 tons, propeller (1856); *Northwest*, 628 tons, barque (1862); *Pewabic*, 730 tons, propeller (1863).

And, as he progressed, he knew he was getting closer to the bulk carrier the nation needed for converting the red dirt from Michigan into Cuyahoga iron for shafts, plates, rods, nails, rails, and destiny.

Peck often stood before his work board reflecting. Irvine Masters often rose from the ledgers to look over his shoulder. He would see light pencil-sketch overlays on drawings of a ship already afloat. Detail changes; a plan for communications, oddly from the bow of the ship to the stern; a rudder that could be operated from more than one station. Sometimes, even as early as this, penciled speculations on the layout of the deck—the engine house and pilothouse far separated.

"What ship is that, Eli? Your great S.S. *Maybe*?"

"Yep. With a new idea added. She may never sail."

"Eli, we didn't get a reputation from Buffalo to Detroit for *old* ideas."

"Well, I should be ready with drawings in two months. Can we raise construction money on her then?"

"Not for a speculative boat, Eli. Our loans are too heavy for the next six to twelve months. But after that . . ."

But they never did built it together. The faithful Masters died in 1864. For five years, Peck carried on alone with the assistance of his now highly trained workmen and, once, a consultant in the person of Captain Gilbert Knapp, who watched over the Government's interests during the construction of two revenue cutters. Although Masters was gone, his name remained in gilt above the offices that prospered under his financial guidance. Eli Peck was a loyal man. He kept Masters' name on everything.

This fairness led him to build speculative vessels for which there were no definite orders:

". . . A working man himself, he was in thorough sympathy with his workmen, and in the slack season, instead of discharging men and thus entailing want upon them, he built vessels [not on order, but] on speculation, merely that he might keep the men busy and their families supplied. Providentially, these speculations were always successful [as we will later observe] thus illustrating the proverb that 'there is he that scattereth, and yet increaseth.'" [Cleveland *Plain Dealer*]

And because of this speculation the Captain's great ship finally sailed.

You see from 1864 to 1869, few ships were built by Peck & Masters. Peck's men operated their well-reputed skills to the repair and upkeep of other men's ships, and Eli took care of administrative and financial matters. In this capacity, he began to diversify. He was active in the formation of the People's Gas Light Company and became president of that organization. He was also made a director of the Savings Loan Association.

This brought to his attention with greater forcefulness than ever the importance of iron to Cleveland, and the need for supervessels to carry enormous amounts of ore.

It was Eli Peck's final examination for destiny. Standing now in his pattern loft, aged forty-seven, amid a clutter of half-finished drawings, he had in his head all the best of history's naval architecture.

He had the confidence of twenty-two successful years of shipbuilding; he had the timidity born of repairing shipwrecks. He had the awareness of need. He had the poise to go after construction money. To raise money, he had to talk his ship.

"It will be propeller. Single screw."

"Single?"

"Yes. Two of them, exposed on the flanks, would damage in the shallows. One, sheltered by the rudder, will give as much power and nearly as much control. The engine will be as far aft as she'll go."

"Aft, sir?"

"Aft. To free up cargo space. It'll be bigger, though—more powerful. That's the trouble with these new propellers. Though they burn only a fraction of what the side-wheelers do, they're not as fast. So it needs engine."

The hull's cross section was to be square. And there had to be some sail area. Three masts, gaff rigged. He wasn't through with sail just yet. If the new engine failed, the wind would bring Peck's boat in. But the masts were to be short. When the sails were not set, they would look like cargo booms. But all this was a combination of existing features.

"But what will make this boat a moneymaker, the pilothouse is to be way forward over the bow."

"Forward, sir!"

"Forward."

A significant thing was Peck's move for much greater teamwork between the docks that loaded and unloaded.

"You see, they've got those loading chutes at Marquette on twenty-four-foot centers now, and everyone's converting their deck hatches to fit. Loading is fast, but *unloading* is where the tie-up is."

"To discharge these boats fast, the pilothouse and other deck structures have got to move out of the way of unloading. Way up forward, over the point of the bow that you wouldn't use for cargo anyway. Then she'd be clear and free, just a big stretch of hatch covers in the middle."

The plans came in before the money did. Peck decided to plunge ahead on speculation. But it occurred to him that *Captain Robert Hackett might be interested.* They had spoken on several occasions, and Hackett had always been partial to Peck & Masters vessels. Peck sent a message to Detroit on an upbound customer's boat.

Hackett arrived on the next steamer. He looked over the plans.

"It's boxy right up to the stern, Eli."

"Yes, Robert."

He looked over the stocks and the scaffolding, indicating a ship of mammoth capacity. He asked questions. Pilothouse to engine room communications? Controls? Where would fuel be stored? What about crew quarters? Calculated draft? Minor changes were suggested and agreed on by both.

Robert Hackett approved.

"Eli, I'll cosign with you."

Captain Hackett now had reason to help sell Peck's new vessel. He had money in it. But he found himself suddenly in a strangely awkward position.

Typical of this awkwardness was the day he made a strong presentation of the vessel to his competitor, Captain Varm Jensen. Jensen listened to the wonders of the new supervessel under construction. He thought a moment, and then he said, "Robert, I'm surprised at you. You've been a tough competitor, but fair (except the time you beat me to the fuel dock by running through the fog). But now for the first time, you lie to me."

Hackett purpled, "Lie? Why say that!"

"Figure it out, Robert. As hard as you and I compete, if that boat would really run faster, load more, and unload quicker, would you *really* offer it to *me* . . . of all people?"

Hackett knuckled his jaw thoughtfully.

"In fact," Jensen continued, "would you offer it to *any* other captain?"

Hackett went to Cleveland. "Eli, we can't sell the boat. We'll have to operate her ourselves."

They formed the Northwestern Transport Company to contract for carrying ore down from Fayette Brown's Jackson Iron Company. An agent for that and other iron companies, Harvey H. Brown (the son of Fayette), bought a minor interest in the Northwestern.

Construction on the boat went ahead. They decided to christen it the *R. J. Hackett*. No doubt Peck's fair nature first proposed this. The hull was closed in and the powerful engine was ordered.

Dockside critics watched with interest and criticism. If the boat was so advanced, why was it not being built with plates of iron?

Peck probably realized that the age of steel vessels was coming. But what kept Peck and other yards from metal was that their men were good with wood. Oak and cedar timbers were strong, and the price was right. Iron members and plating were a somewhat unknown quantity; they were scarce and very costly. Oddly, early wooden ore boats, from the *Hackett* on, accelerated the change-over.

Came the day for launching, many Cleveland mining and transport men were there. They were immediately struck by the great length of uninterrupted deck between pilothouse and after-house. And the masts were sawed off. But the wheeldeck was ridiculously high.

"Why make her look like a giraffe?"

"He did it so the captain can see down over the bow in close navigation."

"What'll keep her from rolling over?"

"Eli Peck's reputation, y'damn fool!"

What the onlookers couldn't see was that although the *Hackett* had rather conventional major dimensions—211 feet long and 33 feet wide—space available for cargo should hold at least 1,129 tons of iron ore. Ore boats of conventional layout prior to this time had been considered large if they could carry 700 tons.

Everything was ready. The *R. J. Hackett* left the stocks bound for history. Bound to keep Cleveland steel mills fed. Bound to leave her mark on the shipyards not only on the Cuyahoga but all along the Lakes.

She drew the calculated amount of draft, when her holds were full, with room left over to clear all navigable waterways. She steamed up to the Jackson mines, the propeller churning up twelve miles an hour. They opened her twenty-four-foot spaced hatches to the loading chutes there and churned on back down-lakes with 1,200 tons of ore for the mills at Cleveland.

Along the Cuyahoga, a lot of loud mouths were silent. With only one trip to her log, plans were being made for a second ship like her.

The *Forest City* was completed by the following year. For one season she operated as a consort, in tow. In doing this, North-western Transport continued a practice begun by oxen and barges, carried on by tugs and schooners operating in restricted waters, and employed later by propellers towing sailers over open waters when the latter became unprofitable to operate under their own power. By the time that season ended, they had already made enough money to purchase a separate engine for the *Forest City*.

There is yet to be found the ore boat built after these, except the picturesque whalebacks, that did not use Eli Peck's design. Boats sprung up all over the Lakes—engine room aft, pilothouse foreward, and a long stretch of hatches in-between.

These were the long ships.

There were, of course, improvements. Thirteen years later, the *Onoko*—out of Cleveland's Globe Iron Works—became the first iron ore boat with a hull built entirely of iron. The 1880s saw development of the Bessemer steel process and a material even better for the naval architect. The *Spokane* of 1886, also built by the metal fabricators of the Globe works, was the first Lakes boat with a hull of the new material. The year 1895 saw one of the last holdouts of resistance to metal boats. Harvey H. Brown wanted a boat in the Northwestern fleet bearing his father's name. Captain Peck designed it and it fitted his earlier boats to a tee. With one change. It was iron above the waterline.

But methods of forming and joining sheets and strengthening metal had not yet really been perfected, so the idea of composite boats never really caught on. It was merely transitional.

The propeller steamer Peck built in 1869 was to be the mold for the modern ore carrier. With engines aft and pilothouse in the point of the bow, nearly the whole hull was left open for cargo. Loading hatch centers were spaced twenty-four feet apart for the convenience of standardized loading and unloading equipment. High sides she had, too, and a square hull section to carry nearly twice the cargo of previous boats the same length.

By this time, the good Captain Peck had retired. Ships carrying the legend "N.W.T. Co." had been sold to the Vulcan Transport Company in Detroit. "Peck's boats" had not retired. They stayed on the Lakes and their image can be seen today in the big ones towed by tugs in the serpentine Cuyahoga.

By that time, ore shipping on the Lakes was over its growing pains. Things got to the point where a landlubber could manage a fleet. Or think it profitable enough to get someone to do it for him.

The stage was set for Rockefeller.

20

Here Comes *The Mather!*

SOME PEOPLE light up with recognition when the S. S. *Samuel Mather*'s bow cuts the mouth of the Cuyahoga. The name is a Cuyahoga name. Beginning with the Mather who was on the executive committee of the Connecticut Land Company, there has always been a sobersided, public-conscienced descendant of Cotton Mather silently and firmly at work for the well-being of the Western Reserve and the Cuyahoga valley. They were thin-lipped men of towering conscience and ability, reclusive during gaiety, tough as iron during trouble. And iron was their business.

The name has always been on one of P-M's best boats: there have been four S. S. *Samuel Mathers*—one afloat ever since '87 when the three-masted, sail-and-steam-powered *Mather* was launched.

I don't mean the S. S. *Samuel L. Mather,* but the *Samuel Mather,* named for the Mather most widely known as "Mister Mather." Thousands who never knew him personally have seen his works, which fanned out like the stern waves off his ships. All along the iron ore route from the Cuyahoga to Port Arthur on Superior you see the name cut into marble on colleges and hospitals; engraved on the letterheads of foundations, being polished in raised brass letters on the fronts of corporations, branches of corporations, and the ownership plaques on vessels running from the Cuyahoga north to the iron ranges.

On the Cuyahoga, the name's part of the spoken language; the inflections range from a groan to a sigh. The sighs must wait for his biographer since this book hasn't time to go inland. But the groans are apt to be from maritime competitors based along the Cuyahoga, which some feel might be just a fat fishing stream but for Mather.

Even his seniors called him Mister Mather, and men tended to step apart to let him through. Closing in after him, they'd recall the mine accident that pinned young Sam Mather under timbers and iron dust, smashing ribs and an arm which he carried bent through the rest of his life, and through several chapters of this book because of his multi-chaptered life. The dignity and lonely ethics of this slight, wiry vessel operator didn't quite conceal his awesome dreams of empire.

He made the Cuyahoga boss over a 2,000-mile steelmaking network, stretching over the water and rail arteries all the way from the West Virginia coal country up through the Great Lakes shipping lanes to the iron ranges of the Marquette, Menominee, Gogebic, and Mesabi in Minnesota. This network involved scores of furnaces, coal mines, iron mines, limestone quarries; and connecting them all, the world's most unusual merchant navy.

Sam Mather built it.

That brings back into the cast the man who made the Cuyahoga shores the nation's oil refinery.

John D. Rockefeller didn't set out to get into the iron business big. But Mather's firm, Pickands-Mather, was deep in the iron business, mining it, smelting it, hauling it.

When the financial panic of 1873 struck like a Lake Superior blow, iron companies were hurt badly. Rockefeller was persuaded to come to the aid of the Merritt Brothers, the seven wild iron men of Minnesota who owned and opened the great Mesabi Iron Range. From that instant, he had to throw so much good money after bad that he felt he had to get into the Mesabi and *manage* it. To manage it, he had to own it.

While the iron world laughed, Rockefeller acquired, piece by piece, control of the little-regarded Mesabi, where the ore was said to be too lean, too powdery, and too distant for lower Lakes mills.

Then a strange message crept over the steel world like the shadow of a cloud. It dawned slowly that he had control of *the* richest ore property known in the world.

The steel world was afraid Rockefeller would build a steel mill. They locked arms against him under the leadership of the then king of steel in America, Andrew Carnegie.

But if they meant to fight, Rockefeller had an advantage—the ore. "I was astonished," he said, "that the steelmakers had not seen the necessity of controlling their ore supply." They had left that in his hands, unwittingly at first, unwillingly later.

Now Rockefeller set out to control his transportation. He wanted the largest fleet of ore vessels afloat. He wanted construction supervised by an expert. To John D. that meant Mather.

Rockefeller, by then living in New York, invited Mather to take on the work. Mather declined; he was not interested in creating a competitor to his own company's vessel fleet nor its iron ore. Rockefeller said he was only going to haul his own ore in these boats. Still Mather declined. Having married Amelia Stone, he'd heard harsh things about Rockefeller from his father-in-law, Amassa Stone.

But when Mather was in New York, a Rockefeller aide asked him if he would come to Rockefeller's house for dinner.

"I'm sorry. I have a dinner appointment."

"Mr. Mather, could you come for just a few minutes *before* your dinner?" Gates asked. "Mr. Rockefeller said even ten minutes would be enough."

"It wouldn't. You don't purchase a great vessel in ten minutes."

"I suppose not," Gates grinned. "But it's enough time for you to say 'no' again, isn't it?"

Sam Mather was ushered through an ornate residence into the presence of the unjeweled, unostentatious, plain multimillionaire.

"Mr. Mather, thank you for coming. I understand your time is very short. We certainly wish you would assume charge of vessel construction for us?"

"Thank you, sir. But I have explained that I have no desire to encourage you into the ore-carrying trade. I'm perhaps your strongest competitor."

"Would I go for help to one of the weakest?"

Mather grinned. "Why go to a competitor at all?"

Rockefeller explained that he wanted Mather's great knowledge and towering integrity.

Mather explained that a vessel was a very expensive construction, costing more than an oil refinery.

"And it would cost *me* even more than it would *you*. But I feel you would spend my money more carefully than your own."

Countering Mather's objection to building a ship for a competitor, Rockefeller said, "If I'm going to build *anyway*, shouldn't you as well have the commission as anyone else?"

"Well, although I'm honored, the commission for superintendence of constructing a vessel is not really interesting to me."

"Of course, Mr. Mather. But I had in mind twenty-four."

"*Twenty-four!*"

Mather walked the carpeted deck of Rockefeller's study.

An unheard of fleet! Or was it an *armada* to conquer the iron world?

Construction of such a fleet would upset the whole balance of the Great Lakes. All the shipyards from Duluth to Buffalo could not produce it at once. If word of this order got out, the price of shipbuilding would go out of sight. No other ore company or vessel operator could afford so much as one vessel, and might have trouble even getting repairs. Competitiveness to this new fleet could vanish.

In this depression, with the mills already on slow bell, iron could remain locked in the geology; miners and mills could idle. If such a fleet was to be built, better that it be built by someone who knew the currents and whirlpools of the Great Lakes marine-iron world. Further, they were to be the largest boats on the lakes—475 feet.

Sam Mather stopped pacing. "A free hand, Mr. Rockefeller?"

"Absolutely."

"I had better build them."

"Excellent."

"One thing. Until I let contracts, don't discuss how *many* vessels I am building for you."

Mr. Gates remembers smiling at such instructions to such a buyer. But Mr. Rockefeller gravely nodded and extended his hand, "Since you can't stay, I hope you are not late for your dinner, Mr. Mather, and that we see you soon."

Mr. Rockefeller dined alone; they never met again.

In under ten minutes, Mr. Mather took the largest single order for vessels ever placed on the Great Lakes. For the knowledge he carried home to the Cuyahoga, any shipbuilder would have paid a king's ransom.

The Great Lakes had ten shipyards, all shut down, except for desultory winter repair work. These yards all together could build twelve vessels simultaneously, if the two largest each built two ships.

When the hull was designed, Mather sent a set of plans and

specifications to each shipbuilder, saying he was "interested in building a ship" and asking for a competitive bid on construction. "If bids are low enough, possibly two ships may be built."

Every yard on the lakes wanted that contract.

Shipyards which had been on hard times for five years sharpened their pencils, trimmed to the bone their production steps; they secured tight-belted competitive bids from subcontractors on engine construction, cabin trim, steel plates, and rented money.

The bids came back to Mather lean and clean.

Mather was a thorough man. He asked all shipbuilders to come to his office in the Western Reserve Building on a Wednesday to go over their bids with him individually to see that they were in agreement on quality of materials and certain construction details and completion schedule.

On the appointed day, ten shipbuilders were seated nervously in Mather's anteroom, each hoping he would be able to answer satisfactorily Mather's questions on his bid. Several, seeing their competitors close up, suddenly wished they had bid even lower.

The first man had been in Mather's inner office twenty minutes when he walked out. All studied him carefully. He had a swallowed-the-canary smile and a jaunty step that took the heart out of the others.

Mr. Mather would no doubt come out now, thank them for bidding, and dismiss them.

But he called in another shipbuilder. He was in Mather's inner office the quarter part of an hour. Those still waiting speculated that probably the two lowest bidders had been called in first. When he came out, they all noted that he walked right out of the office as if embarrassed by his good fortune.

Mr. Mather had suggested there might be a second ship built. It looked as if both contracts had been assigned.

But Mr. Mather called for a third shipbuilder.

Well, by four o'clock several of the ten shipbuilders went to the Weddell House bar to brag about their contract and offer consolation to the losing bidders.

By five o'clock, they had discovered that every yard had got a contract. Each had been bidding only against himself.

It's said that at the Weddell House bar that night any seaman could get all he wanted to drink by just walking in.

By nine o'clock, the news had traveled all the way up to the head of navigation on the Cuyahoga.

When the first twelve vessels neared launching, Rockefeller wrote Mather asking him to run the fleet. Mather felt he couldn't, to be true to some of his complex partnerships. He thus turned down the leadership in 1898 of what became shortly Rockefeller's twenty-eight-vessel Bessemer Steamship Company, largest ore fleet in the world. By 1901, it was fifty-nine vessels, including some five hundred footers and above.

On the east shore of the Cuyahoga now began rising the towering, red brick Rockefeller Building of seventeen stories to house the fleet offices; to house other iron and vessel companies as tenants; and to throw its morning shadows across the crumbling roof of the old Hewitt & Tuttle warehouse which now wore a patina of lichens and green moss.

In the recovery of 1900, American mills produced eighteen million tons of steel. Rockefeller's fleet could carry ore enough for every furnace on the Great Lakes. He raised the rates to $1.25 a ton from Duluth to the Cuyahoga. Mr. Carnegie had to pay it.

But it scorched his Scotch soul. He immediately began construction and acquisition via Henry Oliver of a great fleet of his own, The Pittsburgh Steamship Company, at the mouth of the Cuyahoga.

The war was on.

Bow to bow, the vessels of these great fleets raced for survival.

Their wash lapped the banks of the Cuyahoga night and day, and their spillage reddened the current.

The mills raced each other just as violently. Small mills and small fleets and small mines were getting killed in the fight.

A Mr. Morgan in New York, initials J.P., thought the battle was getting too rough for the good of his holdings, his clients, and the American economy. He set out to bring peace and efficiency by a huge vertical consolidation, putting together a company called U. S. Steel Corporation.

Although J.P. was to pay a multimillion-dollar premium rather than admit it to John D., "vertical consolidation" was the lesson the young Cuyahoga commission clerk had just taught the world.*

---

* Rockefeller got out of iron and the lakes a few years later, but the whole industry had seen the example of organized bigness he and Mather had set. For example, the dozen shipyards which built his fleet soon combined to become American Shipbuilding, headquartered at the mouth of the Cuyahoga.

Rockefeller had seen a rainbow on the river. Following it upstream, it had led him to an industry in chaos, petroleum. He had
straightened it out by establishing "vertical consolidation." It
meant control your raw stock, control your transportation, own
your refinery, make your own barrels, ship it over your own carriers to your own stores. Young John D. had played the lesson out
in a fiery public chapter. But the students weren't all listening. So
old John D. ran a make-up semester for the steel business. The
tuition would be high.

To make a "vertically coordinated" steel company with its own
iron ore mines and vessels and limestone and furnaces and mills,
Morgan raised funds to buy out Carnegie's magnificent mills and
Gates' wire mills; and then he had to go to Rockefeller, the
teacher, to buy his mines and boats.

J. P.'s arrogant pride wouldn't let him walk down the street a
few blocks to talk business with John D.

So they sparred through emissaries, haggling a half year, splitting hairs the size of redwood trees. It was much like the auction
John D. had been in with the three Clark brothers years before.
But the ante was higher. The price went up weekly as the two
delicate dinosaurs coyly dickered. Finally they settled on $88,-
500,000 for John's ore mines and ore vessels.

Putting Rockefeller's boats together with Carnegie's boats,
Pittsburgh Steamship Company became a colossus of shipping—
106 vessels!

John rented them some space for their shore captain's office in
the Rockefeller Building by the Cuyahoga.

As it was then, it is today the greatest fleet on the Lakes. When
a ship from Pittsburgh Steam goes by, it's called "a Corporation
boat."

Corporation boats of this first great Pittsburgh fleet, rebuilt
many times and converted and repowered, still beat the water.
Some sail under other ownerships and other flags.

Many have been towed to Canada and converted to barges,
some have been tied up and converted to floating storage silos,
some are anchored off Great Lakes cities as break walls, some
have been towed to Italy for scrap.

Corporation boats from that great fleet have changed names
ten times, and still haul cargo. Meanwhile the Pittsburgh Fleet,
headed by Admiral Khoury, has gone to larger, newer vessels, 730-
foot supercarriers, and is still the largest fleet.

Across the river from shipping headquarters, Ernie Bohn clamps on a dead cigar and scowls as he watches their upbound stern wash lap the shores of his river.

With the river booming again, there'll have to be more places built for people to live along here.

Interestingly enough, both men will occasionally single out a boat with a P-M stack. And like everyone else, they're apt to murmur, "There goes the *Mather.*"

It's a big name on the river. The Cuyahoga is a man-made river. And one of the men who started two great fleets and made the Cuyahoga shipping headquarters of the inland seas was Sam Mather.

21

Man with a Wheelbarrow

ALL FALL and winter of 1847, visitors to Cleveland had to stop and stare. A lonely shovelman was gravely clearing and digging a straight right-of-way from the mouth of the Cuyahoga south. His progress was slow, but you could tell he was following a line of stakes.

One startling fact was that he worked in all weather, and he worked with a sense of mission.

Visitors always asked the Warren-Cleveland coachman, "What is he doing?"

The coachman always answered, "Building the Cleveland-Columbus & Cincinnati Railroad."

The coachman enjoyed leaving it right there, and feeding the information out as piecemeal as possible.

"One man? Why?"

"To hold the charter 'til they raise the money."

"Why do they have to hold it?"

"If they don't start building the railroad within ten years of getting the charter, they lose it. Time's almost up. So they started one man to work. Legally, the road is now under construction."

"Why don't they really build it like they meant it?"

And in that question lies the story. Railroading on the Cuyahoga is a history of adventures in canniness and contrivance. This is the little known history.

The mechanical part of that history is glamorous and boldly exciting for all to see. Some of it has been preserved for us today by Mr. Mack Lawry of Akron. As the traveler drives north up Route 8 from Akron, away from the river, he is surprised to see several cold but once real steam-snorting locomotives by the roadside. A sign proclaims this to be "Railways of America." They are the same trains that once punished the rails from coast to coast, come to pasture now by the Cuyahoga to serve as a sight for tourists.

Mack Lawry is an Akron businessman, but for years his hobby has been building and collecting model railroads as well as the old retired locomotives, Pullman cars, and cabooses that stand in front of a red brick station house typical of those that bordered the Cuyahoga for fifty years.

Inside the station house is a museum of railroading and a corridor lined with paintings from the heyday of trains. From there, you will come upon the largest collection of model trains in the world. A single table holds eleven thousand feet of miniature track and three hundred switches, all built by Lawry.

Solemn-faced, white-haired Lawry, one of those wiry men of deceptive energy, announces, "It's a piece of America . . ."

The rails are a big piece of the Cuyahoga story, too, because they importantly determined the character of its banks. More important, however, were the people.

This story begins with the group of top-hatted, fine-frocked gentlemen gathered on a sunny afternoon in October, 1847, at the river end of Superior Street in Cleveland. Alfred Kelley, stoop shouldered and frail from his work on the canal seventeen years before, led them, a long-handled workmen's shovel over his shoulder. At a point just beyond the city limits the group paused long enough to survey the peaceful scene of trees and meadows. Then Kelley began to dig, scooping the earth into a wheelbarrow with determined bites. When it was full, Jim Briggs, attorney-at-law, hefted the handles of the wheelbarrow and trundled it a short distance away to dump the contents.

From a fallen log where he had taken a seat, gingerly, so he would not soil his trousers, George F. Marshall laughed. "Bravo, gentlemen," he slapped his thigh. "Another barrowload like that and you'll have it flat enough to stand solid and see which way to aim our railroad."

The others did not pause in the work.

Marshall stretched out on the log, propping himself on an elbow. "How long do you think it'll take us to get to Columbus, Alfred?" He wheezed into another cackle of laughter. "A hundred years?"

Kelley passed the shovel to Mr. Handy and wiped the perspiration from his brow. "Well, George, since it's only taken us ten years doing nothing, think how much faster the job will go with five of us shoveling."

Mr. Handy drove the shovel deep into the moist earth. "If George'd get off those sitting muscles, we might make it faster." He heaved the clod into the barrow and passed the shovel to Mr. Sargent.

Oliver Perry staggered a step from the unaccustomed activity at the wheelbarrow, "Get to it, George. We've got two hundred miles to go."

"Right, gentlemen," said Kelley, leaning against a tree, "and once begun, we can't stop."

Even Marshall sobered slightly, "Well, it's a comic beginning for a railroad. We've hardly enough money to pay for this ceremony, but we're obliged from this moment never to stop construction until the road is finished—or lose the charter." Marshall laughed again, but the smile faded swiftly as he looked at Kelley's determined face.

Kelley said, "Mr. Marshall, I do not intend to be associated with a comic venture." He looked toward Columbus. And he handed the shovel to a bona fide workman, "Mr. Teasely, commence building this right-of-way to the south; and do not leave the job for any reason except the Sabbath, without calling for a replacement." He turned to Marshall. "We have money to raise."

The smiling reporter from the *Cleveland Leader* asked, "Mr. Kelley, do I understand the ground for the Cleveland & Columbus Railroad is now officially broken?"

Kelley's gaze was steady until the smile faded from the reporter's face. "You do," he said slowly, "and there is little prospect of its ever being mended."

Next morning, *The Leader* reported the incident as a "Railroad Accident." The paper took this sarcastic tone because the first charter for the Cleveland & Columbus Railroad had been granted ten years before when railroad fever was running high throughout the land and every city was determined to get rails first. It would mean the making of a city.

The prize was worth it. Cleveland, which the canal had elevated to a New York market, was already a trade metropolis, funneling goods from the Midwest and the middle seaboard which extended west and north to Michigan's shores. Railroads, as they were envisioned by the more worldly, would not only siphon off this trade, but also open up the entire eastern seaboard as a market place. The winner in this pit fight to gain the first charters would be a metropolis even greater than Cleveland at the end of the canal.

Sandusky, archrival to the river's king city, was first to petition the Ohio legislature for a railroad. Their charter to build the Mad River and Lake Erie Railroad was refused, understandably enough, because the legislators were concerned more with paying the debts on the completed canal than with financing a new and so far unproven means of transportation.

Thus began the bickering of a score of Ohio towns that had been ignored by the canal, all trying to attract the railroads and feed on the wealth of a nation's trade.*

Clevelanders, seemingly confident of their position as the lake shore terminus of trade, took a smug view of the petty scrapping around them when they eventually chartered their own railroad to tie together the three major cities of the state: Cleveland, Columbus, and Cincinnati.

Saner heads prevailed among the Cleveland railroaders, and it was soon realized that while the Columbus to Cincinnati route would draw upon the Midwestern markets, a route to Pittsburgh would eventually open the outlets through the Pennsylvania rail-

---

* On January 26, 1832, the first charter was granted incorporating an "Erie and Ohio Railroad," but since no terminals were named and the route vaguely implied as "between Lake Erie and the Ohio River," every city that could conceivably became a part of the route joined the melee to be first with rails. Painesville cited her harbor as "susceptible of as great, if not greater, improvement as that at Cleveland."

It must be remembered that while those giants who spun the steel webs that eventually entwined this nation were just beginning to grow in power in the East, the Midwest thought only in terms of short line roads. *Each city sought to become a rail metropolis by starting first and, hopefully, linking later with other short lines.*

Other cities soon squared off in rivalry. While Painesville was planning a route through Chardon, Salem, and Wellsville, the editor of the Ashtabula *Sentinel* was busy devising a route from his city through Jefferson, Warren, and East Liverpool. Both cities fought bitterly and eventually got their charters.

At this point, Conneaut put in her bid for a railroad, declaring that it was the terminal point of the shortest and least expensive route between lake shore and the Ohio River. On January 11, 1836, a charter was granted for the Conneaut and Beaver Railroad Company.

roads to the Eastern markets. And so it was that on March 14,
1836, the Cleveland and Pittsburgh Rail Road Company was
granted a charter.

Now Cleveland may have been a wolf among the bickering
scrapping dogs around it, but Cleveland also lacked the one thing
that eventually terminated the plans of many short lines in that
day—money.

With the financial panic of 1837 already brewing, Pennsylvania
refused to support her end of a Cleveland and Pittsburgh route.*

While the plunder law was just one more fruitless route to
nothing for Clevelanders, it indirectly applied a pressure to the
railroad builders that couldn't be ignored. It seems that the city
of Sandusky had succeeded in obtaining plunder from the state
and had used it to build their long-delayed Mad River and Erie
Railroad. It may have been a rickety strap-iron, "shake gut" line,
plagued, as always, with snakeheads and shifting roadbeds; it
may have been horse-drawn and only thirty-three miles long, but,
by Godfrey, it was a *railroad*.

Sandusky was out in front.

Now the railroad interests pitched into the race with a vengeance. In the utter confusion of short-line railroads that were char-

* Strangely enough, on an eve of panic, the national treasury was
choked with money and a national surplus revenue was declared. By an
Act of Congress on June 23, 1836, the surplus was divided among the
states, a prize of $2,000,000 falling to Ohio. Clevelanders cast a greedy
eye on the $120,000 alloted to Cuyahoga County. But it was up to the
county officials to designate the money either to internal improvements
which would give the railroad its start, or to private individuals. The dog
fight continued in earnest with only two things positive about the prize:
it was generally agreed that the state would loan the money with the
interest going to support public schools; and, what was most important
as fuel to this bitter fight, the United States would never ask for its
money back.

The compromise law of March 24, 1837, was almost immediately
dubbed, "The Plunder Law." And Cleveland campaigned to raise the
two thirds necessary to match their plunder, expecting Pennsylvania to do
likewise for her end of the road. Valiantly, the editor of the *Cleveland
Herald* exclaimed, "Private investment and state aid combined would
have to raise less than a million dollars." He called for a public meeting
to determine where the county's plunder would go. Unfortunately, words
weren't enough. No meeting was ever held, and the fund commissioners
of Cuyahoga County finally announced that the money would go to
private individuals.

tered during the 1830s, one of them, the Ohio Railroad, rallied enough support to give Sandusky a good run for its money.*

The Ohio Railroad Company set out to build a rail link from Sandusky to Manhattan at the mouth of the Maumee. Unfortunately, this stretch of so-called land had been known from the time of the early frontiersmen as "The Black Swamp." The "walk on the mud" as it was called, was a railroad on stilts sunk in the swamp. It was doomed before it started, but at least it had been started.

The charter for the Cleveland, Columbus & Cincinnati had lain dormant since 1835, and in those days charters were granted with the stipulation that work would begin within a certain period of time and continued uninterrupted. In time, the Big C's charter had quietly expired, but no one seemed to care. Cleveland still had the canal.

Sandusky extended her rails southward while Clevelanders, who knew these puny, strap-iron affairs could never carry the weight of freight that poured over the canal, were content to wait until someone got up gumption enough (and money enough) to build a real railroad.

On the morning of July 27, 1846, however, an incident occurred that shook the Big C to the roots of its complacency. Fifty passengers arrived in Buffalo, intending to travel by lake ship to Cleveland where they could catch a canalboat for Cincinnati. No doubt ship captains were prompted by the additional fares they could collect by extending their passage to Sandusky, but their argument appealed to the sophistication of the travelers. "Why suffer that plodding canal," they said, "when you can take the

* The Ohio Railroad was another dream of Painesville organizers. Originally, the charter described a road to link Buffalo with Toledo (then called Manhattan) along the lake shore. The Painesville people were lucky in securing a share of plunder from the state, but it is hinted quite strongly that their luck was tempered somewhat by shady manipulations.

As required by the plunder law, Painesville sold stock in the enterprise to pay two thirds of the construction costs. The directors gleefully announced that $800,000 worth of stocks had been sold, but perhaps glossed over the fact that this was in land, no cash. It was only after the state had paid out some $249,000 that it was discovered the land was actually worth only about $30,000. By then, the Ohio Railroad had squandered the money on one of the most comic fiascos in the history of railroading.

railroad at Sandusky and get fast, modern transportation all the way to Cincinnati?"

Fifty passengers promptly voted to bypass Cleveland and booked passage for Sandusky.

Clevelanders panicked. It was an omen that couldn't be ignored. In desperation, the old charter for the Cleveland, Columbus & Cincinnati Railroad was revised and the Ohio legislature passed an act enabling Cleveland to subscribe money for the road.

But the directors trying to sell bonds for the enterprise in New York soon found that old canal debts were still hampering investors and the Mexican War was siphoning off most of the extra money available. They returned with a mere $250,000 in conditional stock subscriptions and pledges, hardly enough to begin the project. As far as the discouraged directors were concerned, it would take a genius to make the Cleveland, Columbus & Cincinnati Railroad a reality.

With only a small glimmer of hope, Richard Hilliard of the Big C endured the stagecoach to Columbus and called on Alfred Kelley.

"Mr. Kelley," Hilliard explained, "you're the only man who can do the job. Our second charter is about to run out. If work doesn't start, we'll lose it. There won't be a railroad. There won't be a Cleveland."

No doubt, as they talked, Kelley was remembering the long years he had slaved to bring the canal into reality.

He looked at Hilliard, his firm mouth pinching the words. "I'm sorry, I can't do it."

Hilliard continued the discussion far into the night, but Kelley refused.

Hilliard spent a fitful night as guest in Kelley's house, perhaps dreaming of his report to his fellow directors. At breakfast he greeted Kelley with a bleak good morning and seated himself at the table.

Kelley cleared his throat. Hilliard's eyes snapped up from his plate. He waited, not daring to speak.

"I've reconsidered," Kelley said. "It is a matter of great importance to the interests and welfare of the state. I feel it is my duty to accede to the proposition."

Alfred Kelley returned to Cleveland by stage as the president of the Big C. He would return to Columbus by rail.

Time walked on its hands as Kelley raced to begin construction before the charter ran out. The surveys were made, the estimates totaled, but on deadline eve not a shovelful of earth had been turned.

And so it was, on October 1, 1847, a solemn group marched to a spot just outside Cleveland proper, their top hats and frock coats contrasting blatantly with their shovels and wheelbarrows: Kelley, followed by the treasurer of Big C, T. P. Handy; the engineer, J. H. Sargent; Attorney James A. Briggs; H. B. Payne, Oliver Perry, John A. Foote, and the laughing, slouching, log-sitting George F. Marshall.

And it was that fall and winter that a solitary workman was to be seen laboring forlornly in this remote spot, languidly picking at the earth, loading his wheelbarrow and carting it to a spot where the mounds grew bigger and the task more hopeless.

In one last now-or-never gesture of defiance at the lethargy that had stalemated the Cleveland railroad for ten years, Kelley called a meeting in the Empire Hall on the evening of August 1, 1848. The *Herald* described the audience as "the bone and sinew of Cleveland—Commercial men, Dry Goods, Grocery and Hardware dealers, Mechanics, Capitalists, Bankers, Lawyers, Doctors and even the Rev. clergy."

Kelley took the podium gravely, "Gentlemen, we are here to discuss the condition of the Cleveland, Columbus and Cincinnati Railroad." At that moment, a number of men grouped at the doors, prepared for an early exit, were startled to hear the bolts click. Kelley was taking no chances.

"Yes, gentlemen," said Kelley. "The doors are locked and will remain locked until we have enough subscribers to make sure the road."

Kelley then launched into one of the most persuasive arguments of his very persuasive career.

Murmuring grew as Kelley took his seat and John A. Foote moved forward. He pointed directly at Richard Hilliard.

"Mr. Hilliard. Will you raise your subscription to fifteen thousand dollars?"

Hilliard rose as if to a question. But he said, "Yes."

With every "yes," cheers rocked the hall. All told, they totaled $114,000.

Mr. Kelley had his railroad. And he built it with the same shrewd integrity and hawkeye to the future with which he had built the canal.

"Strap iron, Alfred?"

"No. Solid iron. I'll be in Quebec this June to see that seven thousand tons of English iron are delivered promptly."

"That's not enough."

"It'll last the year. By then, I'll be in Wales. I'll get another five thousand tons. Spread the order in thinner piles. A thinner price."

"But the money, Alfred?"

"We'll pay in company bonds."

"The culverts? We'll build in wood?"

"Stone."

"The bridges?"

"Iron."

"There's not enough."

Kelley bit the words. "We'll find enough. We build in stone and iron so we don't do the work twice."

As Henry Clay had observed years before in the Ohio Legislature, "Alfred Kelley has too much cast iron in his composition to be popular."

A scant year from the historic meeting in Empire Hall, the first locomotive puffed up the grade at River Street. Knee-breeched boys swarmed over the wooden flat cars and slowed the train to a stop.

With such a faltering first run, one wonders if the Big C would ever rival the canal in freight. However, on November 22, 1851, the train made its complete run from Cincinnati to Cleveland carrying a full load composed of the entire state legislature, the mayors and city councils of Cincinnati and Columbus, headed by Ohio's governor, Reuben Wood.

Officially, Big C said good-bye to their man with the wheelbarrow who had worked so diligently through the winter of '47, but he was not to be unemployed long. It is said he immediately went to work on the Lake Shore Line.

Railroad fever became epidemic and men sought new rails to carry their money. The Cleveland & Pittsburgh, whose charter had also lain dormant these past ten years, was revised. Rail lines began creeping into the Cuyahoga valley like the gathering of rain trickles on a cracked earth.

But the Big C Railroad made one decision that was to give rise to a dramatic competitor. It avoided Kent Township's part of the river en route to Columbus. That wouldn't have made much difference except for one thing. That was where Marvin Kent lived.

Kent had settled in Madison Falls where the Cuyahoga's southern course begins its westerly loop toward Akron. By 1850, he was head of a glass works, a woolen mill, and a flour mill. The town changed its name to Kent.

As trains began to roll over the Big C rails, Kent was ready to begin his next enterprise, a cotton mill by the falls of the Cuyahoga. When the Big C avoided Kent Township's part of the river, Kent took it personally. "What's the use for us to build these mills if I can have no railroad to connect us to the outer world!"

Kent voiced the views of thousands of unrailed towns. Kent, however, did something about it, personally. He stormed off to the state legislature at Columbus and introduced a bill chartering a railroad to run east from his home town, through Warren to the Pennsylvania line, and west from Kent to Ashtabula. Kent was moderate in his immediate plans, but not in ideas. To make sure he would have as many markets at the disposal of his mills as possible, he described a route ultimately running to the southwest corner of the state, to the very border of the south itself.

Originally Kent's name for this road was the Coal Hill Railroad, but to understand Kent's next move, we must understand that this was the era of the great rail mergers and the rail merchants, most of them roughnecks like Jim Fisk and Daniel Drew who used every power at their command to gobble up rivals presuming to be any more than short-line, intercity roads. Looking back now, the history of the big lines is corroded with cloudy deals and scandals. Towns and cities that had innocently and sincerely invested money to build rails through their towns often found the charters absorbed by the big roads, their bonds repudiated, their money gone and, in some cases, the rails diverted to other destinations. The merged railroads rushing between the cities made big cities bigger and backwatered the small towns.

But Marvin Kent, with a small railroad charter in his pocket and a big railroad idea in his head, was about to bring the big railroads and the big markets to Kent. Kent's charter presumed a great deal by granting the right to stretch across the entire state of Ohio. It was a juicy plum for the big roads, if they found out about it.

Kent determined that they would not. But the name he had chosen made people wonder about its terminals, and ask. Consequently, Coal Hill was changed to "The Franklin and Warren Railroad," safely mundane. Both towns were well to the east of Kent's prime target on the Cuyahoga. Kent was able to maintain an illusion that his short line was barely long enough to connect two unimportant cities. However, Kent shrewdly kept the terms of his original charter unchanged.

The Franklin and Warren was organized at once and $900,000 raised in stock subscriptions. On July 4, 1853, Kent stood by the banks of the Cuyahoga and turned the first shovelful of earth. Seven days later, work commenced in earnest to extend the road, not east to Warren or Franklin, but south to Dayton where it would connect with the new Cincinnati, Hamilton and Dayton line.

Kent's so-called Franklin and Warren line was well started on its cut across the state when the money markets went berserk again. Drought hit the Midwest farmlands, rail building came to a standstill. Kent decided it was time to bring his road into the open and his plan to its rightful place in the commerce of the United States. In 1855, he made a slight change in the name from Franklin & Warren to the Atlantic & Great Western Railroad.*
Now *there* was a *rail*road!

Over the next ten years, the Atlantic & Great Western grew beyond even Kent's grandiose dreams. Edwin Drake in Titusville brought oil to the road's traffic in 1859.**

By the time the Civil War swelled the railroad's traffic to the

* Although money was tight in the United States, Europe was bursting at the wallet. It was almost easy for Kent to obtain the necessary financing from James McHenry, an English moneymonger who became the guiding spirit of the Atlantic and Great Western.

** James McHenry, never one to let the slightest moneymaking opportunity go by, publicized the oil discovery overseas; and, as a consequence, had English investors standing in line to buy the road's stocks. They say that construction of the Atlantic and Great Western proceeded during this period at a pace even faster than the building of the Union Pacific.

bursting point, the Atlantic & Great Western, connecting with the Erie Railroad, had the first trains traveling all the way from Salamanca, east of Erie, over 369 miles of track to Dayton, Ohio. By this time, however, Kent was thoroughly disgusted with the mad expenditures, the scandals, repudiated bonds, stock manipulations, bankruptcies, forced sales and the extravagant money-sucking construction which clung like a plague to everything that came near the Eastern railroad moguls. In 1864, he resigned.

The Atlantic & Great Western was leased to the Erie Railroad and, although its name remains only in histories and legends told by the railroad buffs of today, it had gone far beyond its original purpose in crossing rails with the Cuyahoga.

Into this fantastic garble of railroads that were conceived, born, built, and often bankrupted during the 40s and 60s, we must add one more road—a rather important one in Cleveland's future which led to rails along the Cuyahoga.

While all other roads could take the products of industry and the Midwest farmlands out of the port city, the Cleveland & Mahoning was the one road that brought in fuel so necessary for the industrial furnaces. It tapped the heart of the best coal country in Ohio, the Briar Hill deposit near Youngstown.*

The question that seemed eminent as far as rail building was concerned was whether or not Cleveland was to use coal and raw materials to become an industrial center or send them out and become a loading dock for the markets of the world.

Quiet voices over the matter were heard occasionally through the 1860s, while the thriving Cleveland & Mahoning hauled coal in two directions, alternating with loads of butter, cheese, and produce from the Midwest farmlands. So much commerce passed over the "Butter and Cheese" road that in 1858, Jacob Perkins, the line's prime mover commented, "If I die, you may inscribe on my tombstone, 'Died of the Mahoning Valley Railroad.'"

As business increased, so did prices; and when coal topped

---

* Of course, Youngstown and Pittsburgh were using most of the coal, much to the concern of absolutely no one. But as ore boats piled the best of Mesabi riches at the Cuyahoga docks to be shipped down the C&M rails to the blast furances of Youngstown and Pittsburgh, the possibility of coal being brought up from Briar Hill to meet the ore occurred to a great many people. "Why should Youngstown be the great Ohio iron center?" asked an anonymous newspaper reader.

$1.50 a ton, Clevelanders woke up. On December 6, 1871, the *Cleveland Leader* commented: "There are millions of tons of coal waiting to be brought to Cleveland over this new route and millions of tons of Lake Superior ore waiting to be smelted here whenever Cleveland can command sufficient cheap fuel to do the work."

The charter for the new line was under the name of the Valley Railroad Company. Unfortunately, the details of the road's construction did not please all the cities along the proposed route.

Akron industrialists wanted broad gauge so that they could load freight and connect at Cleveland with the coast-to-coast railroads without discharging freight and reloading on ordinary gauge lines. Clevelanders, on the other hand, were only interested in the coal the road could bring. They were also interested in freight profits as long as the road never fell into the hands of the big lines. However, that eventually could be offset by building to narrow gauge.

The controversy waged politely in meetings, and the year 1871 closed quietly on a stalemate.

Professor J. S. Newberry, state geologist, offered a suggestion: ". . . the only way to prevent the Baltimore & Ohio from getting control of the road is to have the stockholders hold onto their stock."

By 1872, every town along the proposed route had sold its share of stock in the enterprise, all except Cleveland.

On February 23, the *Leader,* almost with a sigh of relief, but certainly without enthusiasm, reported the decision of three hundred men "representing the capital of the city" who met at City Hall. Standard gauge would be built, which "closes definitely, we suppose, all the debate on the question."

In April, the newspapers were still prodding. Cleveland businessmen just wouldn't get off their wallets. By November, a bond issue was proposed to finance Cleveland's share of the road. And the citizens voted No.

Finally the panic of 1873 crimped business money in an unrelenting grip and the Valley Railroad project silently closed its books and drifted into history's file of abandoned projects.

But it was not the end. After seven more years of rising coal prices, private capitalists gathered enough money. On February 2, 1880, ten years after its charter was granted, the first train rolled over the Valley Railroad overlooking the banks of the Cuyahoga.

The Valley Railroad finally brought the coal to Cleveland blast furnaces. It stirred the great hearths and fanned the flames which marked Cleveland as one of the great cities of the world during the 80s and 90s.*

Today, time has forgotten the little railway along the Cuyahoga. But against the sky stands the vigorous steelmaking silhouette it fueled.

---

* It seems anticlimatical also that so much time and argument was wasted on the question of gauge and whether or not the road would ultimately be absorbed by the sprawling Baltimore & Ohio. The private capitalists who finally built the road voted in favor of the wider tracks which could eventually connect the road's traffic with the rest of the nation's, but they did so with the stipulation that they would do all they could to keep the road from the hands of the big lines. Yet, all breathed a sigh of relief on January 12, 1890, when the story of the acquisition of the Valley Railroad by the B&O appeared in the *Cleveland Leader*. During its ten-year existence as an independent short line, the Valley Road was a loser. It never earned more than its fixed charges.

22

The Home Place

THERE'S A HOUSE by the side of the river, in Bath, that's been building for 141 years. It's the way a house should be built, and I hope it's not finished in my lifetime. They call the house "Old Brick."

Five windows across, three stories high, red brick with white trim, it compels that second and third look. But everyone sees it a little differently. With the sun glancing off rippled glass, it gives back to every man a reflection of what he set out to be.

Having outlived many builders, it's a house which should be studied by all architects and builders who want to know what their business is all about, and by anyone who wants to know the architecture of a love story.

The next to last builder on the job was a lady named Clara Belle Ritchie. Her first move in 1938 was to buy some more of the land around the house. Then she had some workmen replace some bricks that were crumbling, and replace the old stone floor in the basement. The basement mantelpiece was rotting. She had that replaced.

Some newcomers around town thought Miss Ritchie would do better to tear it down and build a modern new ranch. Easier to heat.

"She'll put a lot of money in it."

At first very few knew she was putting back together a love story. She was a single woman for whom love was a fresh and wonderful thing, and she had a lot left over.

The story is there in the structure today to read. It starts with the river road in front of the house, which looks as if a thousand miles of tributary roads were built only to bring someone to this door.

On August 14, 1810, Jonathan Hale, an eagle-faced giant, wrote a letter from this valley back to Glastonbury, Connecticut.

Dear Wife,
    This is my fourth letter that I have wrote you since I left home . . . and the last one was dated 30th stating my safe arrival, my success, of my Land, etc.
    Purchase such articles as you want for yourself in wareing apparel . . . medicines, Essences of peppermint, opium which is good in fever & ague. Get a Copper Kettle and get a Plow Share . . . a few pounds of nails . . .
    The best way for you to come, to take Lenox Turnpike to Albany from there to Skenectady & then on to Utica & then to Canandaigue, & then to Buffaloe & put your things on Board a vessel, and come on the shores of Lake Erie. . . .
    Send us word if you can when you get to Buffaloe we will come with oxen and horses [to the mouth of the Cuyahoga] to help you. I'll try to write again before you set out if I can . . .

                                                        Adieu

                                                        J. Hale

To my beloved wife, Mercy Hale

So Jonathan Hale needed a road into his clearing. He went to the County Seat at Ravenna. The record in the county books contains the item:

    Jonathan Hale presented a petition signed by Timothy Bishop and others praying for a road beginning at Pontey's Camp on Columbia Road, thence on the most eligible ground to the Cuyahoga Portage . . . and said Jonathan having given bond to pay costs . . .

The road they cut came down along the river and is called River Road; it turned off to become the present Oak Hill Road that runs past the house now called Old Brick, then turned back to the river at Botzum.

The road was ready in time for the three wagons which were coming on from Glastonbury, Connecticut.

Mercy Hale was in one ox-drawn wagon with Sophronia, six; William, four; and one in lap, Pamelia, two. Jonathan's sister,

Sarah, was along and her husband (and cousin), Elijah Hale, with two children, Eveline and Mary. And there were three chickens. The third wagon held the Hammonds with their children, Rachael, Mary, Lewis, and Horatio.

Jonathan had a cabin ready for them. The cabin has quite a lot to do with the construction of Old Brick—and why it is made of brick.

Out of a snug house in Connecticut with a store close by, Mercy came into a wilderness where she must raise five children with just what she found on the land, with her hands and the copper kettle and needles and thread she had brought. A year from her arrival her son, Andrew, was born, the first child born to settlers at this place. In 1813, she had a daughter named Abigail who lived only ten days, and in 1815 she had a son named James Madison.

That translated into fast deepening lines in a soft complexion and premature stiffening of the fingers and swelling of the knuckles of a gentle young woman lugging a huge copper kettle of water and acting as if her husband had brought her to the kind of paradise he had described.

She didn't register the shock of seeing her husband thinned down by the ague, with his Connecticut clothes already worn out, and his friends needing clothes and looking to her to make them out of brittle strings of flax they brought her.

She acted very pleased when things improved by 1817 to where she could get imported cloth, a little of it. She was good with the needle and shears and the valley needed her and kept her bent over her sewing many hours; for example.

- a great coat for Mrs. Miller—$1.25
- a jacet for a squatter's son—$3.00
- a wedding coat for a groom—$2.50
- two pairs pantaloons @ $1.00
- two jacets @ $1.50

She was good to the Indians and the squatters and the neighbors and taught her children some reading, but she lost weight.

She saw her husband working from sunup to sundown. In addition to farming for survival food, he had found limestone on the place, a deposit of lime-bearing rocks washed down by the streams that fed Hale Run. John J. Horton, the author who knows this story best, writes that Jonathan piled these rocks up, covered them with dead timber cut by himself and his boys; then he burned the rick for twenty-four hours, pulled off the debris, sifted the lime from the ashes, packed it in tierces and swapped these casks of lime up and down the river for cloth for Mercy and for iron nails and bar iron, and for glass, some livestock, and for hard money when he could get it or when he was willing to sell that cheap.

Translated into dollars he was doing this work for about three dollars a barrel, and delivering up to Hudson and beyond. But he was better off than most of his neighbors because he *was* getting a little cash ahead.

All the while he was watching his wife go from a handsome young woman in 1810 to a work-brittle invalid by 1825.

He wrote her a note:

Mrs. Mercy Hale, she is my true and loving wife
She's been a slave to me a great part of my life.
I hope she'll be rewarded here before she dies
And then receive a mansion in Heaven above the skies.

But actually he meant the mansion to be under the skies right there in Bath by the Cuyahoga River. Therefore at a time when it was a big thing just to plaster between the logs of a cabin and puncheon the floor and plank the loft, Jonathan Hale set out to build a mansion.

In 1825, at a time when there was not a brick house on the Cuyahoga south of Cleveland and many people were moving back East, Jonathan Hale took his sons across Oak Hill Road to dig clay.

Jonathan had built only log sheds. But there was a Colonel Lemuel Porter going to build a brick building up at the school in Hudson. It would be nice if Hale could wait until he could afford to hire a contractor like Porter. But if Mercy Hale was ever to have a mansion on earth . . . Well, Jonathan and his sons, Andrew and James soaked the clay, puddled it into large frames, let it partly dry then sliced it and fired it.

Some of these bricks came out light and powdery, some glassy blue and brittle from too much fire. But a few out of each batch

seemed all right. The sides of some bricks bowed out, many had
cracks where the clay pulled apart when wet. But the mortar
could cover a lot of learning.

Meanwhile, up on the slope they thinned out the woods, cutting large timbers that they squared up with the ax. The family's
cash money went to a sawmill on Yellow Creek for sawed planks
for flooring.

For heavy jobs like cutting stone for the cellar walls, Jonathan
hired some neighbors.

They cut a cellar into the side of the hill, put four great corner-
stones in place, and laid up stone to the grade level. Then the
heavy timbers went into place.

Because of the slope of the hill, the front of this excavation
required no digging. To observers who didn't know Jonathan's
pretensions, it looked merely like a one-story house cut into the
side of the hill to get the warmth of the ground on three sides.

"Jonathan, you're putting too much weight in those ceiling
beams. You don't need it to support the roof."

"But they're not roof supports. They're foundation timber."

Then a surprised settlement saw the frame go up two stories,
then three.

Jonathan Hale traded lime to Captain Thorndike of Tallmadge
for iron nails. And he traded to Dudley Griswold and Mr. Jerrod
for raw iron. He had some iron hinges cast in Tallmadge.

The canal came by and Jonathan was able to sell a lot of lime
to Samuel Cozad, the lock contractor, for Johnnycake Lock and
the Double Lock and the Pancake Lock. And the Irish canal
workers had to be fed, from Hale's farm. It was to become important in time that one of the contractors was a man named Cozad
from Cleveland, who had a sister, Sarah.

Jonathan Hale erected a three-story brick mansion. Even before it was finished, land jobbers took new settlers by it on Oak
Hill Road.

It stood out in the valley like a man's declaration.

Jonathan Hale took Mercy Hale out of the cabin into the mansion. It had the clean unnatural smell of wood shavings and
slaked lime.

The second and third floors were still building. But the "cellar,"
which wasn't really a cellar but the first floor, was livable. It was
a giant stone-floored room, with a cooking fireplace, a dining

room and living room area, and a root cellar cut into the hillside in back. The back wall, of course, was blind, cut into the hill. But the front had four large windows and a door opening to the valley.

John Horton's book supposes the whole family moved into that floor the first year. It would not have been too crowded because Sophronia moved out. She married Ward K. Hammond of the Hammond family who had driven with the Hales from Glastonbury and worked beside them for seventeen years in this clearing.

Meanwhile a small section of the canal opened for business between Akron and Cleveland. What most settlers had not been able to see came true overnight; a steady commerce opened immediately from Akron to New York City.

A bushel of corn jumped from twenty-five cents to seventy-five cents.

More important, a heavy export traffic floated north carrying Hale's lime. And there was some call for brick, special kinds of timber, and for flax and wool and whisky. Hale produced these.

There was even a call for some homemade money, which was being manufactured a half mile from the Hale farm by Hale's friends, the Mallett Brothers and Latta and Brown at Moneyshop Hill.

The wall of hardship was breaking down. But Mercy Hale had a feeling about herself.

"Jonathan, I would like to see our kin in Glastonbury once more."

Hale went out and watched his son, William, at work. He was grown now.

To Mercy, he said one day, "I'll finish off the upstairs parlor for William's marriage and we'll go."

So today in the Hale house one sees a small upstairs parlor. Jonathan Hale could now afford milled boards from Yellow Creek. Mercy liked the room. That's how you design a house.

They liked sparkling Sally Upson whom William was to marry.

"She'll sit and talk with us, Jonathan, but not as a guest. She'll want to be hostess."

"I'll build a family living room that belongs to all."

So at the rear of the house, the walls of the root cellar were raised with brick. A living room was built above grade with a small attic over it.

Jonathan Hale went to see Captain Thorndike about transportation to the East. He came back to the house to explain to Mercy. She answered, "But Pamelia and William Oviatt will be married."

"I'll plaster the upstairs parlor and partition a bedroom on the third floor."

That's how a house is designed.

Sally and William Hale moved to the basement. They had now been married long enough to be out among the rest of the family, and the basement was a rather public place. The whole family cooked and dined there. And Sally was the kind who could be hostess all day to the whole family. Pamelia and William Oviatt had the privacy of upstairs.

Jonathan and Mercy packed the new clothes which Mercy had tailored. As the settlers watched, he took her by the arm and stepped aboard the canal packet to Cleveland. There they transferred to the schooner *Eclipse*. Jonathan wrote back to his son-in-law, "Mr. Oviatt":

> My dear children:
> Your mother has stood this journey better than I expected. Still she is subject to those painful turns. She is impatient to get into the salt water country which I hope by the day after tomorrow . . . We feel very troubled about Sally [illness] and the rest of our children. I hope they will see to all things. I know not how they will manage affairs, but have reason to believe they will get along. . . .
>   Jona. Hale

Jonathan and Mercy Hale reached Glastonbury apparently on the fifteenth of June. Near the end of July, he received the letter from his son, William, announcing Sally's death. It was a sad letter; but in the way of the eldest son in charge of the home place, he felt it important to report: "The wheat looks very well, but the corn, oats and grass will be very high. Our meadows are light." When Jonathan broke the news to Mercy, she wanted to go back to Bath. On the way she worsened. They were coming across the New York canal when Mercy needed some water in the night. Jonathan went topside to fetch it, slipped on the deck and gashed his thigh on an iron boat hook so seriously that, when they transferred off Lake Erie onto a southbound Ohio Canal packet down the Cuyahoga valley, both were ailing.

In October, Mercy died. Jonathan could not get up to attend her funeral.

As you look at Old Brick, you find some interesting reeded mantelpieces. They are there because the house had a prematurely old man in it, puttering around. Six-foot, 180-pound Jonathan Hale stopped being the driving force in this part of the Cuyahoga valley. Right in front of everyone he grew old; and they all knew he was planning to leave the valley.

And if you look at the land titles to Old Brick, you see that two months after Mercy's death Jonathan Hale sold all of his Lot 13 to Sophronia, his eldest, and her husband, Ward K. Hammond, for four hundred dollars.

Then Lots 11 and 12, the main farm and meadow and orchard, to his oldest boy, William, the young widower. Jonathan took a trip to Cleveland. The construction of the house would seem to be finished.

But as you look at Old Brick today you'll find a wonderful inconsistency. Even the ornate parts are frontier built from wood and clay and lime and stone right off the land.

But here and there is a carved molding where you can't detect knifemarks at all, a more perfect piece, a milled piece from the city, or a carved pillar head, called for by someone who wouldn't seem to be a Hale or a Hammond.

That brings Sarah.

You'll remember that back when the canal was building a Cleveland contractor named Samuel Cozad built the Johnny-cake Lock near the Hale house. He bought lime of Jonathan Hale, and he brought with him his sister, the widowed Sarah Mather, who boarded and kept house for his Irish construction crew. Her presence brightened the town.

When the lock was finished, Sarah went back to Cleveland with her three children, George, Jane, and Betsey, all carrying-size, plus an adopted niece, Harriet.

Back in Cleveland at Doan's Corners Sarah taught school and raised her family.

She was still there when the widowed Jonathan Hale arrived.

To our knowledge there is no record of the next events, but we do know that in the parlor of Sarah's father's house, on what is now Western Reserve University, Jonathan Hale and Sarah Cozad Mather were married.

They returned to Old Brick.

Today, visitors note that the bedrooms upstairs in the Hale House are strangely partitioned. But it's not really strange at all. You see, Old Brick tried hard to welcome the new couple. But

this was not an easy homecoming.

Old Brick was now more of a barracks, peopled by men, the widowed William, and the maturing Andrew. Even young James Madison Hale was four years older than Sarah's oldest child, George Mather. Jane and Betsey Mather were nine and seven.

These were difficult ages under one roof; but even more difficult was Sarah Mather Hale. Frankly accustomed to the sophistication of Cleveland society, a now quite real and exhilarating one, she was a city woman. And she was surrounded by the sons of Mercy Hale, a hard woman to follow.

Jonathan Hale was aware of Sarah's loneliness at Old Brick and the reason for her coolness. He wrote her a poem:

To A Stranger

Far from the land that gave the (e) birth!
Oh! Cans't thou find a spot on earth,
So fondly dear to the (e)
As the heart-woven land thou left behind?

Thou'st left behind thy social train;
Will thy fond spirit rest again,
And feel security
In the bosom of strangers thou ne'er has tried,
By the ebb and flow of prosperity's tide
Or will it retreat on the soft wings of regret
To that frequent bower where so lovingly met
All by friendship made sacred to me.

Believe me here are friends as kind
As those whom thou has left behind.
But cans't thou not the fairy chase
Which binds the (e) to thy native place;
Rather than be unblest,
To the friends of thy children—thy country—thy home
Go—go and be happy, tis folly to roam.

Then something happened. William Hale fell in love with
Sarah's niece. They were married in the parlor; then as man and
wife they moved to the "cellar" which had been the bridal suite
twice before. Within two years they had two children.

Jonathan Hale and Sarah also had two boys and a girl. And
now we see what a woman Sarah was. She named the girl Mercy.

Jonathan Hale's powerful body healed. He worked the farm
with the strong help of Andrew. Andrew, he could see, was the
one who would stay.

In 1836, something stranger still. Andrew Hale married Sarah's
daughter Jane—in the parlor. It was Andrew's turn to have the
bridal suite. William and Harriet built a frame house across the
road. Andrew and Jane moved into the basement.

And Sarah Hale, now deeply involved with both her families
became actively the matriarch of the house.

Old Brick was back in order. But construction wasn't finished.

In Old Brick you will see a set of ledgers.
Young Andrew gradually took over the farm, and changed the

accent some. He hired more hands, and changed some of the crops from large staples to smaller, higher-priced specialties: honey, vinegar, wool, onions, in addition to the old staples of corn, beef, potatoes, apples, flour. He had a decided bent toward apples.

Andrew's family was outgrowing the basement. Therefore, he built a story and a half clapboard wing onto the basement on the south.

Old Jonathan meanwhile had moved heavily into wool. He built a large barn across the road to house their increasing flock of sheep.

In 1854, at the age of seventy-seven, Jonathan Hale wrote to Sophronia that he didn't think he would stay much longer, and he died. Sarah followed him.

Construction of Old Brick would seem to be over. Old Jonathan had felt he must divide up his land among his sons and daughters fairly. He left the heart of it to Andrew who had stayed on the farm and was working it. But he willed land to the other sons and daughters.

Therefore Andrew began to buy back these lands and put Old Brick back together again. He loved this place.

He moved the wooden wing he'd built around to the rear of the house, attaching it to the living room. He built a wooden north wing for storage of coal, with a corn room above it, and on the front a delicate, highly trimmed porch with a hipped roof. On this porch, his family watched the valley develop in the evenings. The Valley Railroad came snorting down by the Hale House.

Years rolled by. Andrew grew sick with a painful illness. A series of operations failed to relieve the pain. One day Jane found him trying to shoot himself, and was able to stop him. In a second attempt in 1884, he wounded himself seriously, and died soon after.

Jane lived on in the front room for twenty years to see the century turn.

Like Jonathan, Andrew divided up the farm in his will.

Old Brick was quiet and lonely. Grass grew up in the driveway. Older people in town watched it ruefully, "Shame to see it run down like that."

"Yes. But it's too big. A fortune just to heat it."

The Hales were strong men. Although they indulged in flashes of humor and some music, they were for the most part hawk-faced earnest pioneers, hard-working, effective leaders. Life was work.

Suddenly, unexpectedly, came a happy-hearted Hale.

Andrew's son, Charles Oviatt, inherited the heartland of Old Brick. Like Andrew, he began to buy back the fringes from his brothers and sisters and cousins.

Now C.O., as he was called, was not a man to make life hard; and he was not a working farmer. He was a hobby farmer, flowers and the like. For the real staple crops, he brought onto the home place his wife's nephew, Carl Cranz, a man who knew what the land was about.

C.O., with a more sophisticated education than any Hale thus far, went into the affairs and politics and industry of the valley.

But he loved the home place.

So viewing Old Brick today one wonders about the large number of small rooms in it. Well, C.O. began to turn Old Brick into the showplace of the valley. He planted the grounds beautifully and he invited paying guests from Akron and Cleveland for weekends.

Then families began coming for summer vacations from Cleveland. It was a fashionable thing to do.

C.O.'s wife, Pauline Cranz Hale, cooked and served meals in the south wing with the help of her daughters, home from college.

As the crowds increased in the summer, the stove had to be moved to the adjoining north wing in summer and back in winter.

The place had an easy manner. It was hard to tell the proprietor's family from the guests. And, in fact, the host and hostesses seemed to be the ones on vacation.

The affection for the place was amazing and the guests distinguished: W. T. Holliday, Seiberling of tires, Hoover of vacuum cleaners, Severance of Severance Hall, Judge Day, Victor Morgan, Rabbi Gries.

A tally-ho party of horses from Akron would be likely to charge in for breakfast at 7:00 A.M. of a Sunday.

C.O. Hale sold timber to an aggressive young man named Samuel J. Ritchie, who cut it himself off the Hale slopes. Watching him was Andrew's daughter, Sophronia. They married, but did not move into the basement. Ritchie went on out into the world to great lumber enterprises, then copper, iron, land. He became wealthy. Ultimately he settled in Tallmadge. But he was away a lot. That's important to this story, because it meant that his daugher Clara Belle Ritchie was home with her mother, Sophronia, listening to stories of life at Old Brick.

When C.O. Hale, "The Squire," died, Clara Belle bought Old Brick. She named it The Hale Farm, and she began to repair it. People said it was too much house for a single woman. She'd find it hard to heat.

But Clara Belle Ritchie was putting back together a love story.

In the middle of her work on it, she died in 1956. In her will she gave the house to the Western Reserve Historical Society to be open to the public.

To many it is a museum of the Midwest frontier. But actually Old Brick is a love story.

23

The River's Genial Monster

IF YOU CAN imagine riding on a dinosaur's head while he's feeding, you can imagine how it feels to operate a Hulett. In repose, this monster is the ugliest, ungainliest machine ever made. In action, it's sheer poetry.

A small Hulett chomps ten tons in a mouthful. The adult of the species can slurp up seventeen tons of ore from the hold of a ship in a single bite. An occasional Hulett with the right rider will often grab twenty tons in its maw. More than 2,200,000,000 tons of iron ore have come to Lake Erie ports since the first shipment of six barrels in 1852. Of this amount, the four Hulett unloaders at the mouth of the Cuyahoga's old riverbed have handled over 175,000,000 tons.

Huletts have become the dominant species of ore unloaders along the Cuyahoga. Their towering necks arch over ships whose bows and sterns come close to scraping their paint on the river bends. They look like rows of prehistoric mechanosaurs dipping their ore-reddened beaks deep into the whalelike ships. They smack their steel lips with a clatter that shakes the whole of Whisky Island, which is the island of land between the old river bed and the new.

A Hulett's main action is often described as a monstrous grasshopper's leg, which is very descriptive if you can picture a five hundred-ton grasshopper leg with very neat knees. But that's only the top part of a Hulett. The knee action part rests on another five hundred tons of machinery. It is a massive leviathan standing ten stories high, its legs straddling several hopper car freight trains, while its neck juts out over water and ships. At feeding time, when a herd of four of them are bobbing their beaks deep into the holds of a ship, they look like an outsized flock of those toy birds that sit on the rim of a glass, incessantly tipping forward to drink then upright again; but they are ten stories high.

The Hulett is a mechanical impossibility surrounded by disbelief, yet it reigns supreme as the fastest, most efficient ore unloader in the trade today.

Unloading iron ore used to be the bottleneck on the Cuyahoga. In the heyday of the Marquette and Mesabi, when mountains of ore piled into the mouth of the little river, the problem of getting down into that hull to get out that iron became a nightmare.

They tried shovels and buckets, hoists and cables, steamshovels and weird contraptions. But for fifty years, the river remained a

bottleneck. Once you drop ten or fifteen thousand tons of dirt into the hold of a ship, you have the devil's own time getting it out again.

The mind that conceived the Hulett monster, which eventually dug out this bottleneck, could only have been a genius. Engineers say it must have been dreamed up by a man with nightmares. Those who knew him say that George Hulett was . . . well, eccentric.

One thing is certain; he was a kind of mystery, and no fame seeker. Only the barest biographical traces are recorded about this man who revolutionized ore transportation. The very few men still living who knew him personally are themselves old-timers with memories dimmed to detail, but they all remember one thing. Hulett was a brilliant engineer with a fantastically inventive mind . . . and eccentric.

The stories they tell give the impression of a man who would sit down to a high-level conference table with a Carnegie or a Rockefeller, fish a plug of tobacco from his stained waistcoat and chaw throughout the meeting like a general-store patriarch.

He looked like a bullfrog in a baggy suit, wore steel-rimmed spectacles, and talked as if he were still driving a team of draft horses back on the farm in Conneaut where he was raised. He was a practical farmboy genius whose inventiveness was born of getting the job done, and he didn't care what his inventions or his person looked like as long as they did the job.

Hulett came to Cleveland with his parents in 1860. On the occasional trips to the city from his boyhood farm, Hulett had become familiar with the sweat and strain of ore unloading, but Cleveland was a revelation. In those days Whisky Island (the narrow strip of land sheared off from the Flats by the old river bed and the new channel which cut the Cuyahoga's new course to the lake) was nothing but a great cloud of red dust, filled with men, mules, and dirt. The infant mills on the Cuyahoga were squalling for ore like tiger cubs, while the Marquette was packing boats and piling them through the Soo like floating sausage links. They filled them to the decklines, deepened the canal, enlarged the locks and then built new ships. All this was done just to send ore into a bottleneck of aching backs and wheelbarrows.

The way they tackled a boatful of ore in those days was to put rock-muscled men with shovels into the dirt and they heaved it into wheelbarrows; then more iron-backed men wheeled it to the waiting railroad cars. And when the shovelers got too deep in the hold to throw it out, they built a platform and shoveled to that, while still more men reshoveled it to the decks.

George Hulett wasn't the first one with an idea to unplug the bottleneck. The first was a man who rigged a block and tackle from the mast into the ship's hold. After that, it was a short step to hitching a horse to the block and tackle.

By 1867, they had forty horses employed with the shovelers on the south bank's Nypano Docks, and possibly no one will ever know how many more horses contributed to the melee of Whisky Island just across the river to the north. The Cleveland firm of Bothwell and Ferris ran the Nypano and it was J. D. Bothwell himself who first stuck the corkscrew into the bottle's neck by replacing the horses with a steam engine.

The little donkey engines began to multiply along the wharves at Whisky Island. The neck of the bottle began to clear. It looked as if the fifty thousand tons of ore a year cramming through the Soo could at last be handled with ease.

Now although the neck of the bottle had been unplugged, the inevitable happened. The bottle got bigger. Youngstown and Pittsburgh added their demand for ore and the 50,000-ton torrent soon swelled to an 831,000-ton deluge. The bottleneck was right back where it started, only tighter.

Captain Thew of the steamer *William P. Thew* was next to design an ore unloader. The device that he outlined was a long-armed steam shovel. The cab of the shovel where the operator controlled the beast, swiveled around like a big giraffe on a turntable. Instead of a block and tackle attached to the mast of the ship, Captain Thew designed a self-contained shovel that took the ore directly from the hold to the dock. This was the day of the whirleys.

As steam was replacing horsepower along the unloading docks, George Hulett had embarked upon a career as proprietor of a general store. Later, he went into the commission business where he began to apply his ingenuity to unloading shiploads of grain.

Another young man, however, was applying his talents directly to the ore industry. Alexander Brown's father, Fayette Brown, was one of the original financial backers who tapped the Marquette iron ore range. So the boy, Alex, had a good education as an ivy-league engineer plus firsthand knowledge of the drama that was taking place along the Cuyahoga's docks.

Brown's nimble mind eliminated the whirleys by envisioning a fantastic skeleton of steel girders that straddled the entire railroad yard on one side and jutted out over the ships at the other. The bucket could now be lowered from the "hoist," into the vessel's hold, filled, raised, carried along the skeleton to any one of several tracks and dumped directly into the selected car.

For the next twenty years, the Brownhoist was the marvel of the Cuyahoga. Ore boats grew still bigger, the Soo got bigger, and the demand for more ore never stopped getting bigger. Self-closing buckets were added to the rigs so they could bite out their own ore rather than needing shovelmen to fill their buckets.

The Hoover-Mason bucket came out with an ingenious set of blades that could scrape ships' holds clean. But it wasn't enough to calm the clamor for more ore.

All this while George H. Hulett was the manager of the Cleveland Steam Cooked Food Company.

That was 1886. Two years later, Hulett switched from food to manufacturing derricks. As the skeleton-like Brownhoists were breeding all along the waterfront, Hulett was playing with coal, literally playing. One of his first inventions was a gargantuan machine that clamped an entire railroad car in a viselike hand, lifted it like a toy and upended it to spill 120 tons of coal into a mammoth funnel. Hulett was always pretty direct in his approach. His methods usually followed suit.

To Hulett, unloading an ore boat would be a simple matter of building a thousand-ton posthole digger—and then putting a man in the shovel.

No one really knows whether or not Hulett was influenced by the posthole digger of his farm days, but there is a certain similarity in the way the giant leg jams the shovel down into the ore, clamps it shut and lifts it out, opens its jaws to release the ore.

With the designs under his arm, Hulett began the rounds of engineering companies and financiers. He was asking them to gamble on an unproved nightmare, and no one was buying. Hulett was well into his second and third calls when he approached Sam Wellman of the Wellman Seaver Company. Hulett hiked a chair up to the machinery tycoon's desk and fished out his lint-encrusted tobacco plug.

"Sam, you build this machine, it'll make you." Hulett usually dispensed with the time-consuming preliminaries.

A smile tickled the mouth of prosperous Sam Wellman.

"I've seen the plans, George. It looks like a monstrosity."

"But it works."

"How do you know?"

"The coal unloader worked, didn't it?"

"How much would it take to build one?"

"Forty-six thousand dollars."

"All right, George. If it works, we'll buy all you can build. If it doesn't, you get nothing."

"Fine. Sam, where'd you hide the spittoon?"

It took two years to put the monstrosity together. If boat captains profaned the horses, steam engines, and Brownhoists as their introduction, they were speechless at the sight of this incredible beast that reared its head along the docks. In 1898, it devoured its first boat of ore. By 1900 it was king of the Cuyahoga.

The first Huletts were steam operated. In a cab the size of a phone booth there were pipes over the operator's head, dripping constantly, making a steambox in the wintertime and an impossible torrid zone in summer. It was like a Turkish bath with a leaky faucet.

By 1912, the Huletts had been converted to electricity. Since then, the basic design of the monsters has remained unchanged to this day.

We walked out on the Cleveland docks at the western tip of Whisky Island to watch the agile monsters feeding on one of the modern twenty thousand-ton ore boats. They are still all that history and the veterans of the docks claim. But a siren sounded across the railroad yard—one blast, then two short ones. A clattery little pig skimmed over the tracks to number two Hulett, its massive beak frozen in the hold of the ship. An electrician was already clammering up the ricketty old ladder to the control house.

"The Hulett's are getting old," he commented later. "There's nothing to do the job as fast or as well. But they're getting old and stiff in the joints." The original forty-six thousand dollar price has rocketed to two million dollars now. There are no new Huletts on the river today.

The old monsters are growing extinct. The ones that remain will reign supreme until the cost of their maintenance outweighs their ability to create time. The cables and buckets of the Brownhoist, which could never keep up with the nimble Huletts, are once again gaining dominance over the machines that rule the Cuyahoga.

A new breed of ships is building, too. Their holds are built as hoppers, and to unload, they open the bottoms and let the ore flow onto built-in conveyor belts.

Yes, the Huletts are getting old. But their towering hulks with lights on their moving arms and legs still claw the darkening sky. Every man and woman should go down to the Cuyahoga and see the monsters feed, before the species is extinct.

If the Huletts ever go, there'll be an empty place against the Cuyahoga sky.

24

A Long Way

Going Somewhere

WHO BUT Henry Thoreau gets a whole week to travel up a river? So I'll settle for two or three days of your time and promise you the thrill of discovery.

The first six miles, you should go by boat; *The S. S. Goodtime* leaves every two hours from Cleveland's Ninth Street Pier. If you're not courting (and it's a good trip for that, too), you will not be able to take your eyes off the river that was the home of the men and the fleets who built the American steel industry and freighted the raw materials that made middle America an industrial power.

And in this twentieth century, the companies these men founded have opened up the great iron fields of Quebec and Labrador, retaining the leadership with far-ranging ships and minds.

As you come into the river, from Lake Erie, past the Coast Guard station, I believe you will be compelled by the dance of the twenty-one bridges. To let you through, some lift, some jack-knife, some swing, pivot, rotate, and some arch so high across the valley that they have other bridges under them.

I hope you're lucky enough to be just behind or ahead of an ore vessel churning upriver so you can gape at the closeness of the navigation as the boat cat-whisker's its way around Collision Bend where the fireboats are stationed. If it is mealtime, you'll see the diners in Jim's Steakhouse leave their tables and come out to watch this maneuver. Clearance is tight below the vessel, too, which is why you will see the dredge operating twenty-four hours a day in the first four months of shipping season.

High to your port side, you'll see the Standard Oil Building, just a few rods away from the site of John Rockefeller's first wooden office on the riverbank. And if you look upstream, you'll see the towers of the crackers at the refinery, doing business at the same location.

Perhaps you'll be lucky enough to see some drunken pigeon who has fed on the fermenting grain at the elevators.

At the Republic Dock, you'll see a black and red and white mountain range rise out of the river, coal, ore, and the largest

limestone stockpile in the world. But when the mills have a good winter, you're hard put to it to scrape up a wheelbarrowload by spring thaw.

Your stare at the crews of unloading vessels will be returned with friendly interest. They see few people during shipping season.

When the S. S. *Goodtime* returns you to the dock, you will want to start upstream by car.

First, you should get lost a little around the mouth of the river and Whisky Island, under and over the bridges and along the docks.

After that get to West Eleventh Street down in the flats near the New York Central movable bridge at the mouth of the river and head upstream past the marine supply houses. Their launches come alongside the ore boats to deliver the steward's food order, the ship's laundry, and other supplies.

The harbor master's office is the small cube of bricks on a postage stamp of grass under the High Level Bridge. It does not have the vacant look of municipaldom because of the harbor master's cultivated garden of sunflowers.

The white building in the middle of a large parking lot is the Great Lakes Towing Company dispatch office where the tug crews stand by for calls from vessels.

Samsel Rope and Marine Supply Company is the lake sailor's hardware store. From the traditional hemp and manila to the new no-rot nylon, from unfinished cast fittings to shinny brass lanterns.

As you drive along past skeletons of small boats, retired tugs and launches moored or resting on the shore, piles of anchors and rotted-out hulls, you'll come to Merwin Street, then Columbia Road. Take a right turn. Because of the curves, the river is a long way going somewhere.

Cross the bridge, turn left onto Franklin. Actually, as you will see shortly, it is Lorenzo Carter's old road, Carter Road. Signs are kept to a minimum, and they're sometimes wrong. On this road, and others, you will get the feeling that you are driving right through somebody's plant. But you are on a public road which you share with railroad trains.

Turning right where Carter Road meets Scranton, drive under a railroad bridge, left onto University and up the hill. This becomes Railway Street along by a variety of interesting salvage yards, and some nice, old, weathered warehouses.

The dead end is at Literary Street. Left across the railroad tracks, jog right at the next dead end. This will be West Third Street, home of Sohio, Republic Steel, Jones & Laughlin and other heavy industry. With the lights on at dawn or dusk, it is quite beautiful.

Beautiful to some, too, would be the graphic economic equation seen here. In the shadow of the steel mills are thirty acres of obsolete and junked automobiles. And the one feeds the other.

When Clark meets West Fourteenth Street turn left even though the river will go out of sight behind a complex of industry; it will come into focus again on your left. Look for Bradley Road just before a hill. It is alternately called "Van Epps Road." Turn there and go to the end, which is Schaff Road. Make a left here and keep bearing left when you get to Granger Road, which is Route 17. This will take you to Canal Road where you turn right.

Finally you are paralleling the river and the canal, which is right next to the road. Here the valley takes a sharp turn in mood and pace.

Abruptly, you're in the country.

From 1827, the canal was the main street of the West, and was singly responsible for the early economic development. Youngsters will ask, "Why was the canal built when the river was so close?" The river is not level and it has too much current.

Beyond Stone Road, near an establishment called "The Old Boat House," you'll see a canal lock, one of four in plain view from here to Peninsula.

Just beyond the intersection of Fitzwater and Riverside Roads, there is an interesting log cabin to the right-hand side of the road. Here the road is elevated, giving you an aerial view of the Cuyahoga valley and River.

Station Road, right after you cross Chippewa, is an interesting one to explore, sometimes literally inches from the river. In here, you'll think you have turned the calendar back one hundred years.

The quaint old B & O train station at the town of Jaite received its last freight in 1963. But it is a charming classic in railroad gothic. You'll be tempted to buy it and convert it to a small restaurant, "B & O's Last Stop."

Two of the Cuyahoga valley's skiing areas are nearby, Brandywine with seven skiing trails and the Boston Mills ski area with man-made snow.

To the south, you'll pass through a picture town—Boston. Then you'll come to another, Peninsula. If you look carefully you will see raging here a fight between progress and nostalgia, perhaps the same one which goes on in your own heart.

Monuments of Yesterday

Sleeping on the banks of the Cuyahoga where it crosses Route 303, the town of Peninsula watches the decades roll by. For over a hundred exciting years, the whole world passed through here on the Ohio and Erie Canal.

This is where the canalers brawled and fought their way to first in line for the locks to Akron. Here's where they washed their tow horses while waiting for the packet jams to clear.

Then the railroads came. To keep the river from blocking their path with its loops and twists, they straightened its bed. They took the trade from the canalers and left the town alone with its memories.

Today, two jet-streamed highways, 21 and 8, skirt Peninsula east and west, losing the town in one of the swirling cloverleaves. But if you can get off the superhighway and swing down Route 303 from Riverview Road, time stands still. The square, white houses are unmistakably early Western Reserve, standing proudly in their functional storm shutters defying thermopane progress.

Yet the tranquillity here is sometimes shattered by a fight that would command the attention of canal captains.

Peninsula is fighting for its status quo.

The day the wrecking crews came to take away the old Wood store, one of the crew cupped his hands and called to the woman in a red raincoat crouching in the midst of the ruins, clutching two children to her. "Lady, you're gonna get hurt if you stay there!"

Lily Fleder tossed her head defiantly and pulled the children tighter. The little girl stuck out her tongue.

"Lady, yer kids'll get tetanus on them rusty nails."

Lily withered them, "I had them inoculated so if they get hit it won't make any difference!" Laughter—for the streets of Peninsula had begun to crowd with townspeople.

At this moment, another woman entered the scene, a woman whose bulk and voice labeled her unmistakably as the owner of the building.

"What do you think you're doing?" the lady roared.

"I'm not going to let you tear down this old building," cried Lily. "It's a landmark . . . part of our town."

There is no telling what would have happened to little Lily Fleder at this point if it hadn't been for the tall young man who drove up in the long car. He wore a corduroy jacket and sport shirt, but he approached the stalemate with the air of a country squire about to make a law. Lily breathed a sigh of relief. The crowd grinned and edged closer.

"Look down there," he said, pointing to the river. "Over a hundred years of history have flowed right by this door."

"What's that got to do with this crummy old building?"

"Why, everything," the stranger answered. "Do you realize this was the first store built in Peninsula? Right here in these show windows they displayed the first jewelry this section had ever seen." He pointed to the building across the street. "That church," he said, "was built in 1835. Your ancestors probably worshiped there."

"Not mine," the owner said, but she listened.

The stranger indicated the row of white houses stretching up the hill. "Every one served as a rooming house for canalers. Some were taverns. It would be shame to destroy this history."

The woman was calmer now, but the reverie was broken by a voice in the crowd. "So Hunker finally got here!"

Anger exploded in the woman's eyes. "Are you Robert Hunker?" The man nodded. "Then you can just get the hell out of here you . . ." Quite a long speech followed.

The reason for this outburst is quite understandable. There are groups at work to transform the town of Peninsula into a sleek and modern center—progress. Hunker, on the other hand, is leader of the opposition. He is a designer with a feeling for the preservation of historic architecture. He is also a keen business-man, coupling his talents with an almost arrogant self-confidence which frequently gets him his own way. The argument pro-gressed in public to what seemed a stalemate. Finally Hunker asked, "What would you take to sell the store?"

He bought it.

But this is everyday fare for the people of Peninsula. For five years now, they have witnessed the drama of progress vs. history. In the first act, it was the church.

The Bronson Memorial Church stands opposite the Wood store, square and sturdy with a truncated belfry perched precari-ously on its roof. By 1960, the church had been closed for ten years, while the weather marred both exterior and interior. Squir-rels had chewed far enough through the roof beams to make it hazardous. Several miles down Riverview Road, in Everett, is the Jonathan Hale Homestead where the Western Reserve Historical Society is assembling and restoring a typical village of the early days.

The Hale Homestead wanted the church. The Episcopal Diocese of Cleveland, who owned the church, did not want it.

The only thing that stood in the way of the move was Lily Fleder.

Lily is small, quiet and friendly, but she knows her own mind explicitly.

Marching a committee of umbrella-armed ladies into the Bishop's Cleveland office, she demanded that the landmark church stay home. The Bishop eyed the ladies with a twinkle that turned to a frown. "The Diocese is not interested in restoring the church," he explained. "The church is being moved to the Hale Homestead."

Lily filed an injunction to halt the move.

Peninsulites added voice to the battle. The Bishop and his trustees became aware that this little woman was backed by a sentimental army. In the town of Hudson just ten miles east of Peninsula, the local bank which had occupied a quaint brick building for years decided to tear it down and rebuild. They suddenly found many an important savings account withdrawn.

The Bishop did not want to defy sentiment. On the other hand, it would cost a great deal to restore and maintain the church. But Peninsula was determined. They banded with Hudson to save not just the town's buildings, but the entire Cuyahoga valley there from industrial invasion.

They appealed to the National Trust for Historic Preservation in Washington. Helen Duprey Bullock, Director of the Department of Information, made a special trip to see the valley. Robert Hunker drove her through the two towns, pointing out the landmarks. Late in the afternoon, they stopped at a restaurant, and imagine the coincidence, they met there the curator of the Western Reserve Historical Society.

After a series of rather frigid introductions, Mrs. Bullock commented, "You realize that the church is not really Western Reserve on the inside. Although it was built in 1830, it was completely renovated in 1880 to Victorian style." Mrs. Bullock set her glass on the table and asked, "What are you going to do with the church if you move it out of Peninsula?"

The curator looked at her confidently. "We'll get it," he said, "and put it back the way it was in 1830."

Silence.

"If you do that," said Mrs. Bullock calmly, "you might as well build a new church."

The restaurant where they met was situated at the river bridge almost precisely on the site where the old canalers used to fight for the locks. It was a good place for a fight.

"Now just a minute," Mrs. Bullock said. "Just because 1830 was a little before 1880, by fifty years, doesn't mean that 1880 isn't going to be an important part of American History. The real value of this church and Peninsula is that you can see the collective age, all the way from the Indians to the canal to the railroad."

Nothing was settled in the restaurant, but Mrs. Bullock's visit brought about the formation of the Peninsula Valley Heritage Association. Charlie Conger stood up in the first meeting and said: "This was a canalers' town. They fought. Now it's our turn to fight for the things that made our town!"

Lily Fleder chimed in: "The Church has always led people. Now our church is gathering the people of our town together. Let's see that it stays a part of Peninsula!"

By October 1964, 650 residents of Peninsula had contributed $18,500 to restore the Bronson Church and establish an endowment fund to provide maintenance. Only one thing seemed curious. At the time, the population of Peninsula was only 645. The Summit County Historical Society brought the total to $20,000. The church was saved.

But the fight continues.

Proposed superhighway, Route 271, aimed its six-lane speedway directly at the little town. Galen Rousch, president of Roadway Express; Charlie Conger, vice president of Bender Louder Freight Company; J. Kubinyi, engineer; George Fischer, Mayor of Peninsula; Mr. Sarison and Mr. Hunker stormed the office of Director of Highways in Washington, D. C. "Your highway will split our town in two. We think you're making a grave mistake."

The Director of Highways rummaged through his desk for a rubber band. He broke it into one long length and stretched it across the map the men had spread on his desk. "What's wrong with that line?"

"Up a little," said Hunker.

The rubber band moved up. "All agreed?"

"Fine."

"Thank you, gentlemen. Glad to have met you."

Route 271 cuts across the Cuyahoga valley in a line as straight as a stretched rubber band.

Then came the hot wires. The plan was to cut a mile-wide swath across the valley for high-tension wires. But Peninsula won't conduct electricity. No wires.

Turn south once more on Riverview Road. On your left, look down into the old quarry where they cut the Berea sandstone for the canal locks; farther down in the woods, reached by the walking trails of Metropolitan Park, is the deep lock, part of the old canal.

As we wind into the countryside of the Cuyahoga valley, a sharp ridge, hirsute with tall trees, cuts in and out of sight—the towpath of the canal.

At the corner of Everett Road and Riverview, you can catch a glimpse of famous Johnnycake Lock, now a backyard playground. On the hill is a cemetery for sixteen Irish canal construction men, near Locks 23 and 24.

As the miles roll under us, the river loops toward the road and away like a playful snake.

From Botzum, Riverview Road merges with several others, and if you turn instinctively to follow the river, you will find yourself on Old Portage Trail where the Indians left the river to portage their canoes over the divide to the Tuscarawas.

The river turns east, looping away from Akron to Cuyahoga Falls.

In the Metropolitan Park which borders the river, you can walk a short half mile to the rocks of the Mary Campbell Cave. If you ask the old-timers here about the cave, they'll smile and say, "Oh, you mean Old Maid's Kitchen."

Mary Campbell was only eight years old when she was brought to the cave, captive to a tribe of Indians who raided her home in Pennsylvania.

As you watch the river here, a ghost from the past shimmers the vision. Spray from the big power dam of Ohio Edison mists over the area enough to diffuse the present and reveal solemn-faced warriors grouped around watching a white trader beach his canoe on this side of the river and climb hesitantly toward the bluffs of the Indian encampment. Blink and the image is gone.

The dam is still here and the woods are thinned to a white man's park.

Cross Route 5 on foot, there is an entrance to the gorge, apparently the only one here. Few ever explore this section of the river, even though it is almost in the center of Cuyahoga Falls itself, so few have ever seen "Old Chuckery."

It was on the main Cuyahoga that Dr. Crosby, the restless champion of the Akron race on the Little Cuyahoga, tried to repeat his success with water power to make a city here. He

designed an aqueduct to carry water from the big Cuyahoga to a point north of Akron where the mills would be built. He called the power point Summit City, but it ran into financial grief.

A detractor of the project was once asked the population of Summit City. He shook his head. "Population is one thousand. One human being and nine hundred and ninety-nine wood-chucks."

The story spread and it buried Summit City under damaging laughter. So the big stones sunk in the south bank of the Cuyahoga here in Cuyahoga Falls have always been called "The Old Chuckery."

Upstream Gossip

At Akron, you can split off from the Cuyahoga River bed and follow the Little Cuyahoga a short way to its source if you like; but if your time is short, I'd rather take you into Akron alongside the bed of the Ohio and Erie Canal.

You will keep losing it under Akron streets, bridges, factories, and fenced-in backyards where the grand concourse of western commerce has been filled in to make a barbecue place or a tulip bed.

For a starting place, go to the old Portage Hotel; ask where the great staircase of locks begins. They will direct you to a place under a mile away.

With the weeds and small trees growing up in it, it will be hard for a moment to visualize two thousand men chopping these locks into the great divide to build a stairway to economic survival. But if you get out of the car and walk up alongside the lock beds, still so perfectly intact, you'll marvel at the craftsmanship of pioneer engineers.

When locking through Akron, Captain Guard Jamison of the *Western Star* would spread himself a lot by treating the passengers to a program of name dropping.

Just after he'd pass the Old Stone Mill, he'd point up west to the crown of the pleasant hill to some scowling mansions. "That one beside Colonel Conger's belongs to Lewis Miller. They call it Oak Place. Lew made Akron big in farm implements. He was handy with hardware. Got work over at the Aultman Company at age twenty-two, making stoves and plows. In sixty-four, he lashed together a mower with special rakes and droppers attached. He named it the Buckeye. They changed the name of the Aultman Company to Aultman-Miller and they built a new plant opposite Fred Schumacher's oatmeal works. Then Lew built that big house up there.

"Then in sixty-five a farm boy named John F. Seiberling came to town with a reaper contraption he'd made called the Excelsior. Built a plant next to Miller. In seventy-three, he lost the business and the plant. Came up with a better reaper he called the Empire, bought back the plant, hired six hundred men and went to working around the clock. Then he built that big house on East Market.

"Now that house I said was Colonel Conger's—what he did, he sold parts to both Seiberling and Miller, also to McCormick and John Deere. Then he built a house up on the hill, too, and settled down to enjoy his money.

"He financed Bishop Vincent in founding Chautauqua. His daughter, Mina, went there, met that young electrician, Tom Edison. The wedding was right up there on that hill at Oak Place."

Canalers liked to point out the factories and homes and names that were already beginning to belong more to the nation than to the Cuyahoga valley. They liked to see the amazement on the faces of their listeners that these national names were just people, living up here at the head of the Cuyahoga.

Captain Jamison would point out about General Lucius V. Bierce, who led a crusading war north across the Great Lakes to free the Canadians. A heroic type from youth, Bierce walked eighteen hundred miles to Yorkville, South Carolina, because he wanted to study law under a certain master. When he heard that his father was in failing health, he walked eighteen hundred miles back.

Years later, he began getting the idea that the Canadians wanted to be free like the United States. And in 1838, he led a force across to free Canada. Canadians did not join his crusade. His army was defeated in two battles, and he withdrew to Akron.

The Canadians were trying to extradite him, but Akron elected him mayor, then re-elected him five times. He served as state senator, brigadier general of militia, Union Army officer, and defense attorney for James Brown of Moneyshop Hill. His home on Market Street became Akron's library.

Rightly enough, Akron people today like to point out along the canal the homes of the Firestones, Seiberlings, Ben Goodrich, the Perkinses, the Aultmans—pipemakers, millers, and tire builders for the world.

Upstream along the Cuyahoga, Route 14 through Monroe Falls, Kent, and Brady Lake gives you the best view of the winding river.

North of Brady Lake you must use a lot of small field roads to follow the river. It gets marshy along about Auburn Corners.

Near the headwaters in Geauga County, mansions crown each hill that rises out of the watershed.

The river forks. You'll lose the west branch in a swamp. Only from a plane do you see that it's a hundred little rivulets flowing together to start the river near the intersection of Routes 6 and 608.

East Branch contains a dream scene reservoir with an island in it. The whole jewel is mounted in a man-made pinewoods.

The source of East Branch, you'll find in the woods on a dairy farm near the road close to the intersection of Routes 6 and 86.

Mile for mile and drop for drop, as pretty a little river as you'd ever want to see, all the way from the source—downstream past the rubber factories, oil refineries and steel mills under their halo of red air—to the mouth where the white Coast Guard station at the breakwall sparkles like bucket-flung water in the sun.

25

Men at Work

THERE'S A marine population on the Cuyahoga working just below the public eye level. It's a race of great skill and anonymity and professional pride. They're visible only from the water or occasionally in the all-night restaurants alongshore. A few know about them, however. You can see men and women in tuxedos and evening gowns there some early mornings who have come down to view marine life—respectfully, not as a side show.

There are salvage men, Coast Guard men, longshoremen, warehousemen, tugmen, bridgemen, crane operators, and ship chandlers.

Ship chandlers are a big part of this population. Ever since large ships have sailed, ship chandlers have been meeting ships at port to furnish the thousand things it takes to keep a ship in action. But on the Cuyahoga, ship chandling is a little different because of the pressures under which the fleet operates.

Striving for the most cargo turn-arounds per season before ice closes the river, a ship coming up the Cuyahoga hopes to be unloaded in three to four hours and out again. And while the vessel is tied up, the crew is busy. It leaves little time to service the ship with laundry, food, tools, marine parts. And whenever the vessel needs a *special* part, some heroic feats are performed by ship chandlers scouring northern Ohio for hard-to-get items.

Since ships are not mass produced, the interchangeable part is not a matter of course; and on a half-century-old vessel the original manufacturer of the component may be long out of business. A ship may have been rebuilt four times, and there's little tracing the source of the part. So many a blacksmith or machinist is called out of bed at 2:00 A.M. to study a worn part and a chief engineer's sketch and to open up his shop.

Sometimes of course the chandler gets advance notice by ship-shore radio telephone. But if he suspects there may be complications, a ship chandler will send out a launch to meet the approaching vessel far out in the lake, then scurry back to shore while the vessel lumbers in. He can sometimes get nine hours that way, counting the time it takes the ore boat to go upstream, unload and come back down.

The chandler knows the captain will usually put out whether the part is ready or not, so many a ship chandler launch chases a ship far uplakes to deliver on the run in choppy seas to a line dropped from the ship's stern.

Another part of this riverside population is the bumboat that comes along and ties to the outboard gunnel of ships at the unloading dock. She's a floating drugstore carrying candy, cigarettes, sundries, work clothes, and a large stock of etceteras.

The bumboat is loyal. In gratitude for the fair-weather business, she comes out in foul weather, nighttimes and holidays. More interesting than the cash trade is the bumboat's steady commerce in personal matters: letters for mailing, messages for men on other ships, shopping errands involving affairs of the heart.

At work on the Cuyahoga is a precision artist whose job is to thread a needle-straight ship through a crooked river. It's a thing of beauty to watch a Cuyahoga tug use the ship's momentum jujitsu fashion to bend it around the U-turns.

Because of the cramped waters, a Great Lakes tug is essentially an enormous engine packed into the smallest practical hull. When it moves, the thrust is immediate. That's essential, of course, because when the stern of an eight or nine million dollar ship is swinging toward the shore, with perhaps ten feet to play with, the action needs to be fast. When the tug pushes the stern around, the bow may be heading for the opposite bank, so the tug moves forward fast to work the bow.

In the early days many independent tugs fought for the available business, racing each other to each approaching bow. In the event of a tie, a battle resulted and towing prices were cut. Falling prices prevented tug owners from maintaining their equipment.

The delays suffered by the shippers from cobbled-up tugs became so costly that they stepped in to form Great Lakes Towing Company, merging the more efficient tug operators. Great Lakes Towing covered all the Great Lakes iron ore ports. The tugs were named for states.

But today the vessels need less help from tugs because bow thrusters are being installed by several fleets. The thruster is a transverse propeller in a hollow tube in the bow of an ore boat. It pushes water left or right so the captain can swing his bow fast, giving him back a lot of control of his own vessel.

A tug veteran waiting for a call explained, "With the new variable-pitch main propulsion propellers in the rear, the captain can reverse the ship, too, without changing the turn of the engine shaft. It's a lot quicker than the old way; gives 'em better maneuvering, too.

"If a ship's got both of these, it stands a fair chance of getting up the river on its own."

There was a awkward silence while he listened apparently to some echo of his own words.

" 'Course we've got progress on the tugs, too. All diesel now. And . . . why even coming aboard is different. Time was when the tug just slowed down and came close to the shore. The old crew jumped off and the new one on.

"Some missed the boat and couldn't swim. After that we used taxicabs. At seven in the morning, three in the afternoon and eleven o'clock at night he'd take us to what bridge was nearest our boat and we'd change crews at the bridge."

"That's changed though now?"

"We've got our own dock right here. You just step aboard, like you'd go in an office in the morning and out at night. It's a better life now . . . I guess."

The Cuyahoga Bridges

Another part of this 'round-the-clock river population is the bridge operators.

Traveling twenty-three miles upriver from the mouth you pass under eighty-four bridges to reach Akron—over three and a half bridges per mile. Twenty-one of these are concentrated in the navigable section of the river where both water and land traffic are high, so many of them are movable. The variety of action in the first twenty-one bridges is interesting. There are vertical-lift bridges, of course, and drawbridges, but the jackknife, side-swing and rotary bridges are worth a trip just to watch.

Every day, without fanfare, a kind of drama goes on at the movable bridges. It starts with an ore boat steaming toward the Cuyahoga. The captain checks down from about fourteen miles an hour to about four at the wall, and winds her around a quarter turn at the lighthouse and breakwater. He picks up his tugs and heads upriver. About three hundred yards from each bridge he blows it open with one long blast that rattles windows all the way to Public Square.

Then he listens very closely for a long and a short from the bridge. He has 132,000 tons in motion and if the bridge isn't going to open he must put on full reverse soon enough, or carry away the bridge. If the bridge can't open, it answers with three shorts. The captain can't wait long for the answer.

But the bridge operator has multiple safeguard systems. Before the bridge can swing open—or tilt up or lift—traffic lights turn red and a gong rings. Warning gates with flashing lights lower, and, finally, a cable-net barrier blocks the road. Safety still depends on the bridge operator's judgment. But if he should have a stroke or faint, the whistle signal may be safeguard enough. It's up to the ship to leave enough time for stopping if the bridge doesn't blow back. If the operator is incapacitated after the bridge begins to open, however, it will lift all the way open until a limit switch stops it. If the operator can't bring it down, it stays up until help arrives.

In an emergency, road traffic can turn around and use some other crossing, but the ships have only one road.

In heavy storms, a power failure can be a threat. So two power lines run to each bridge. If both lines are out, there is an engine-generator set to operate the bridge. If this fails, a direct gasoline drive comes into play or a compressed air motor. Some Cuyahoga bridges have gears for manual operation with a hand crank. Despite the tremendous weight of the bridges, counterbalancing makes hand operation possible. A measure of the systems' effectiveness is the fact that, outside of a railroad watchman, bridge tenders were the only men down on the river during the great storm of 1913.

Some bridges go unscathed, but during the 1913 spring flood the steamer *Mack* knocked the south span off the lower West Third Street bridge into the Cuyahoga. Inventive engineers replaced it with a secondhand span from Michigan. Three years later the north span was clipped by a runaway streetcar and knocked over onto the B & O tracks. Not to be stopped by lack of a bridge section, the railroad adapted a girder span, only slightly used, which it cut down to length and installed.

This bridge, lashed up wholly of secondhand and jury-rigged parts, lasted without further repair until replacement twenty-four years later.

When it was time for old bridges to come down, corporate executives and government officials discovered that the bridges had a place in the hearts of the people.

Several years after the Lorain-Carnegie bridge was in use, the fifty-two-year-old Central Viaduct was closed, even to pedestrian traffic. A Reverend Mr. Stark of the Viaduct's west end made it plain that "This community was developed as a result of that bridge and there is a definite need for it."

The old bridges doomed by a 1944 project—with the exception of one swing bridge—were all of the Bascule or jackknife design. Counterweights shoreward of the bridge helped pivot the span up into the air.

Small boys of all ages were sorry when they were torn down. On a hot summer day, you could sit by the river and watch those graceful Bascules by the hour. But sentiment will not widen the river, and captains needed room for bigger boats.

Crews felt differently. Wives and sweethearts of lake sailors were sorry when wreckers took away that little swing bridge near the harbor mouth. The central pier stood right in the river so that ships had to glide within twelve feet of the east bank. At this spot was a park area like a giant widow's walk. There the women waited, to see their men pass by or to welcome them home from the inland seas.

Today, in addition to the tugmen, ship chandlers, dock personnel at work on the river, there is a contingent of U.S. Coast Guardsmen stationed at the mouth who worry about the safety of vessels and inspect them on a regular basis.

These are the men at work . . . on the Cuyahoga.

26

The Noonday Club—

and the Nation

THE MOST exclusive lunch club in the world meets at 1200 hours sharp daily at the mouth of the Cuyahoga.

The food is good, but very plain, and the men are neither rich nor sociable (how would you like to eat with the same fellows five days a week for ten years?). But it's highly exclusive in membership: A man must know the shipping business backwards and forward, and his word must be his company's bond—because at the lunch table he may buy $100,000 worth of coal just with the spoken word; and his company must pay the invoice when it comes, or this lunch club couldn't work.

These men are also carrying out the Cuyahoga's role as boss of the Great Lakes fleet from Duluth to Buffalo.

No guests. The men who run the vessel-coal-and-iron-ore complex have long ago developed a cold stony eye for laymen who want to hear about "the romance of the business," because while they're talking romance they can lose their shirts. And anyway, the interviewer isn't likely to understand the split-second tension in a business where ships move eighteen miles per hour.

Besides, the chessboard they play on like the back of their hands is so big nobody really believes it, and the names they name, nobody recognizes. I get to this lunch club only because I've been scrivening around the vessel business 150 years.

Though the lunch club is exclusive, the intricate and crucial chess game these men play affects the lives and incomes and well-being of thousands of people in a seven-state belt from Minnesota to Pennsylvania and south to West Virginia and Kentucky.

You see, the most ticklish rendezvous in economics today is the moment when a train is scheduled to meet a ship at the mouth of the Cuyahoga or anywhere along the south shore of the Great Lakes. If either is late, the cost is gigantic. If early, same problem.

Now when a ship starts downlakes from Duluth, Minnesota, to meet at the mouth of the Cuyahoga a train that is rolling north with a hundred cars of coal from Beckley, West Virginia, you have a precision high wire act that may keep fifty men on the edge of their nerves for seventy-two hours.

They have planned this meeting precisely, because if the train gets to the dock and sits idle, somebody pays. Likewise, if the ship sits empty, or waiting for dockage, it's eating raw money.

Despite this planning, though, the ship captain can't control a storm on Lake Superior, a delay at the Soo Locks, a strike on the dock unloading equipment, or an eight-hour fog in the Cuyahoga. The railroader can't control a flash flood in the mine or a burnt-out journal bearing. And one of these things or something like it *is* going to happen.

But the train and the vessel continue relentlessly toward the original meeting place, even after it's impossible for them to connect.

Now with telephone and radio communication being good, obviously traffic management could get on the phones and re-coordinate this rendezvous with the dock, the shipper, the customer, the vessel, and the train. But if eight docks, seven railroads, four vessel companies and ninety shippers tried to do this in a 190-million-ton year, it would jam every switchboard in the Great Lakes trade.

What you need is a man sitting up so high he gets an eagle's-eye view of the railroads from West Virginia, and all the vessels from Lake Superior to Ontario. He should also be able to see the docks to know if they're ready, and which kinds of empty cars they have. In the case of iron ore, some mills accept ore from hoppers, others from flat-bottoms. This perch sitter needs to be able to scan the whole south shore of the Great Lakes to see where the right kinds of cars are to come from.

Well, there *is* such an eagle's nest. It's on the eleventh floor of The Terminal Tower at the mouth of the Cuyahoga. "Room 1101" is what it says on the door. It's known as The Ore and Coal Exchange, Gordon Walker, Manager.

The three dispatchers there are locked to their desks by telephone and ship-shore radio. They each have a complex ledger in front of them. The way these three dispatchers keep the Midwest economy coordinated is this: Each shipment of coal gets a consignment name (i.e., "Holiday," "Red Dog," "Blue Sky," etc.). The coal is usually going to be transferred from a train from West Virginia to a vessel upbound for the electric power stations on the upper lakes. Coal from West Virginia makes toast in St. Paul, Minnesota.

So the shipper then tells the Exchange the plans for each consignment. It's a code language all its own, but in English it tells: what's in the consignment by grade; when depart mine, over what rails; to which dock; for which customer; how mix at dock when loading in ship.

The vessel company then tells the dispatcher which of its ships will pick up this coal.

When the train and the ship are seventy-two hours away from the rendezvous, the dispatcher receives calls from shipper and/or railroad and vessel company as to the location of each. At sixty hours, another call. Again at thirty-six hours; again at (and now it's touch-and-go) twenty-four, twelve, and three hours away from port.

The dispatcher is the one man who can see whether or not they're going to connect.

Since it doesn't always work that neatly, the dispatcher also uses other sources of information. Every morning, his first calls are to Detroit, Buffalo, Port Colborne to see if any of his named-in ships have cleared these points last night, and at what times. And which ships did not clear those points. He's familiar with the speed of each vessel, loaded and light.

"Why can't they just ship the coal up early so it's here well ahead of the ship?"

Demurrage.

Demurrage is the penalty for sitting around blocking the Great Lakes trade. It's a charge that begins on each car of coal after 120 hours on the dock. The space is needed by a relentless column of coal coming up behind from West Virginia, Kentucky, Pennsylvania, and lower Ohio. The whole secret in coal is to keep it in constant motion. Never let it rest—from the mine face to the customer's furnace blower—or it costs like gold.

"Well, why not at least mine it earlier, so no production stoppage can delay the train's departure?"

That's the other jaw of the same vise. You must mine it as *late* as possible so you load it right from the preparation plant into the train, to avoid piling and rehandling. This coal has been in motion from the moment the coal mole chews it out of the mine face sending it out behind it on a moving belt into railroad mine cars that carry it above ground to the top of the preparation plant where it falls across classification series, and down through washers and graders and separators into railroad hopper cars that immediately roll north to Cuyahoga and Lake Erie docks to meet boats.

Now on the dock, demurrage is totaled at end-of-season on each shipper's account. And it can well tell the story of his ability for the year. For every day that a car of coal sits at port beyond 120 hours, it picks up one debit (about $3.00 per car per day)— or it picks up a credit for every day *under* 120 hours.

Toward the end of the season, a shipper who has piled up heavy debits works hard to erase them with credits.

So if the train bringing "Red Dog" is seriously delayed en route, a new cargo must be found quickly for the S.S. *Western Star*. If the vessel is delayed, a new bottom must be diverted to meet "Red Dog" which is racing north.

Since you're talking about 3,000,000 carloads per season, 16 ships, and eight ports on Lake Erie alone, emergencies like this happen several times a day, at the mouth of the Cuyahoga.

By midmorning, every vessel dispatcher on the Cuyahoga, every railroad, every dock and coal shipper may have a white hot slip of paper in his pocket—an emergency getting closer by the minute. A dispatcher in a vessel company is somebody you don't chat with casually while he's on duty. While you're talking to him he is dying, trying to see the clock over your shoulder, and watching the three buttons light up on his phone. He hopes they are three solutions to problems he just sent out; but he suspects they are three more problems.

If you don't get to the point before the sweep second hand comes around again, he will grab the phone without apology and you won't get his attention again all day. He can't help it. He has 79,000 tons of ore bearing down on him, needing dockage.

At 1145 hours, they each walk out of their offices down to the Cuyahoga to the Noonday Club. There, among ninety others, each hopes to find a man who has an emergency which fits with his like the other half of a solution. So you'll see men get up and circulate to other tables, leaning down to talk to other diners here and there.

You'll see some just walking through the room searching the tables. They are men looking for solutions—before one o'clock. The problem they're seeking to solve has probably been building up all morning, and they have possibly called or visited the Exchange in person previously this morning.

Let's take Mike Bonnard, bulk vessel dispatcher from Ardco Fleet.

He had been down here early this morning to see the chief dispatcher at the Ore and Coal Exchange. "Al, will *The Orion* have a clear dock today when she gets in?"

The chief dispatcher, here for a hundred years, smiles and consults his vessel sheets. Although he sits in the ulcer chair, and he's watching six major problems graduate into top grade emergencies, he approaches Bonnard's problem as if it were absurd even to think that everything won't come out all right.

Anyone not used to his job would be sweating bullets. But the three Exchange dispatchers stay calm by assuming the best laid plans will fail, and by having in their minds alternate plans for nearly every situation, the way a pilot's roving eye is always selecting an emergency landing field.

Right at this moment, the chief dispatcher has an alternate plan for Bonnard's big vessel. But before the morning is over, his alternate may have alternates on it.

"Can't say for sure yet, Mike. She might, if the sun comes out in Toledo."

"When can you give us a firm answer, Al?"

"I hope by eleven A.M."

Bonnard leaves.

The dispatcher's phone stops ringing thirty seconds, so we ask a fast question: "What's the sun got to do with it, Al?"

He steps to the map and outlines the problem building up in the case of *The Orion*. This vessel has cleared the Soo downbound with eighteen thousand tons of ore for Toledo, where she's to pick up coal.

Now it happens that Vessel B is still at *The Orion's* scheduled dock in Toledo, taking on coal. But loading is slow because the coal is frozen. Even with the hot dogs turned on, they're only dumping seven or eight cars an hour into that hull.

Next, Vessel C is just now clearing Cuyahoga River for Toledo where she was scheduled to load before *The Orion* at the same dock. But she was delayed at Cleveland even longer than *The Orion* was delayed at the Soo.

Fact four: different grades of coal must be available at Toledo for Vessel C from those for *The Orion*. But we don't know yet which vessel will arrive first, nor how long it will take to finish loading Vessel B.

"You see, if the sun comes out," Al explains, "it may loosen up that coal so they can start dumping fifteen-twenty cars per hour instead of seven, which would mean that boat can clear the dock in about half the time."

"But what if the sun doesn't come out, and you can't assure Mike Bonnard at eleven o'clock that *The Orion* will have a clear dock when she gets down?"

"Well, if we can't straighten out by noon, then maybe he can make a deal at Noonday Club today with some other shippers or receivers."

Not all those who come to Noonday Club bring a problem. But

they come anyway. That's part of a bargain made in 1913 when they organized the Exchange to mobilize all the iron and coal in the Midwest against the Kaiser.

But several men will have problems.

For example, one shipper's coal is loading into a vessel right now. But he has got word this morning that he's going to be short eight carloads of making up a full vessel. He can't afford to send the vessel up light. He hopes to find another shipper at lunch who has eight extra carloads of the same kind of coal, sitting at the same dock at the same time. He'll buy eight carloads from him right now, verbally. His competitor is usually glad to help him out if he can, because tomorrow the shortage may be on the other foot.

Or again—a dispatcher from a vessel company has a commitment to put a ship at Cuyahoga's Erie Dock by 4:00 P.M. to pick up a shipper's coal. But the ship has been delayed at the Welland. He looks for another vessel operator who happens to have an empty carrier near the Erie for which cargo is not yet ready.

But the pieces of the puzzle may not fit together so neatly. First the stranded cargo must fit the available vessel. Second, if it's a divided cargo, the vessel must have enough compartments to keep the grades separated. Third, the vessel must fit the port of destination. A vessel which requires twenty-seven feet of water cannot get up to some of the shallow river docks. Fourth, the type of unloading equipment at the receiver's dock must fit the vessel. A straight deck bulker can't unload at a plain dock the way a self-unloader can.

There are other requirements which must mesh.

Now one fellow we see moving around the dining room while his lunch gets cold is Mike Bonnard, with his *Orion* bearing down on Toledo, needing a clear dock to unload ore and pick up coal. You see, the sun didn't come out.

But by the time Mollie comes by with the coffee, Mike has worked out a solution. His ore can be diverted to another customer on the Cuyahoga who can use the same mix. His customer, who is also represented at lunch, can forego this load of ore on assurance that two slightly later and smaller cargoes will be diverted to him tomorrow.

Weather is a major factor. On a stormy day the tables at the

Noonday Club are left covered with uneaten lunch. But today is routine.

Bonnard goes out of the dining room to line up at the dispatcher's desk along with others who have also solved problems at lunch.

When his turn at the dispatcher comes, he takes a slip of paper out of his pocket and says, "Al, changing *The Orion* to Cleveland lakefront at seventeen hundred hours."

"O.K., Mike. The dock and the railroad already gave me their corresponding changes."

Al has before him a pad of vessel sheets a yard wide. It shows every vessel's destination, cargo, estimated arrival. He does not cross out or erase the original figures. He's keeping score on millions of dollars of equipment and material. So no erasures. Changes in red ink only.

When the chief dispatcher goes home, the sheets go home with him. He has five telephones there.

But if it weren't for the Noonday Lunch Club, he'd need about a hundred phones and a hundred operators. When shippers and receivers and carriers meet for one hour at lunch every day, there is assembled in one place all the men it takes to keep coal moving north, iron ore moving south, limestone moving crossways.

And when you've said that, you've just about described the heart of Midwest economy—iron, coal, steel, and stone.

27

Whisky Island

THE HIGH-RENT island in coastal United States, except for Manhattan, is at the mouth of the Cuyahoga. It grows no crop of high-rise hotels and no reef of cabanas or marinas. It has Huletts, salt mines, and a considerable glory. In fact it would be no exaggeration to say that in one sense the gangs of men who worked Whisky Island built the modern iron complex just as Alonzo Carter, on the same site, built Cleveland.

You can hear the story of Whisky Island in the Greenbrier Room of the Terminal Tower and at the Union Club in Cleveland. But if you have better connections and if you can stand the snobbery of Flanagan's Lookout or Old Angle Bar, it's better to get the story there.

"I'll bet you've listened your ears off trying to find out sumpin' about Whisky Island. I've seen you around here a week or so. But people here don't talk about it unless they know you."

The gray stubble hunched toward me over his beer. His grin was battered, but it was also a badge, membership in a quite exclusive group.

Mr. Cohalan matched his surroundings. The double-breasted wide-lapeled pin stripe ran to wrinkles very like the rippled paint on the cafe walls. He wore a new tie and a white shirt with collar tips forced up like butterfly wings by a good rugged neck.

However, I was able to show him enough proficiency in Whisky Islandia—good names like Mr. Kilbain, Mr. O'Mara, Mr. McGranahan—that he considered having a beer with me, but not enough that he'd let me buy.

Mr. Cohalan nodded. He indicated the bundled overcoat propped against the wall. "And you should talk to Tom Mallory over there."

Whisky Island in one way *made* this river. It served as terminal for Indian canoes, ore boats, and railroad trains. The Cuyahoga canyon itself is hostile to shipping with its narrow valley shelf and steep escarpment. But Whisky Island was flat and accessible, making it possible for ships to drop cargo without attempting the trip up past Collision Bend and Irish Town Bend.

Today, Whisky Island is a five hundred-foot wide strip from the mouth of the Cuyahoga to West Fortieth Street, thirty blocks paved nearly solid with railroad tracks, dock surface, and modern salt-mining equipment.

Like the Cuyahoga, Whisky Island is man-made. The Cuyahoga flows under Superior bridge bound straight toward Lake Erie, but just five hundred feet before reaching open water, it veers sharply west, cutting a deep bed parallel to the lakeshore as far as East Fortieth Street, where it finally flows north to the lake. This is the old river bed.

But man changed that, as we'll see.

The Cuyahoga loops in a series of S's as it approaches the Erie shore. Within five hundred feet of open water, it makes a last huge loop to the west. This loop was holding up Midwestern commerce. It effectually dammed the entire Cuyahoga. Sluggish waters piled sand around the entrance as if to frustrate the most ingenious captains, and the torturous channel along the lakefront denied navigation to anything much larger than an Indian canoe.

In 1825, however, the leading men in Cleveland went to the state legislature and hammered through an appropriation of five thousand dollars to cut the river straight through from the beginning of its last big loop to the lake.

Although this meant the creation of only a five-hundred-foot passage, it demanded more work than could be done for five thousand dollars even in 1825. When you remember that you had to have width and depth, you're suddenly talking about moving a million cubic feet of dirt.

But the U.S. Engineering Corps officer in charge of the work was Major T. W. Maurice, and a man who knew how to use his imagination.

During the dry season, the Major constructed a dam at the angle, cutting off the unnecessary loop. This forced the waters to flood, building up pressure against the land toward the lake. When the rains came, softening the earth, the pent-up river tore its way through the last few yards to the lake, by the shortest route, gouging a straight ten-foot channel to open water.

And there was now an island, instead of a tongue of land, bounded by a new channel and the old river bed.

The new channel sucked in shipping like a whirlpool. As two-way traffic began to plug the river, the old bed became a natural siding for incoming ships. Slips were notched into the island. They widened it with five hundred feet of fill to create more land. Whisky Island thus became the transfer point between lake and land transport.

In the 1850s, it gave birth to a world of dockwallopers and mules surrounded by mountains of ore and studded in succession over the next sixty years with a fantasy of ore unloading mechanisms ranging from the simple wheelbarrows to the monster Huletts.

The men who made their livelihood on Whisky Island spilled onto the angle of land where the old river bed turns west. That's how the Angle, as it came to be called, grew layers of piled-high dwellings to house their families.

The Angle became the rough house of the river, a community of rock-shouldered men who worked together, drank together, and fought together. But they say if you made the grade in this proudly Irish community, your neighbors would never let you go for want.

Even today, the Angle is the country of a laconic group who need no strangers and eye authority with icy hauteur. Old-timers from the tugs and docks and shore installations meet in tiny cafes like this one at the west end of Superior bridge topping the Willow Street hill where it dips down into the Angle.

This is where Mr. Cohalan received me.

"You'll hear a lot of people say Whisky Island got its name from the bootleggers and rumrunners that landed there during prohibition," he said. "And it is true—lotta people made their living through the depression that way, but that isn't how Whisky Island became Whisky Island.

"You'll hear the railroaders say Whisky Island got its name 'cause there's no *water* here. That's a fact; but nobody who worked on the island drank water anyways.

"Twenty-four hours a day, the ore was unloaded and the trains were loaded. They had five saloons on that hunka land. Sold thirty-two barrels of beer a day. When we were makin' up trains, we'd send a kid over to Fat Jack's or Corrigan's four times a day to bring back beer in buckets slung on a yoke around his neck.

"Still, that's not why Whisky Island got its name. Man named Carter had a store here on the Cuyahoga mor'n a hundred years ago, when the Indians were here. And right across the river, right on the tip of Whisky Island, was where they had the still. It was there for a helluva long time. *That's why they call it Whisky Island.*"

When the ore boats were smaller and coming in faster, Whisky Island practically made the city. In those days, the island looked as if a couple of kids had gone wild with a giant Erector set. There were Brownhoists, Hoover-Mason buckets, and whirleys all sticking their skeletons up in the sky. Everywhere you looked, the piles of ore were crisscrossed with wooden catwalks for the men to trundle their wheelbarrows. In-between were railroad tracks. It was hard to tell where the island left off and the man-made part began. The railroads put in fill dirt to extend the island out into the lake. Then they covered it with tracks.

"I've talked to railroaders that worked yards all over the country, 'n' they never could get the hang of Whisky Island."

Mr. Cohalan described the most distinguished saloon on the island, "You walk down Willow Street hill outside here, and you'll come to Willow Street bridge. It's brand-new steel now. Back then it was wood. You cross it now and there's nothing. You cross that bridge back then, and there was Fat Jack's.

"J. C. Dare was his real name, but nobody called him that. He was a good-lookin' fellow and not exactly fat. Just paunchy. Jack ran the only place on the island where you could pick up your change and have a fair chance of getting out with it. Nobody fooled with Fat Jack.

"About a hundred feet down from the J. C. Dare Cafe, right on the river, was Mother Carey's place. Now that was a place I can't tell you about. I was tough back then, but Mother was tougher.

"The poison she served was iron ore and ammonia. But her place was very interesting.

"I'd say Mother Carey was about forty or forty-fivish when I saw her. Good-lookin' woman in a rough sort of way. She sure did get along with men. She pulled the roughest bunch this side of

Sandusky. I say Sandusky 'cause that's how far the Lake Shore Gang operated. Mother Carey's was their hangout.

"The Lake Shore Gang had a thriving business on Whisky Island back in the nineteen hundreds. They had nothing to do with the main business of the island, unloading ships. They were . . . well, crooks. But big. You have to remember that rails were the only way to get anywhere fast, those days. Roads were narrow and crooked, but the rails made clear track to Sandusky or Painesville out east. That's what made the Lake Shore Gang so successful. They'd bomb a safe in Sandusky and time it so they could follow a freight on a handcar. They wouldn't run into anything that way, and it was impossible to catch them.

"There are three entrances to Whisky Island. The west one is dry land, of course, where the old river bed is filled up. The east approach is the New York Central bridge over the Cuyahoga. The other's at Willow Street.

"Most trains went east, over the river. Trouble was, there was also a lotta boats goin' in and out of the river. So, it was always a bottleneck. Every train that came through Whisky Island had to slow down or stop at that bridge, which made it easy for the men riding rods to jump off. That's why the hobo jungle started there on the northeast tip of the island, right by the bridge. That's where the Lake Shore Gang used to break the seals on the box-cars and dump off stuff. Then they'd lose themselves in the jungle. Their hangout was Mother Carey's.

"Mother was kind of a recruiting agent for the boats, too. Those days it took a little time to clear the holds, so the crews would take off for Mother Carey's and Fat Jack's. I guess Mother had some more exciting entertainment for the crews, too.

"Lotta times some of the crews didn't come back, and a vessel was left short-handed. So Mother Carey unofficially helped out with this recruiting problem.

"The other saloons on the island never equaled Fat Jack's and Mother's place. There was Sweeney's—and Corrigan's where the dockmen got their soup. And there was Kilbane's.

"I don't think this Kilbane was any relation to Johnny Kilbane who got to be featherweight champ, although both of them were Irish and both came out of the Angle.

"In a way you *had* to be something of a fighter on Whisky Island. Generally nobody'd bother a guy with a lamp in his hand. That's a railroad man. But even when we were switchin' and had

to walk from one end of the train to the other, we went with a
buddy. Either that, or you got to be a helluva good fighter.

"Johnny Kilbane was the most famous of the Whisky Island
fighters. I remember him when he was just fresh out of the Angle.
His job was to man the big puzzle switch in the center of the
island. We had about ten tracks comin' into this puzzle, so it was
pretty important to have someone there all the time. But that
Johnny Kilbane, he was always jiggin' and dancin' around,

throwin' punches at the moths that used to gather 'round his
lantern on summer nights.

"I remember plenty times the yardmaster, Tom Corrigan,
would holler at Johnny, 'Yuh gonna take care of those switches 'r
keep shadowboxing?'

"Johnny'd fling back, without missing a punch, 'Corrigan! One
day ye'll pay tuh see me fight!'

"I know for a fact that when Johnny got to be featherweight
champ, Corrigan personally went all the way to California to see
him fight. I'd read about his fights in the newspapers, but I
couldn't help laughin'. I remembered him back on Whisky Island
straddling the lever like it was a chinning bar and jumping up
and down, trying to close the puzzle switch. He was little, but
was he fast!

"Lots of times Johnny'd just take off for a workout at the La

Salle Club. They used to warn him, but Johnny didn't care. Once he missed pullin' the switch four nights runnin' and Walt Kramer had to throw it for him. 'Damn it, Kilbane,' he roars one day, 'you get back on time or yer gettin' sumpin' yuh won't like.' Johnny'd just laugh. 'Course later on, he went into politics and that's a different story.

"Lotta important people come outa the Angle. They live up in big houses now in Shaker Heights and Pepper Pike and other parts of town."

"Could you name me a few?"

"Could—but I wouldn't care to."

"Why is that?"

"We-ll, it's a kind of a—unspoken deal. They're not eager for people to know they cut their knuckles on Whisky Island."

"Isn't that kind of irritating?"

Mr. Cohalan looked at me to see if I'd understand. He wasn't sure. "It isn't quite like that. The other half of the deal is—we need something, we ask. They come back and help. I mean real big help."

"But I also hear some big men brag that they came from Whisky Island."

"True. But those are the medium-sized big shots. And not ones that stayed in the iron business. And that kind didn't really work here. More like sons of men who did. Or men that only spent a year or so here.

"There are a lot of guys you never heard of, too, and probably never will. But there was one—Doughbelly Garlock—was boomer on a line of cars we was feeding into the switchback one time. The switchback is a kind of dip in the tracks with a switch at the bottom. The engine shoves boxcars one at a time down the incline, and the momentum carries it up the other side aways. Before it rolls back down, the switcher throws the track over so it coasts on the other track to the coal unloader.

"Well, Doughbelly's riding the first car down the dip, but this time the engine coupling breaks. Before you know it, Doughbelly and twelve cars is riding down the dip and up the other side. They've got more momentum this time and the whole string goes over the top headed straight for the river, forever.

"There's not awful much you can do with twelve runaway box-cars but watch 'em. We just stood there looking at the bubbles comin' up from where all those cars had disappeared in the river. Then someone pipes, 'Gee, Dough's a good old plug. We oughta dive down and see if we can find him.'

"I don't think any of us were too willin' to jump into that mucky river and pull him up, but it was a kind of bond among islanders.

"Turns out we didn't have to, though. Here comes Dough, crawlin' outa the weeds alongside the switchback, his pants all slits and slavers and mouthin' language fit to boil that river into live steam.

"I remember Bluenose Heller runnin' up as Doughbelly wipes the cinders out of his eyes. Bluenose shakes a finger under Doughbelly's chin. 'Garlock,' he says, 'no doubt you'll be discharged over this. Why the hell didn't you use yer head to stop those cars?'

"That was railroadin' Whisky Island in the ore-unloadin' days. It lasted about twenty years, until the Huletts beat out the Brownhoists and the Hoover-Masons.

"Me? I got bounced out with the wildcat strike in nineteen twenty. I always felt like Whisky Island was my home, though. Lotta guys felt that way during the depression. Remember that hobo jungle I told you about? Well, after railroading moved out and the island started to fall apart some, a lotta guys moved in there. That whole strip fronting the lake was a jumble of boards and corrugated iron scrounged outa junk piles. The guys put together shacks, open on the side away from the lake with the backs and sides banked with dirt. Hooverville, we called it.

"The smells on Whisky Island never were choice, but whenever I smell liver and onions frying, it brings back those days with the tin cans over the open fires. There's something about outdoor cooking, right?

"We even had a mayor. John Grady. He elected himself.

"Couple guys used to spot a hunk of scrap at the same time and there'd be all kinds of cussin' and fightin'. Grady'd step in and settle the argument. 'Arbitrate' is what he called it. I think he just liked to argue louder. He used to make three hundred dollars a week as a lake diver. But he'd get paid on Friday and be broke by Monday. That was Grady.

"Grady was kind of a last-ditch stand for Hooverville. The city police and the railroads got together one day in nineteen hundred and thirty and marched down on the shacks like an armored tank division—with bulldozers. I heard Grady was right out in front, throwing bottles like he was fighting for his life. They say the language he used soured the ground. Why not? They were destroying a way of life. After they wiped out Hooverville, he just hung around the cafes. It took twenty years more before he really died.

"Whisky Island had a couple of mayors, but after Hooverville there were no people. Mickey Kane lived on a houseboat, called the *Titanic*, underneath the old Willow Street bridge. Mickey practically had to duck his head every time they swung the bridge open. He left when they announced they were going to put a garbage incinerator on the island. All the waste from every factory south of Cleveland flowing right underneath his house, sea gulls perching on his clothesline, but the thing that makes him move is the thought of a garbage incinerator in his front yard.

"Bill Hoey struck oil. He was pumpin' crude outa Whisky Island. It was nineteen fifty-two before anyone found out about it. Funny part was that Bill had been pumpin' oil for fifteen years. See . . . another reason we don't talk to strangers.

"They say for all those fifteen years, Standard Oil was sendin' a truck around to pick up something like a hundred twenty barrels a month. That guy was pullin' over five thousand bucks' worth of oil a year outa that junk pile."

I left Mr. Cohalan at his club.

The sinking sun was just setting fire to the high level bridge when I hit the open air, so I sauntered down Willow Street for another look at Whisky Island. The Angle has changed since Mr. Cohalan's days when the streets were mud and the houses looked like something a kid might draw on a blackboard.

Now you look up at low, lean apartment houses that give it a thrifty residential atmosphere. Down near the river, the apartments give way to great piles of bluestone, sand, and ore.

The old Willow Street swing bridge is gone now. In its place is a towering lift bridge so new it's still structural-iron orange.

I stood looking over the loneliness that is now Whisky Island after quitting time. To my left, stretching west, is an old dirt road running alongside the old river bed, which is really a deep and navigable channel. Wasn't that where Mother Carey's used to be? And Kilbane's and Sweeney's? All I could see now was weeds.

I wondered if Mr. Cohalon had made it all up.

I walked back to the little cement building that still stands in the curve of the road where it angles in front of the new bridge. It stood like an old, lonely guardian of the river's history. And very faintly, in faded whitewash on the dirty wall, I could make out the peeling letters: "J. C. Dare Cafe." It stood right across from where Alonzo Carter had built Carter's Tavern.

Twice, this strip of land had been the birthplace of the Midwest, once when Carter made it the headquarters of the Western Reserve, and again when the boomers made it the center of the Midwest economy—transfer point for iron, coal, and limestone . . . foundation of mid-America.

28

Bohn's Palisades

THE CUYAHOGA is a man-made river; and if you sail up it or drive across the mouth of it and look up to the west bank above the escarpment, you'll see even the palisades are man-made. Brick.

They begin at the mouth, looming above Whisky Island, and continue upstream along the west bank, intermittently to the big bend at the old Russian Orthodox Church with its turnip spires.

Few who live along the Cuyahoga know that from all over the world, men travel to see these brick palisades. They bring notebooks and cameras and questions.

You see, these are the nation's pilot model of slum clearance, urban renewal, low-rent public housing, and especially designed housing for the elderly. Few know that they led a nation out of the world's worst depression. A handful of Ohio journalists like Louis Selzer, Phil Porter, Norman Shaw, Wes Lawrence, Gene Segal, and Marie Daerr have watched the story grow. But even those who live in these palisades don't yet know that their houses are a chapter in U.S. history.

Beyond that, these palisades of brick are a swashbuckling story in American politics. It is a story of startling paradoxes.

The very river that floats millions of tons of ore in to feed the furnaces and the families on the Cuyahoga also washes ashore human problems. Some shanty towns grow, and bars and game rooms, an army of spot labor, overcrowding, disease, crime—and some fairly desperate riverbank poverty.

That is no different from any other industrial river. But from the Cuyahoga came a sweeping answer for such ghettos.

Before Bohn, the sociology of slums had been peopled by relays of bleeders, talkers, planners, writers, who went down yelling, loud and righteous, under waves of advancing slums. What the job needed was a tough and inventive lawyer with a prag-

272

matic understanding about moving ponderous bodies of government, population, and attitude . . . coupled to an armor-plated sense of mission.

Bohn's was no simple frontal attack. He hit slums from the flanks and the rear. It has not been obvious, because it has taken a third of a century to make its way across the nation; and it is complex.

But then Ernest J. Bohn is a complex man. On the one hand, he's so deeply religious and scholarly that new opponents, hearing him argue with quotes from Cicero or the Bible, feel they are contending with a lamb; then yowl in outrage to find they have been mauled by a lion.

Cynically tough and tenderly idealistic, Bohn is a battle-scarred old lion who guards the riverbank with gravel-voiced warnings and a rapier intellect.

Although that's a character held in some degree by many effective men, the two characteristics are in such daily combat in Bohn that they both appear within the same hour. In the same day, the same newspaper quoted him on page one arguing with a contentious committee of divers membership for some unified action on housing for the underprivileged. His tone is gentle, "We've got to get together on this thing, bury our differences and do a little something for God for once. He'll forgive us our trespasses if we forgive those who trespass against us."

Page two: Ernie has just learned the Supreme Court has declared five to two against an Ohio Housing law which Bohn needs to get bond backing for hundreds of new housing units. Bohn: "If those guys think we're going to take that lying down, they've got another think coming!"

Nor did he take it lying down.

Bohn's latest victory is the towering bank of Riverview apartments overlooking the Cuyahoga. They rise on the former site of acres of bars, shacks, dumps, and misery. And they are being studied by visitors from afar.

That's because they are designed so that there are old people mingled with young people. The tower apartments contain elevators, safety features, and special rooms for sociability, crafts, and the defeat of boredom. The young couples with children are in low buildings with as many as six bedrooms, with playgrounds,

easy in-and-out design, off-street parking, and recreational buildings.

There is a clinic in one of the high-rise buildings staffed by the
nearby Lutheran Hospital, and with someone on duty at night.
The U.S. Department of Health, Education and Welfare partic-
ipates financially in response to the Housing Authority's request.
When older people move into the apartments, they get an examination; and besides, the neighbors of Riverview can use these

facilities. There are public dining areas so the elderly don't need
to eat alone.

In the face of all the concern over Medicare and in the face of
housing designed especially for segregating old people, reporters
for architectural and sociological quarterlies seek out Bohn to get
the story. Organizations give him awards and honorary degrees
for vision and sociological pioneering and new concepts.

Actually he appreciates these awards very much; but if it's late
of an afternoon, and he's petulant with the slowness of progress
he's making in about ten other areas, he may explain it with a certain dispatch.

"Hell, old people like to be around young people. Is that sociology?

"Young couples need baby sitters for their kids. Is that a new concept?

"Young kids got to have a place to dig in the dirt and make castles and stuff, so you put them in apartments near the ground. Is that sociology?"

He'll sign a stack of letters for his secretary. She'll smile pleasantly at you, but studying to see if you understand. She's worked with Ernie since the days when they called him not a sociologist, but a Republican socialist.

"Old people have all kinds of sickness; some they don't even know about. So you put in a clinic, not to *cure* 'em, just for emergencies—like their own daughters should do for them if they were there. Is that a new concept?

"You check 'em over when they move in so you got some idea what kind of pills to have around in case of trouble. Is that socialized medicine?"

Today Bohn sits on two single-spaced pages of housing boards and advisory and planning committees and congressional and presidential advisory groups.

But a third of a century ago, the name *Bohn* would get you a fight.

It's 1932. The nation is stunned economically. On the floor of the Cleveland City Council, Bohn is a prodigy, even prodigious enough to conceal it. He arrives here from the Ohio Legislature where, like Alfred Kelley, he was the youngest.

He is also highly religious and humanistic, but careful that it doesn't show in his proposition to council, "Mr. President, my proposal for a council committee to study the housing blight along the Cuyahoga will lead to savings of millions for this city. I am convinced that one particular blighted area which pays us two hundred twenty-five thousand in taxes, costs us nearly two million dollars in fire fighting, crime detection and other services, not counting relief, and sickness from unsanitary, crowded, and unsafe housing."

They let Ernie have his harmless little committee, and in fact they made him chairman. Few knew they had launched a tidal wave that day which would roll from the mouth of the Cuyahoga across the United States.

Bohn immediately began a full-fledged study of slum areas in

Cleveland. He held open hearings with architects, investors, labor, renters, landlords, developers, police, realtors.

Alarm set in. At a time when we were faced with a make-or-break depression, Bohn's hearings were stirring up dust. The committee was calling attention to ghettos, parading before Ohioans a horror story.

It would be all right if Bohn were some kind of wild man that you could dismiss. "But this guy's too canny."

He was getting people upset with talk about tearing down slums. Some councilmen naturally would lose voters by removal of constituents they had already won over. Groups of owners of substandard dwellings blinked in the incandescence of open hearings, which recited five dollar fines against major fire and safety violations, with even those costs suspended on promise of repair. And the repairs were never made nor inspected.

Developers didn't like this either, remembering on second thought that they had stated they couldn't possibly build housing for the kind of rent money available in those sections.

Bohn's committee report to city council made seventeen recommendations; but the big one was that the council urge the State of Ohio to adopt a housing law for the formation and regulation of limited dividend corporations to sponsor rehousing and with power of eminent domain to condemn and demolish slums under the supervision of a State Housing Board.

Ernie Bohn just happened to have a draft of how he figured such a state law should read. He asked for speed.

"What's the hurry, Ernie?"

"There's an emergency session of State Legislature coming up in October. I want to get this bill before them."

The council approved. They might not have if they could have foreseen that Ernie Bohn was about to put together a patchwork quilt of enabling legislation by borrowing some from existing laws, amending some existing laws, and writing some new ones. His trail will be as hard to follow as rabbits through briars.

When the special session of the Ohio Legislature convened, it was surprised to be getting pressure from other cities across the state, which Bohn had contacted.

"What's the hurry, Ernie?"

"There's some federal money available for reconstruction projects, now, which will expire June 28, 1934."

Opponents of Bohn's idea were not too alarmed. Bohn was referring to the Federal Emergency Relief and Construction Act of 1932, which made loans available to private limited dividend corporations formed for the purpose of furnishing low rent housing under certain highly controlled conditions. The law intended to stimulate industry and furnish jobs. This money was only a loan, and this federal law had only stimulated *one* housing project in the entire nation.

Bohn's law to enable the formation of private limited dividend companies passed in Columbus, Ohio, October 3, 1932; *but* it granted no tax relief to limited dividend companies, which meant no incentive existed to make the law work. So those who were opposed to slum clearance and government getting into it still didn't worry much about Bohn. He was standing there with his bare hands and a law in his pocket that left him a million miles from replacing a hundred acres of slums with good housing.

The old-timers knew that one man against a massive slum is like a woodpecker cutting down redwood trees. For centuries slums have devoured and demolished thousands of bleeding-heart crusaders who died early while the slums grew two blocks each month. Bohn knew this too.

The job needed not a local voice in the wind; it needed a national uproar. Bohn set out to create one.

He went into his Cleveland Council with a resolution calling for a National Conference on Slum Clearance to be held in Cleveland July 6 and 7, 1933, under the auspices of the government of the City of Cleveland. Councilmen looked at each other, shrugged and voted "Aye."

Ernie Bohn went over to the library. He looked in various kinds of who's who's and professional journals to find the names of five hundred men in the country he thought should be interested in slum clearance and low-rent housing. He sent them official invitations, not knowing whether they would come or not.

Meanwhile, Ernie kept his eyes open for a financial method of getting action. The Ohio limited dividend law would not attract private builders or investors because it gave them no incentive and left them with the same risks that had kept them out of slum districts before.

But on June 16, 1933, the United States Congress enacted the National Industrial Recovery Act. It established the Housing Division of the Public Works Administration and provided for a 30 per cent capital grant for housing developments adjudged to stimulate industry. The seeds of a solution seemed to be lurking in here. Of course, there was still no administrative machinery set up to activate it. Even then it would be hard to convince Washington that the place to start was on the shores of the Cuyahoga.

But suddenly 428 men from all over the nation accepted his invitation to Cuyahoga country and arrived for his National Conference on Slum Clearance. They were welfare people, architects, public officials, and private citizens interested in slum clearance, housing, better cities.

The timing was excellent. They would be Ernie's national uproar—and the noise would come out of Cleveland from the banks of the Cuyahoga.

Ernie lighted the opening of the meeting with a short fuse, "Years of academic discussion have reached a climax. The time to strike is now!"

Many good ideas on ways and means to get rehousing came out in the meeting; but out of the meeting also came a set of initials, NAHO, National Association of Housing Officials, first president Ernest J. Bohn.

Now on the second day of the conference, Ernie heard the news that Harold Ickes, PWA Administrator, had appointed the past president of the American Institute of Architecture, Robert Kohn, as Housing Director of PWA.

Ernie excused himself from a meeting saying he was going for a drink of water. Instead he went to a pay station and phoned Kohn in New York. He introduced himself by name and as president of NAHO, "Wouldn't it be wonderful for the nation, Mr. Kohn, if on your first day on the new job you could announce a big slum clearance and rehousing project."

"Well," Kohn said, "there's nothing like starting off with a success."

"I have one that would be a perfect beginning, Mr. Kohn. I'd like to come to see you."

The night his conference closed, Ernie Bohn boarded the B & O with a roll of blueprints under arm.

In PWA headquarters building in Washington, Ernie asked the guard, "Where's the Housing Division?"

"Never heard of it."

A cleaning woman spoke up, "I believe I saw it. Follow me."

She led Ernie under the grand stairway to where the brooms were stored. There was a door with a small penciled card on it, misspelled, "Cohen."

Ernie entered and a young woman looked up, studied his face, and said, "Come in, Mr. Kohn. Here's your desk."

So Ernie knew he would be the first in line. He sat down to wait.

The blueprints he had under his arm were for Cleveland Homes, Inc., the limited dividend company created under the wing of Cleveland's Industrial Recovery Commission.

When the Housing Administrator arrived on the job and found Ernie had arrived before him, they had a good laugh and Mr. Kohn told the story with relish for many years.

Even supposing the federal government should act on slum clearance, why would they ever select the Cuyahoga for a start? And even supposing the federal government would lend them 70 per cent for the specific projects, where would Bohn get the other 30 per cent in a depression-beaten area?

To get action on the shores of the Cuyahoga, Ernie Bohn felt he must offer Washington a model city in slum clearance. If he could offer them a city in which the people were loudly interested in the program, perhaps they would use Cleveland to show the rest of the nation how a massive urban redevelopment could spark recovery across the land, beautify our cities, and effect human rehabilitation. He called more mass meetings of leaders and also just people living in the neighborhoods.

Those opponents who became fully aware of Bohn's intention to use parts of the revised Emergency Relief and Construction Act coupled with the Ohio Limited Dividend Housing Act as a means to housing were somewhat relieved by the massive job it would be to prove to the federal government that part should be spent in Cleveland. And even if that barrier was cracked, "which part of Cleveland" would start an equally tough battle.

But the plans for the project were well regarded in Washington, and would be approved if Cleveland Homes, Inc. could raise only two million dollars in private funds. Unfortunately they were unable to do so.

This was discouraging. Ernie Bohn decided that private enterprise was unable to clear slums and furnish rehousing.

The first step was to get the federal government to do the job itself by resorting to the use of the private limited dividend company. So now with a grass fire of commotion started in Cleveland, Ernie Bohn went back to Washington with five specific plans in mind, to ask for action. And he begged for a fast approval for slum clearance in Cleveland and for a shortening of the paperwork.

In his answer to PWA Administrator Ickes and President Roosevelt, Bohn carefully kept sentiment out of it. He knew *their* problem, and he said, "No form of expenditure spreads its effects for recovery so broadly to every branch of industry as new housing.

"Not just brick, plaster, lumber. But when you put the roof on and the people move in, they buy new furniture. They don't bring only the old." And Bohn was not just talking. He had studied housing so much now that he was truly the national authority on the subject.

"New housing gives business to all material suppliers, but also to appliance manufacturers. And, believe it or not, clothing manufacturers. New housing makes people dress better. New housing makes people want . . ."

With unprecedented swiftness, government lawyers cut through the paperwork.

Encouraged, Bohn went on to the next step. He wrote a new law to be introduced in the Ohio Legislature, HB 19 Ohio Housing Authority Law. It was to be the turning point in the nation's housing history—the first public housing law in the nation, and the model for other states. All but two states now have such laws modeled after the Ohio law. It made slum clearance and providing housing for low income families a public responsibility.

This law made it possible in 1933 to create The Cleveland Metropolitan Housing Authority, the first in the nation. There are now over *two thousand*. With such a body created, Bohn then hoped to get it into slum-clearance action by making a financial patchwork of loans and grants from RFC, PWA, and private revenue bond purchasers.

He was starting over again, but now his ways and means were more apparent, and the passage of the Ohio law alerted local opponents of public housing. They could see that Bohn might be getting a little closer to clearing those slums. You couldn't shrug him off so well now.

Ernie felt he would have to be backed up with a grassfire of public opinion.

Returning from the legislative halls in Columbus, he went immediately to a radio station and got on the air, with a challenging thought:

> *The most important piece of progressive social legislation that was passed by any law-making body in the United States in recent years became law last week. I refer to the state housing act.*
>
> Section One says: "It is hereby declared necessary in the public interest to make provisions for housing families of low income and to provide for elimination of congested unsanitary housing conditions which are a menace to . . ."
>
> *The answer to most social problems is environment.*

Bohn then explained his plan for slum removal in Cleveland and the construction of new public housing.

> The idea is opposed by conservatives who say it puts government in an additional activity. And on the other hand it is opposed by the more socialistically inclined who say it doesn't go far enough.
>
> I reply to the conservatives that the slums cost most in services and bring least in taxes.
>
> To the others I say, "Though the first spade of dirt has not been turned, *the spade is available!*"

Bohn was issuing a call for broad support to make Cleveland the nation's leader in slum clearance and rehousing. But what he reached first was an alarmed local leadership. "This Bohn is a socialist."

At thirty, Bohn was a thousand years old. He knew that before he could get the support of the leadership along the river, he first had to let them all take a crack at him. He called a meeting of the heads of fifty organizations having anything to do with housing in the area. He called for their suggestions, criticisms, ideas. He got all the fights right out in the open.

But what he wanted was enough noise to reach the White House and Congress. He wanted it to look as though a thousand leaders in Cleveland were concerned with slum removal.

Well, some were, and some were out for Bohn removal. But the noise was loud, very loud. Bohn intended to make it louder still.

The job of forming the housing authority* in Cleveland (authorized by the Ohio law), and then getting the right to condemn a specific slum area, and raising the money from private investors for this new public activity made old pros tired just thinking about it.

Ernie's moves in this direction now generated enormous resistance from some councilmen who didn't want their voters to move, land and apartment owners who lived on slum incomes, powerful development and read estate groups.

An advisory committee was required which would assist the federal government to administer the slum clearance and construction.

Who was chosen would be important. It had to be someone the whole city and Washington would respect and trust with the spending of miles of money. Harold Ickes was a suspicious alumnus of Chicago politics.

I don't know whether it was Ernie Bohn's keen sense of history —or just a coincidence. But the man he recommended to head the committee was Leyton E. Carter, forty-one-year-old direct descendant of Lorenzo Carter, the man who built the mouth of the Cuyahoga in the first place.

Carter was conservative, thoughtful, resourceful and efficient, and an admirer of Bohn.

Oversimply, thus began the first such slum-clearance and public-housing action in the United States. Cedar Apartments in Cleveland were the first, followed close second by the $2,800,000 Lakeview Apartment just above Whisky Island, twenty-two acres of redevelopment at the mouth of the Cuyahoga.

Now once things had started, a lot of people with other causes, seeing Bohn's piercing way of getting action, tried to hang their causes onto his.

One councilman moved to stop the action until special guarantees of bi-racial occupancy were built into it by the federal government.

Certain interests attempted to use Bohn's momentum to carry

---

* This housing authority was in itself a unique animal. It is not government; it is not a private corporation; it is not an individual proprietorship in the law. It's a special public entity, a new kind of being.

their causes. Suddenly a prominent congressman attacked the plans to install iceless refrigeration, "forcing tenants to accept a type of refrigeration which may be objectionable to them and damaging to their health."

Bohn disposed of these shortly, but then the very people suffering in the slum area above Whisky Island had pangs of tenderness. Demolition of the old "Angle" and the bars in the Flats where police had to walk in threes now bothered people. "That's where champs John L. Sullivan and Johnny Kilbane trained for their fights," some said. "We got to have slums to build men."

This was boss Brick Masterson country. He ruled from his saloon and dealt with governors and senators in his own establishment. He could deliver votes.

The Sixth District U.S. Court ruled that the U.S. had no power to seize property for housing.

There were warnings to Bohn to hold up the project. Bond buyers scare away quickly at any shadow of legal doubt. But Bohn was by then highly skilled in the art of using the laws of the land.

"We'll keep moving ahead," he said to the government attorneys. "You appeal it to the U.S. Supreme Court. If you lose there, then request local housing authorities to use their unchallengeable condemnation rights over slums. Same result."

The real trial of major leadership is the knowledge that to get your own job done, you have to carry a lot of other people's freight. Bohn bit his tongue and tried to accommodate sentiment, councilmen, manufacturers, U.S. courts. But he would not stop.

There isn't time to see Bohn fight each fight. The resourcefulness required each time is typically demonstrated by the time he was leading a city council bipartisan coalition opposition to the then-mayor's annual city budget which contained no help for Ernie's programs.

The mayor retaliated with a very effective move. It happened that the muddy Cuyahoga was muddier than usual this season. The siltation was so heavy that ore boats would not be able to get up the Cuyahoga to the docks to bring in ore, stone, and coal for the mills when the thaw came.

The Lake Erie Dredge & Dock Company would not commence dredging the Cuyahoga without a signed contract with the city. The mayor refused to sign a contract giving as his reason, "How can I sign a firm contract with *anyone* when I don't have a budget O.K. from council?"

Mayors had many times let contracts before budget approval, but technically his position was quite correct. The strength of his move was that the Cuyahoga valley is steel country. And anyone holding up the steel business is threatening the livelihood of thousands.

The mayor knew the headline pressure this would bring down upon Bohn: BOHN HOLDS UP STEEL JOBS.

That would get a quick capitulation from many councilmen. But Bohn was gaining the extraordinary powers that come to men with a mission who are asking nothing for them*selves*. Councilman Bohn went to the United States Government via Senator Bulkley to suggest that rivers and harbors are traditionally a federal concern. Result: The United States dredged the river. Bohn could go back to his budget battle in peace.

But when Lakeview Terrace was completed, the nation had a model of what could be done. From all over the country, they still come to look.

Bohn became, in the eyes of most, one of the nation's leading authorities on housing.

In 1935, Bohn was one of the young men who helped Senator Robert Wagner of New York write the Public Housing Act, which was finally enacted in 1937, defeating one of the most powerful lobbies in the history of lawmaking. This law gave the Cleveland and other housing authorities the guarantee on their bonds through annual contributions from Congress. This then made it possible for local authorities to function *and the federal government went out of the housing construction business.*

Bohn was then able to move down the river to build Valleyview on seventy-five acres on the bluff below Walworth Run, a $3,500,000 development. This was the first of a dozen developments subsequently built by the Cleveland Metropolitan Housing Authority.

Years went by with Bohn rebuilding the slums. A man who lives in the world of abstractions, he nevertheless became expert on brick, structural iron, electrical panel boards, concrete, elevators, sinks, financing, and what kind of soap is best for scrubbing floors.

Most of all, he became expert in humanity.

By 1943, the nation was depending upon him so heavily that he had to be much away from his office at the mouth of the river. His own towering reputation now began chipping away at his empty desk.

Ernie was working to construct some kind of shelter along the river for an army of warworkers who had moved in to man the defense factories. They were living in slums, garages, empty stores, or doubled up with others. Now it wasn't that Bohn felt hardship inappropriate in wartime; but sheer roof coverage was needed over the people, and with both parents needed in the factories, there had to be safe places to leave children.

Bohn was also trying to provide for returning veterans who would need 150,000 homes. Private construction could initially furnish only 3,000 dwellings per year, and the area would rapidly build new slums with the intensified doubling up that would occur.

At the same time, he was haunted day and night by a horrible vision recurring more and more in his dreams. Lonely old men and women, sitting in single rooms in the river valley slums, hour after hour in unutterable boredom and squalor, some hoping to die before pains became worse. He saw them in life. He saw them in his sleep.

Bohn can dress down a legislator in a public hearing with a rapier intellect that will leave the victim bleeding. But he cannot square eyes with an old man staring out a broken window.

So he was already working on his biggest dream—beautiful high-rise apartments on the west bank of the river looking over the Cuyahoga valley, a proper view for elderly men and women. He planned to call it Riverview; it would rise, he hoped, halfway between Lakeview and Valleyview.

But while he was away from the river helping the President with national war-housing emergencies, a news story broke back home:

President of Mortgage Bankers Association says the city needs to put a new watchdog on Bohn to see that he doesn't socialize all residential property.

Bohn's method only *moves* slums, it doesn't *remove* them. We

must watch the city planning commission (of which he is chairman) closely. It is controlled by the outstanding public houser in
the nation.

A cartoon showed Bohn at the head of the conference table in
a chair marked "Director, Cleveland Metro Housing Authority."
In a talk balloon coming from his mouth, the words, "Now these
houses. Let the public build 'em, and I'll manage 'em. Right?"
Seated around the table were five other Ernie Bohns, each
voting "Yes." Their chairs were labeled:

Bohn, Chairman, Office of Civilian Defense Housing Committee
Bohn, Director, Regional Association
   (A citizen's planning organization)
Bohn, Chairman, City Planning Commission
Bohn, Agent for Federal Housing Authority
Bohn, President, NAHO's Regional Housing Officials.

The cartoonist didn't know it, but he could have put fourteen
more chairs around that table, some with *bigger* titles than
those.

But men who have strictly personal ambitions never understand the power that comes to a man who has lost personal
ambition in a cause a thousand times bigger. The surge of anti-
Bohnism played into Ernie's hands. He resigned as many chairmanships as they'd permit. "Why?" he was asked.

"I want these other guys to get bit by it. I want them to *see*."

It took a dozen leaders to fill Bohn's vacated chairmanships.
But they *were* bitten. They saw. They smelled. They hurt. They
had some of the bad dreams that had haunted Bohn—and they
joined the fight.

Bohn's bad dreams spread out to more and more people. Some
had nightmares so badly that the population, the press, and the
Republican party asked Bohn to run for mayor and repair the
whole Cuyahoga valley.

Bohn declined. He said it would sidetrack him. He had housing
to build for returning veterans and the aged wandering along the
Cuyahoga slums. But it helped him get more help, and to get out
from under the "socialism" tag.

Then, in the late '40s, Senator Robert Taft asked Ernie's help to
project public housing into a national program of redevelopment

of American communities. Taft was pressing a housing bill for $75,000,000 in public funds. Senator Dirksen had offered a crippling amendment, cutting it to $5,000,000.

Why did Mr. Republican feel that the providing of annual subsidies for public housing was *not* socialistic? Mr. Taft pointed out, "Much of the private financing for *private* construction is *already* being guaranteed by the federal government through FHA anyway." Further he pointed out that no one had come up with any other solution to the problem of providing decent housing for families unable to pay their own way because of substandard incomes.

Ernie had said it many times. But coming in Mr. Taft's strident twang, it cut through to those who had hardened their ears to Bohn's droning bull horn.

While Taft carried the fight in the Senate, Bohn came back to carry it along the river and in other communities. The result was the Taft-Ellender-Wagner Act of 1949 which declared that a decent home in a good environment for every American was the national policy.

It took him until 1961 to get his Riverview dream for elderly people started. By now, Ernie was sixty and many of his associates from the old brawls had retired or died or gone on from the river to assume leadership in other work.

Over the years, Ernie always received the cooperation of presidents, senators, and administrations in Washington. More than one federal administration offered him a post heading up an important housing agency. He, however, respectfully declined, firmly believing that *action* in housing reform had to be carried out in the local community with federal financial assistance. He continued, however, to serve on housing and welfare advisory committees to the President, Senate, cabinet heads, and agencies.

But in 1961, he was faced on the opposition side by a herd of powerful new young bulls. Even as the plans for the magnificent eight hundred-unit Riverview were about to be converted to action, opponents in city council were preparing to kill it.

On page two of an issue of the *Cleveland Press* in 1961, Ernie is being congratulated at a testimonial affair on the magnificent Riverview apartments about to rise. And Mr. Bohn modulates the gravel out of his voice, holding it to a very civil rumble, "If I have had any success in this, it is due solely to the fine cooperation I received from business and from public officials, both Republican and Democrat."

On page eight of the same paper, it explains, "Upon learning that two able young councilmen were forming a coalition drive to kill Riverview apartments, Ernest J. Bohn, master of the brawls, moved swiftly backstage so fast they didn't know what hit them, and he brought off a crushing victory vote in council on a zoning change for Riverview."

It's these Riverview apartments, just completed, which are now bringing the most visitors to the Cuyahoga to ask questions and to learn. Bohn is hard put to it to find the time to talk with the visitors. The pace he keeps is legend in Cleveland.

"Now that Riverview is finished, Ernie, what's the hurry?"

"Hell, we aren't even started. One thing we got to do, we got to change this crazy thing about putting nonpsychotic elderly people in asylums.

"Say an old widower has a little trouble remembering one of his ten grandchildren when they come to call the first time in three years. Right away, 'his mind is going.' We pack him off right away to some mental institution because there's no other place.

"Baloney. When you get old, you forget. Is that psychiatry? I couldn't even remember *your* name 'til you crossed the threshold. So am I crazy?"

Ernie Bohn and the governor are now at work on housing for the nonpsychotic elderly.

The Cuyahoga is a man-made river; even the palisades along its shore.

The Cuyahoga is a man-made river. There was no reason, by virtue of length, width, current, or location, for this red creek to become headquarters of mid-America's steel, oil, and rubber economy. But men leveled it out with the great canal, straightened it with the cut at the mouth, dredged it to let in deep draft ore bulkers, dammed it to take off power and build empires of rubber and flour.

And this in the end is really the better kind of river, forcing man to reach farther than he can reach, leap farther than he can leap.

Some rivers are so mighty and overpowering they force conclusions on men and nations—the Ohio, the Columbia, the Mississippi—and diminish the men.

But the crooked little Cuyahoga, no larger than many a good fishing stream, required of men their best effort and magnified them. It turned them into giants who could force the valley unnaturally into the pivotal position in mid-America's economy. Sailing out of her mouth, they opened first the Upper Peninsula mines in Michigan, then the Mesabi. Digging upstream alongside with a flat track of slack water, the Ohio Canal made this valley the main freight road from New Orleans to New York.

The Cuyahoga is still challenging men to works so vast that mile for mile and drop for drop it can't be matched by any river I have ever heard of in the world.

Acknowledgments

FIRST, to my colleagues in Editorial Services, Inc., who work with me daily writing the stories of this region in documentary films, television and radio programs: Everett Dodrill for the stories of the underground railroad, the geology, the Huletts, Whisky Island, the railroads and other portions; Pauline Fanslow for the Kingsbury Run story, the index, and for research and general work throughout the text; Carl Goodwin for Captain Peck, the tugs, storms and bridges; D. L. Couzens for assistance in cutting the manuscript down to publication length.

To Carl Carmer, editor, and Jean Crawford, associate editor of the Rivers of America series, for guidance and encouragement.

To Janet Coe Sanborn, History Department, Cleveland Public Library, and Editor of *Inland Seas,* Quarterly Journal of the Great Lakes Historical Society, for extensive bibliographical assistance.

To Katherine Wilder, Rocky River Public Library, and to librarians along the Cuyahoga: Carolina Afflect, Cuyahoga Falls; Margaret Babbit, Independence; Margaret Zearley, Kent; Harriet Johnson, Chardon; Carmen Gordon, Peninsula; Grace Goodale, Hiram; Mary L. Schubert, Brecksville; and to R. Russell Munn, Akron, for reading certain chapters.

For facts, we're in the debt of three grand pioneering regional writers of the past: Henry Howe, Charles Whittlesey, Sam'l A. Lane; and to distinguished modern writers of the region: The late William Ganson Rose; Harlan Hatcher for his works on the Western Reserve; Walter Havighurst who has written something about most Midwestern waters; and to the works of Lee Templeton and Frank Siedel, valued colleagues of mine, who contributed also some of their wonderfully prejudiced regional enthusiasm.

Those wishing to explore the Cuyahoga further will find a bibliography at the end of the book.

Our thanks to Great Lakes Historical Museum in Vermilion; the

Perkins Museum in Akron, Western Reserve Historical Society, Ohio Historical Society and Ohioana Library in Columbus.

Thanks to Richard J. Wright and to Captain Tom O'Donnell and his tug crew; and to Thomas Hawisher, research geologist at Ferro Corporation, for checking over our geological chapter.

Absolutely no thanks in general should go to the denizens of Green's Cafe on the old Angle's border who maintained top security about Whisky Island's exciting past. Therefore, very special thanks to Matthew Quilter, a retired railroad man who was one of the few to break security on the early days of Whisky Island. He was extremely helpful and informative; and we hope this acknowledgment doesn't get him in trouble at the club. Thanks should also go to his long-time friend, Walter Kramer.

To the late Willis Thornton, to David K. Ford and Jack Hollister for special reference materials lent to us, and to Frank Trevorrow for a detailed map of the Canal and to Lew Richardson, editor of *Towpaths*.

To Ross C. Durst, retired professor of engineering, for use of his *History of the Cuyahoga* and book of news clippings; and to the members of the Cleveland Police Department and the Office of County Coronor for assistance.

We're also indebted to a long list of people, especially older people, who spent many hours with us reminiscing about the history they helped make.

W.D.E.

Bibliography

Alburn, Wilfred Henry, *This Cleveland of Ours*. Cleveland: S. J. Clarke Publishing Company, 1933.

American Monthly Magazine, The. Vol. 38, Jan.–June. Edited by Mrs. Elroy M. Avery. New York: The National Society of the Daughters of the American Revolution, 1911.

Annals of Cleveland, 1818–1935. Cleveland: WPA Project 14066, 1937.

Barnholth, William I., *The Cuyahoga-Tuscarawas Portage*. Akron: Summit County Historical Society, 1954.

Cherry, Peter Peterson, *The Portage Path*. Akron: The Western Reserve Company, 1911.

——— *The Western Reserve & Early Ohio*. Akron: R. L. Fouse, 1921.

Cleveland Topics. Cleveland Topics Company.

Clipping File. *The Cleveland Plain Dealer*.

Clipping File. *The Cleveland Press*.

Coates, William R., *A History of Cuyahoga County*, Vol. I. (3 vol. series) Chicago and New York: The American Historical Society, 1924.

"Cuyahoga River," "Moses Cleaveland," "Cleveland, Ohio—Morgana Run." Clipping File, Cleveland Public Library. History, Biography and Travel Department.

Downes, Randolph Chandler, *History of Lake Shore Ohio*. Vol. I. New York: Lewis Historical Publishing Co., Inc., 1952.

Doyle, William B., *Centennial History of Summit County, Ohio*. Chicago: Biographical Publishing Company, 1908.

Early Settlers' Association of the Western Reserve, Annals, Vol. I, III, and VI. Cleveland, Ohio. (Published by order of the Executive Committee.) n.d.

Fairchild, Thomas B. (Reverend), *Cuyahoga Falls*. Cleveland: Cleveland Herald Print, 1876. (A history of the town of Cuyahoga Falls, Summit County, Ohio. An address delivered by Mr. Fairchild, July 4, 1876.)

Fowke, Gerald, *Archeological History of Ohio*. n.d.

Grismer, Karl Hiram, *Akron & Summit County*. Akron: Summit County Historical Society, 1952 (?)

Hatcher, Harlan Henthorne, *The Western Reserve*. Indianapolis: Bobbs-Merrill, 1949.

Havighurst, Walter, *The Heartland*. New York: Harper & Row, 1962.

―――― *Wilderness for Sale*. New York: Hastings House, 1956.

History of Portage County. (General history by R. C. Brown; local history, J. E. Norris). Chicago: Warner, Beers & Co., 1885.

Hodges, Orlando John, *Reminiscences* Vol. II. Cleveland: The Imperial Press, 1902–10.

Howe, Henry, *Historical Collections of Ohio*. Vol. I (Published by the State of Ohio.) Norwalk, Ohio: The Laning Printing Co. Public Printers., 1898.

"Inland Seas," Quarterly Journal of the Great Lakes Historical Society, 1955–56.

Johnson, Crisfield, *History of Cuyahoga County, Ohio*. Philadelphia: D. W. Ensign & Co., 1879.

Kelley, S. J., "Clippings from Cleveland Plain Dealer, Vol. I & II," Cleveland Public Library. History, Biography and Travel Department.

Kennedy, James Henry, *A History of Cleveland*. Cleveland: The Cleveland Printing and Publishing Company, 1889.

―――― *A History of the City of Cleveland*. Cleveland: The Imperial Press. MDCCCXCVI (1896).

Lane, Samuel Alanson, *Fifty Years and Over of Akron and Summit County*. Akron: Beacon Job Department.

Magazine of Western History, Vol. II, Cleveland (1884–88). New York: Magazine of Western History Publishing Co. (1888–1891).

Ohio Guide, The. Compiled by workers of the Writers' Program of the Work Projects Administration in the State of Ohio. American Guide Series sponsored by The Ohio State Archaeological & Historical Society. Oxford University Press, New York: First published in October 1940.

Pioneer & General History of Geauga Co., Ohio. Burton (?) Ohio: Historical Society of Geauga Co., 1880.

Post, Charles Asa, *The Cuyahoga: The Crooked River That Made A City Great* . . . Cleveland (?): Privately printed 1941.

Rose, William Ganson. *Cleveland: The Making of a City*. Cleveland: The World Publishing Company, 1950.

Siebert, Henry Wilbur. *The Underground Railroad From Slavery to Freedom*. New York and London: The Macmillan Co., 1898.

―――― *The Mysteries of Ohio's Underground Railroads*. Columbus, Ohio: Long's College Book Co., 1951.

Vietzen, Raymond C., *The Immortal Eries*. Elyria, Ohio: Wilmot Printing Company, 1945.

Whittlesey, Charles, *Early History of Cleveland*. Cleveland: Fairbanks, Benedict & Co., Printers, 1867.

Wilcox, Frank N., *Ohio Indian Trails*. Cleveland: The Gates Press, 1933.

Index

* Correction: Ref. pp 262, 271, should be Lorenzo Carter, not Alonzo as shown in text.